Bowles and Gintis Revisited

Correspondence and Contradiction in Educational Theory

Edited by
Mike Cole

The Falmer Press
(A member of the Taylor & Francis Group)
London · New York · Philadelphia

UK The Falmer Press, Falmer House, Barcombe, Lewes, East Sussex, BN8 5DL

USA The Falmer Press, Taylor & Francis Inc., 242 Cherry Street, Philadelphia, PA 19106-1906

First published 1988

Library of Congress Cataloging in Publication Data available on request

ISBN 1 85000 173 1

ISBN 1 85000 174 X (pbk)

Jacket design by Caroline Archer

Typeset in 10½/12 Caledonia by
Imago Publishing Ltd, Thame, Oxon

Printed and bound in Britain by
Redwood Burn Limited, Trowbridge, Wiltshire

Contents

Acknowledgements

I would like to thank Routledge and Kegan Paul plc and Basic Books Inc for permission to republish an excerpt from Samuel Bowles and Herbert Gintis' *Schooling in Capitalist America*. I would also like to thank Routledge and Kegan Paul plc, publishers of *The Sociological Review*, for permission to republish my article 'Contradictions in the educational theory of Gintis and Bowles' which appears as chapter 3 of this volume.

I would further like to thank the British Council for two research grants which made the job of editing the book easier.

It was Herb Gintis who initially encouraged me to undertake the project by responding favourably to the idea. My thanks to him and Sam Bowles. Special thanks to Catherine Tyler for secretarial support.

Preface: Why Revisit Bowles and Gintis?

We live in reactionary times, the hard right is firmly entrenched at the time of writing in Britain and America. At the same time Britain has given birth to a number of progressive forces — the left-wing borough councils, the anti-nuclear movement including its impact at Greenham Common, an established women's movement, the miners' strike, the uprisings in the inner cities and the anti-racist struggle, while in America we have seen the advance of the Rainbow coalition and other progressive movements. Whatever the way forward, for the left, there is a fundamental need for a re-evaluation of basic Marxist scholarship but in the light of the significance of these historical and current realities. This book aims to play some small part in that process. The central focus is, of course, education but the issues raised range far wider.

Mike Cole
October 1987

*Prologue: The Correspondence Principle**

Samuel Bowles and Herbert Gintis

> In the social production which men carry on they enter into definite relations which are indispensible and independent of their will; . . . The sum total of these relations of production constitutes . . . the real foundation on which rise legal and political superstructures, and to which correspond definite forms of social consciousness. (KARL MARX, *Contribution to a Critique of Political Economy*, 1857)

The economy produces people. The production of commodities may be considered of quite minor importance except as a necessary input into people production. Our critique of the capitalist economy is simple enough: the people production process — in the workplace and in schools — is dominated by the imperatives of profit and domination rather than by human need. Profits are made through hiring workers and organizing production in such a way that the price paid for the worker's time — the wage — is less than the value of the goods produced by labor. The difference between the wage and the value of goods produced is profit, or surplus value. The production of surplus value requires as a precondition the existence of a body of wage workers whose sole source of livelihood is the sale of their capacity to work, their labor power.

Opposing these wage workers is the employer, whose control of the tools, structures, and goods required in production constitutes both the immediate basis of his power over labor and his legal claim on the surplus value generated in production.

The US economy is a formally totalitarian system in which the actions of the vast majority are controlled by a small minority. Yet this totalitarian system is embedded in a formally democratic political system which promotes the norms — if not the practice — of equality, justice, and

*Adapted from BOWLES, S. and GINTIS, H. (1976) *Schooling in Capitalist America*, London, Routledge and Regan Paul, pp 10, 53–4, 129, 130–3.

reciprocity. The strongly contrasting nature of the economic and political systems can be illustrated by the diametrically opposed problems faced in maintaining their proper functioning. For the political system, the central problems of democracy are: insuring the maximal participation of the majority in decision-making; protecting minorities against the prejudices of the majority; and protecting the majority from any undue influence on the part of an unrepresentative minority. These problems of 'making democracy work' are discussed at length in any high school textbook on government.

For the economic system, these central problems are nearly exactly reversed. Making US capitalism work involves: insuring the minimal participation in decision-making by the majority (the workers); protecting a single minority (capitalists and managers) against the wills of a majority; and subjecting the majority to the maximal influence of this single unrepresentative minority. A more dramatic contrast one would be hard pressed to discover. High school textbooks do not dwell on the discrepancy.

The undemocratic structure of economic life in the United States may be traced directly to the moving force in the capitalist system: the quest for profits.

The initiation of youth into the economic system is facilitated by a series of institutions, including the family and the educational system, that are immediately related to the formation of personality and consciousness. Education works primarily through the institutional relations to which students are subjected.

To reproduce the social relations of production, the educational system must try to teach people to be properly subordinate and render them sufficiently fragmented in consciousness to preclude their getting together to shape their own material existence. The forms of consciousness and behavior fostered by the educational system must themselves be alienated, in the sense that they conform neither to the dictates of technology in the struggle with nature, nor to the inherent developmental capacities of individuals, but rather to the needs of the capitalist class. It is the prerogatives of capital and the imperatives of profit, not human capacities and technical realities, which render US schooling what it is. This is our charge.

The educational system helps integrate youth into the economic system, we believe, through a structural correspondence between its social relations and those of production. The structure of social relations in education not only inures the student to the discipline of the work place, but develops the types of personal demeanor, modes of self-presentation, self-image, and social-class identifications which are the crucial ingredients of job adequacy. Specifically, the social relationships of education — the relationships between administrators and teachers, teachers and students, students and students, and students and their work — replicate the hierarchical division of labor. Hierarchical relations are reflected in the vertical authority lines from administrators to teachers to students. Alienated labor is reflected in the student's lack of control over his or her education, the alienation of the student from the curriculum content, and the motivation of school work through a system of grades and other external rewards rather than the student's integration with either the process (learning) or the outcome (knowledge) of the educational 'production process'. Fragmentation in work is reflected in the institutionalized and often destructive competition among students through continual and ostensibly meritocratic ranking and evaluation. By attuning young people to a set of social relationships similar to those of the work place, schooling attempts to gear the development of personal needs to its requirements.

But the correspondence of schooling with the social relations of production goes beyond this aggregate level. Different levels of education feed workers into different levels within the occupational structure and, correspondingly, tend toward an internal organization comparable to levels in the hierarchical division of labor. The lowest levels in the hierarchy of the enterprise emphasize rule-following, middle levels, dependability, and the capacity to operate without direct and continuous supervision while the higher levels stress the internalization of the norms of the enterprise. Similarly, in education, lower levels (junior and senior high school) tend to severely limit and channel the activities of students. Somewhat higher up the educational ladder, teacher and community colleges allow for more independent activity and less overall supervision. At the top, the elite four-year colleges emphasize social relationships conformable with the higher levels in the production hierarchy.[1] Thus schools continually maintain their hold on students. As they 'master' one type of behavioral regulation, they are either allowed to progress to the next or are channeled into the corresponding level in the hierarchy of production. Even within a single school, the social relationships of different tracks tend to conform to different behavioral norms. Thus in high school, vocational and general tracks emphasize rule-following and close supervision, while the college track tends toward a more open atmosphere emphasizing the internalization of norms.

These differences in the social relationships among and within schools, in part, reflect both the social backgrounds of the student body and their likely future economic positions. Thus blacks and other minorities are concentrated in schools whose repressive, arbitrary, generally chaotic internal order, coercive authority structures, and minimal possibilities for advancement mirror the characteristics of inferior job situations. Similarly, predominantly working-class schools tend to emphasize behavioral control and rule-following, while schools in well-to-do suburbs employ relatively open systems that favor greater student participation, less direct supervision, more student electives, and, in general, a value system stressing internalized standards of control.

The differential socialization patterns of schools attended by students of different social classes do not arise by accident. Rather, they reflect the fact that the educational objectives and expectations of administrators, teachers, and parents (as well as the responsiveness of students to various patterns of teaching and control) differ for students of different social classes. At crucial turning points in the history of US education, changes in the social relations of schooling have been dictated in the interests of a more harmonious reproduction of the class structure. But in the day-to-day operation of the schools, the consciousness of different occupational strata, derived from their cultural milieu and work experience, is crucial to the maintenance of the correspondences we have described. That working-class parents seem to favor stricter educational methods is a reflection of their own work experiences, which have demonstrated that submission to authority is an essential ingredient in one's ability to get and hold a steady, well-paying job. That professional and self-employed parents prefer a more open atmosphere and a greater emphasis on motivational control is similarly a reflection of their position in the social division of labor. When given the opportunity, higher-status parents are far more likely than their lower-status neighbors to choose 'open classrooms' for their children.[2]

Differences in the social relationships of schooling are further reinforced by inequalities in financial resources. The paucity of financial support for the education of children from minority groups and low-income families leaves more resources to be devoted to the children of those with more commanding roles in the economy; it also forces upon the teachers and school administrators in the working-class schools a type of social relationship that fairly closely mirrors that of the factory. Financial considerations in poorly supported schools militate against small intimate classes, multiple elective courses, and specialized teachers (except for disciplinary personnel). They preclude the amounts of free time for teachers and free space required for a more open, flexible educational environment. The well-financed schools attended by the children of the rich can offer much greater opportunities for the development of the capacity for sustained independent work and all the other characteristics required for adequate job performance in the upper levels of the occupational hierarchy.

Notes

1 BINSTOCK, J. (1970) 'Survival in the American college industry', unpublished PhD dissertation, Brandeis University.

2 ROSENTHAL, B. (1972) 'Educational investments in human capital: The significance of stratification in the labor market', unpublished honors thesis, Harvard University; and FRIENDENBERG, E.Z. (1965) *Coming of Age in America* New York, Random House.

Part I
The Context of the Debate

1 *Correspondence Theory in Education: Impact, Critique and Re-evaluation*

Mike Cole

Traditional sociology of education owes much to Durkheim and to functionalism. It was centrally concerned with accounting for the selection and allocation of individuals and, in the case of Britain, social classes to their future roles in society. Its underlying assumption is a broad acceptance of, and commitment to, the values of capitalist society. Individual failure is explained by problems with socialization. Social class differential in educational achievement is attributed to an unequal distribution of resources rather than to structural inequalities in the system. As such, it was an inherently conservative tradition.

In the early 1970s many radical sociologists of education became seduced by the New Sociology of Education (NSE). Its promise was to reveal the political character of educational knowledge which was conceived as a construct of 'underlying meanings'. The task of NSE was to explore the construction of these meanings. Methodologically ethnographic, its concern was with individual social actors rather than with social structures.

The construction of meanings was to be sought in classroom interaction. It was indeed a radical departure from traditional concerns. However, as Robert Moore points out in this volume, it represented radicalism within the discipline, rather than political radicalism. It was not so much that NSE rejected political radicalism; rather it was unable to make the connections upon which a politically radical analysis depended. In this sense it was fundamentally flawed. While it recognized the centrality of notions of power and control, it was unable to make the link between the micro (the school and the classroom — whence meanings — including power relations — were thought to be constructed, defined and redefined) and the macro (the capitalist economy — where economic power, control and ownership ultimately resided). For many then, the publication of Samuel Bowles and Herb Gintis' *Schooling in Capitalist America* (SCA) in 1976 was seen as a breakthrough — at last a resolution to the shortcomings of NSE — in particular its inability to link micro to macro. NSE's commitment to the centrality of notions of 'control' and 'power' rendered many of its protagonists sympathetic to the 'political economy' approach of Bowles and Gintis. To the discipline as a whole, political radicalism became central.

Although, as Michael Apple points out in this volume, Bowles and Gintis didn't start left criticisms of schooling, their achievement was to focus attention directly, in a structural fashion, on the capitalist economy per se. 'In so doing, they provided a more coherent lens with which to view the schooling process'.

The key concept in *SCA* is 'the correspondence principle' — the reproduction of the social relations of production is facilitated through a structural correspondence between the social relations of the educational system and those of production (see the Prologue). 'Correspondence' provided both the key to the problem of the interpretation of classroom interaction for the New Sociologists of Education and a point of reference for Marxist appraisal and critique. The appeal of *SCA* for socialists was fundamental and compelling:

> A revolutionary transformation of social life will not simply happen through piecemeal change. Rather, we believe it will occur only as the result of a prolonged struggle based on hope and a total vision of a qualitatively new society, waged by those social classes and groups who stand to benefit from the new era. This book is to be a step in that long march. (p. 17).

However, the vision of a socialist society and the correspondence principle were seen by many as contradictory. As I argued in *The Sociological Review* (August 1983 and reproduced in this volume as chapter 3) whereas and Gintis Bowles suggest that the 'correspondence principle' implies the need for democratic socialism, an unquestioning acceptance of its applicability can produce a reactionary rather than progressive response:

> Some of my student teachers have even looked upon the principle as reassuring in its promise of stability and the maintenance of the status quo, while others, with a more radical mind, have despaired at the seeming lack of space for individual and collective action.

This is not to suggest that at the time of writing *SCA*, Bowles and Gintis did not favour democratic socialism. On the contrary, their commitment to a socialist transformation led by a mass based party is unambiguous:

> We support the development of a revolutionary socialist movement in the United States. However arduous the path to success, a socialist alternative can provide the sole access to a future of real progress in terms of justice, personal liberation, and social welfare . . . The development and articulation of the vision of a socialist alternative . . . requires a mass based party . . . committed to a revolutionary transformation of the US economy (pp. 282 and 288)

The problem lies more with their (then Marxist commitment but) essentially functionalist account of the schooling/economy relationship. This necessarily entailed a passive view of humankind, a view epitomized by their assertion that schools are *destined* to resign youth to their fate (p. 266).

Understandably, this spawned a series of writers who set out to stress student and teacher resistance.[1] As Dennis Carlson puts it in this volume:

> . . . teachers have too often been treated in a deterministic fashion in the dominant structural-functional theory of schooling, leading to an overly-pessimistic appraisal of their real or potential role in the ongoing conflict between the two great camps in capitalist society: capital and labour. Structural-functionalism has presumed, simplistically, that questions as to the political role of various strata of workers in the labor force can be answered primarily through an analysis of their 'objective' class location and function. In contrast, I have argued that while this is a needed line of analysis, it is less important strategically than an assessment of the cultural conditions and circumstances which encourage teachers to define their interests in an expansive rather than restrictive way: that is, as part of a majority movement for social change that seriously challenges existing structures, ideologies, and practices.

If the correspondence principle does not automatically herald the need for the transition to socialism, what is its potential in interpreting the present and the past? Much has been written on the extent to which it is useful or correct to posit a current direct structural correspondence between schooling and capitalism. Many have argued that such a claim is too crude. Some have suggested relative autonomy between base (the capitalist economy) and superstructure (in this case — the schooling system) where the base determines in the last instance but this in itself presents problems as to when the last instance arrives. Still others have moved outside the realms of Marxism and have suggested total autonomy between base and superstructure. In addition to providing an extensive review of the sociology of education since NSE, Robert Moore, in this volume, proposes an alternative solution to this dilemma.

He suggests that

> Once the theoretical separation (both conceptual and ontological) is made between the *social relations of production* and the *system of social relationships within the process of immediate production* (or simply 'the occupational system'), then both the educational and occupational systems can be approached as distinctive sites of production (under the social relations of production) with their own intrinsic principles and possibilities.

The social relations of production under capitalism are the prior conditions for the process of capitalist production as a *whole* and construct wage labour as a *social category*. The *social relationships in production* refer specifically to *the immediate production of goods*. Education can be seen as a 'site' *in its own right* — but based in the social relations of *knowledge* production. He develops this thesis using Bernstein's *Class, Codes and Control* arguments.

As far as its use in interpreting the past is concerned, specifically the genesis of the common school movement, this is a problem addressed by Peter MacDonald in this volume. Again, the spectre of Bowles and Gintis' Marxist commitment and a non-Marxist account is raised. As MacDonald puts it, although operating within Marxist theory at the theoretical level, at the empirical level, Bowles and Gintis rely, albeit knowingly, on a revisionist theory of periodization. Revisionism, he stresses, centralizes industrialization, urbanization and poverty rather than the (Marxist) concepts of capitalism and class conflict. Revisionist theory, he goes on, is not only a questionable procedure but, with a dispute over appropriate periodization raging within revisionism, the evidence itself is rendered problematic and the procedure appears even more questionable.

Analyzing the common school movement in the concrete comparative context of nineteenth century Ontario, New England and England, he continues that it is only through an analysis of periodization, centred around changes in the organization of the labour process (based on Marx's *Capital*), that we are able to satisfactorily assess revisionist history and hence Bowles and Gintis' empirical case. He suggests that

> a reasonable rating of the three systems of education in terms of developmental level would be Ontario, Massachusetts, and England in descending order. But when the extent to which each society is urban-industrial capitalist is assessed, the opposite order appears to be the case. In other words, the least advanced society possessed the most advanced form of education. The fact that the most industrialized, urbanized, capitalistic society was characterized by the most 'archaic' system of education points to the difficulties faced by the interpretations produced by the correspondence principle.

Educational formation was relatively autonomous of production relations both in upper Canada and Massachusetts, he concludes, and Marxist theory must take this into account.

Another major response to Bowles and Gintis has centred around their omissions — quite simply their relative neglect of gender and 'race'.[2]

Bowles and Gintis argue that 'like the education system, the family plays a major role in preparing the young for economic and social roles'. 'Thus', they claim, 'the family's impact on the reproduction of the sexual division of labour, for example, is distinctly greater than that of the educational system'. As AnnMarie Wolpe puts it, in this volume

> According to Bowles and Gintis both boys and girls are affected by

> the ideological inputs they receive but differentially: ideological formations are derived from the family situation for girls but boys from their schooling ... More specifically the ideologies which have specific reference to work and the development of specific characteristics of future workers which are all attributed to schools must, therefore, affect males. Girls' ideas have, according to their analyses, been formed in the family. Schooling cannot be as important for women because of the greater power of the family structure and its teaching on sex-roles... In one fell swoop they eradicate any importance of education in girls' lives... They do not offer an account of why this should be so, why girls are relatively unaffected by their schooling. Why should girls escape the ideological pressures which, according to Bowles and Gintis, constitute the main effect of schooling on pupils? Such a claim is obviously difficult to sustain.

Their relative neglect of 'race' is equally problematic. As Gloria Joseph argues in this volume:

> The American dream has never worked for Blacks, and that is a truism that must be remembered whenever analysis and discussion concerning the future of the nation's population are in progress. To say [as Bowles and Gintis do] that '... the creation of an equal and liberating school system requires a revolutionary transformation of economic life', is to disregard the dynamics of the racial dimension. The absence of a sharp focus on racism inhibits the social change desired. I am in agreement with the statement that the role of the educational system in America today is to produce a work force willing and able to staff occupational positions in the capitalist system. However, this statement is basically applicable to the white population in America. There exists a significantly large body of Blacks and Latinos who are not in the economic work force at all. A most radical approach to dealing with the problem of radical educational change would be to focus on the Blacks, Latinos, Native Americans — the domestic Third World people — as the vanguard. Historically in this country those fighting racism have been in the vanguard of social movements. The struggle for racial equality, which serves as a generational linkage, provides the nation with a focus that is the antithesis of the avaricious, necrophilic, aggressive, materialistic, selfish attitudes that characterize the dominant Western perspective.

My own work in England[3] has argued for the crucial necessity of an anti-racist, as opposed to a multicultural, approach to education both in terms of structure and content — since racism is reproduced through both. Briefly, I have suggested that all institutions draw up and implement an anti-racist policy which works and that the content of teaching reflects the interests of the Black community. Similar arguments would, of course, apply to an anti-sexist approach. Gloria Joseph in this volume has advocated a

> Black feminist pedagogy as a philosophy of liberation for humankind . . . designed to enable students through the social, economic, cultural, moral and religious history of Third World people to re-examine and see the world through a perspective that would instill a revolutionary conscious liberation ideology.

while Michael Apple, also in this volume, has argued the case for a parallelist position which 'should not automatically assume the primacy of class relations over those of gender and race'.

As he puts it:

> These latter two dynamics, and the complex and immensely *contradictory* interconnections among all three, must be given equal weight in the analysis of any concrete situation. Of course, we may find that class has primacy in a situation, but it would have to be proven, not assumed at the outset.

So far, my attention has been directed at the impact, critique and evalution of *Schooling in Capitalist America*, in particular the efficacy of the correspondence principle and the book's relative neglect of gender and 'race'.

The first two chapters of Part 3 of this volume address themselves specifically to the relevance and impact of the writing of Bowles and Gintis to the *revolutionary* transition to socialism. According to John Freeman–Moir, Alan Scott and Hugh Lauder, while most criticisms of *SCA* have been directed at the explanatory structure of the correspondence principle, rather than at the issues raised regarding the socialist struggle, the two points are not unconnected (as my earlier arguments would suggest also). However they go on to argue that Bowles and Gintis are prominent exponents in the USA of anti-revolutionary 'socialism'. They certainly have moved towards a pluralist theory of the state. As I argue in chapter 3, 'the tendency in *SCA* towards a worrying 'faith' in the liberal democratic state has become [in 'Contradiction and reproduction in educational theory' — reproduced as chapter 2] a fully fledged pluralism'. This is taken up by Rachel Sharp when she asks, if the state is not a site of class domination, 'what then are the armies, police forces and judiciary of liberal democratic states *for*?'.

> Do they not observe any connection between the existence of liberal democracy and its rhetoric of 'person rights' in countries like the USA and the lack of it in much of the periphery and the use of the coercive power of the liberal democratic state wherever

> capitalist social relations are under severe challenge? Only from a provincial nation-state perspective which takes no account of imperialism and which ignores the role of state coercion in cementing the social order in a class society, can the liberal democratic state be defined as not itself a site of domination.

In a similar vein, John Freeman-Moir, Alan Scott and Hugh Lauder argue that:

> It is a central tenet of historical materialism that the state is a class state, prepared long before the last instance to use every means of physical repression to ensure the conditions of accumulation. Even a cursory understanding of labour history in the USA, not to mention the proclivity of late imperial America to prop up anti-socialist dictatorships, attack and even bomb unfriendly régimes, and to demand access throughout the capitalist world for its nuclear ships and weapons is enough to dispense these naive notions to the wind. To a very large degree American freedoms at home are materially maintained by unfreedoms elsewhere on the globe. We do not deny of course that the state is, to use the language of Bowles and Gintis, a site of struggle. But we also insist that this struggle is determined by the vicissitudes of accumulation — most directly by the rate of profitability.

Referring to the British miners' strike of 1984–85, they remind us that

> When the miners attempted to picket effectively in support of their claim for the right to work (which incidentally, Bowles and Gintis state as the second proposition on which post-liberal democracy should be built) then they were met by the full might of the state. Put simply, the capitalist state resorted to force once it realized that the miners were pressing their personal rights away from the bargaining table and were refusing to accept the state's definition or description of that right. They wanted that right on their own terms (as their class right we would argue) and for that they payed the price.

In part, in reply in the last chapter of this section Samuel Bowles and Herbert Gintis argue that to suggest that their recent critique of Marxism as the basis for a theory of democracy means that they have embraced liberalism as a political philosophy is misplaced. They stress that a viable theory of education in a democratic society requires the rejection of the fundamental liberal partition of individuals into learners (those who for reasons of age, incapacity, or citizenship are excluded from the privileges of the rational agents whose intentions and choices are the subject of the explicit political and economic theory of liberalism) and choosers (these rational agents). The liberal position they suggest, needs to be replaced by a theory which takes account of the manner in which class relationships, the state, the family and other structures regulate our own individual and collective projects to shape who we are.

My own position is that there should be no ambiguity in terms of the rejection of liberalism *nor* in terms of the advocacy of socialism. The state in capitalist society is indeed a capitalist state. It is also a patriarchal state and a racist state. Human liberation and our very survival depend on the building of a socialist world. As Sharp argues, Bowles and Gintis are ambiguous on this point. As she puts it: 'whether socialism implies a movement beyond capitalism or its humanization and democratization, whether it is simply a question of finding a more equitable mode of surplus labour extraction or bringing to an end all coercion and exploitation is unclear'.

We cannot afford to be unclear. While it is true that we live in reactionary times, there are hopes for the future. The United States is witnessing an unprecedented class polarization and an extraordinary intensification of class voting[4] which may well indicate a socialist future. As Barbara Ehrenreich puts it with simplicity and clarity:

> Karl Marx predicted that capitalist society would eventually be torn apart by the conflict between a greedy bourgeoisie and a vast, rebellious proletariat. He did not foresee the emergence, within capitalism, of a mass middle class that would mediate between the extremes and create a stable social order. But with that middle class in apparent decline and with the extremes diverging further from each other, it would be easy to conclude that the Marxist vision at last fits America's future.[5]

In Britain there are Marxist Members of Parliament and by the time of publication of this volume possibly black socialist feminist MPs.[6] At the level of the local state, boroughs like Brent are actively attempting to implement socialist, anti-sexist, anti-racist policies. In the Soviet Union, there is a leader who appears to have a vision of a non-nuclear world and a freer and more democratized Eastern Europe.[7]

Notwithstanding its shortcomings, *Schooling in Capitalist America* was an inspiring book with a clear commitment to socialism. Whether Bowles and Gintis' later and current work represents progression or regression is for the reader to judge. Similarly, whether their critics, including the contributors to this volume have made valid and pertinent appraisals and critiques can be more fairly assessed in the light of the contents of part 4 where Samuel Bowles and Herbert Gintis make their reply.

Acknowledgements

I would like to thank Peter MacDonald for his comments on this chapter.

Notes

1 See for example APPLE, M. (1982) 'Curricular form and the logic of technical control' in APPLE, M. (Ed) *Cultural and Economic Reproduction in Education*, London, Routledge and Kegan Paul, APPLE, M. (1980) 'The other side of the hidden curriculum: Correspondence theories and the labour process', *Journal of Education*, 162, winter; ARONOWITZ, S. (1978) 'Marx, Braverman and the Logic of "Capital"', *The Insurgent Sociologist*, 8, Fall; BURAWOY, M. (1979) 'Towards a marxist theory of the labor process: Braverman and beyond', *Politics and Society*, 8, 3/4.

2 While the term 'racism' clearly has substance, 'race' as a concept is problematic and for this reason is in inverted commas. Robert Miles argues against the notion that there exist distinct 'races' since: (a) the extent of genetic variation within any population is usually greater than the average difference between populations; (b) although the frequency of occurrence of different alleles (possible forms taken by genes) does vary from one 'race' to another, any particular genetic combination can be found in almost any 'race'; and (c) owing to inter-breeding and large scale migrations, the distinctions between 'races' identified in terms of polymorphic (dominant gene) frequencies are often blurred (MILES, R. (1982) *Racism and Migrant Labour*, London, Routledge and Kegan Paul P. 16). A good example of Miles' last point can be demonstrated in the Black population of the United States (HERSKOVITS, M. (1958) *The Myth of the Negro Past*, Boston, Beacon Press).

3 COLE, M. (1986a) 'Teaching and learning about racism: A critique of multicultural education in Britain' in MODGIL, S. *et al*, *Multicultural Education: The Interminable Debate*, Lewes, Falmer Press; COLE, M. (1986b) 'Multicultural education and the politics of racism in Britain', *Multicultural Teaching*, 5, 1, autumn; COLE, M. (1987) 'Schooling and the politicization of "race": The need for an anti-racist response', unpublished.

4 EHRENREICH, B. (1986) 'Is the middle class doomed', *The New York Times Magazine*, 7 September.

5 *Ibid.*

6 This is not to suggest or advocate the 'parliamentary road' argument merely to indicate an increasing consciousness among *sections* of the British working class.

7 At the time of writing his commitment to an eventual non-nuclear world seems genuine. The extent to which basic freedoms including the freedom to travel can or will be restored in Eastern Europe remains to be seen.

2 *Contradiction and Reproduction in Educational Theory**

Herbert Gintis and Samuel Bowles

We are often asked how our ideas on education have developed since the publication of our book, *Schooling in Capitalist America.*[1] More specifically, what would we change if we had it to do over again? We must confess that, due to competing research commitments, we have not submitted this issue to a sustained investigation. Thus, in this paper we will limit our treatment to a single question: that of our handling of contradictions within education and contradictions in the capitalist social formation resulting from the specific nature of the eductional system. This question is absolutely fundamental. For as we suggested in our book, creating a truly egalitarian educational system geared toward the full development of students' cognitive, critical, and personal powers requires fundamental social change. But such fundamental social change, involving as it does overcoming the inertial tendencies in social development, can be achieved only by understanding and exploiting the contradictions already present and operative in society.[2] We feel that one of the weaker aspects of our book lies in its weak and possibly voluntaristic political prescriptions for educational change. This weakness flows from an inadequate treatment of the systemic contradictions of advanced capitalism. We shall here sketch how this fault might be repaired.

The Correspondence Principle

In *Schooling in Capitalist America* we began by asking what might be expected of an adequate educational system. We found that three goals were central to the traditional liberal conception of the social role of

*Extract from: (a) Barton, L., Meighan, R. and Walker, S. (Eds) (1980) *Schooling, Ideology and the Curriculum*, Lewes, Falmer Press; and (b) Dale, R. *et al.* (Eds) (1981) *Education and the State: Volume 1: Schooling and the National Interest*. Lewes, Falmer Press.

schooling. First, education should be *egalitarian* in the sense of acting as an effective force for overcoming the natural, social and historical inequities that tend inexorably to arise in society. Second, education should be *developmental* in the sense of providing students with the means to develop the cognitive, physical, emotional, critical, and aesthetic powers they possess as individuals and as human beings. Third, education should be a means of what John Dewey has called the 'social continuity of life'.[3] That is, education should promote the smooth integration of individuals as fully functioning members of society. We then endeavored to show, using a variety of descriptive, historical, and statistical sources that education in advanced capitalism actually *reproduced* social inequality, rather than attenuating it, and acted rather more as a force for *repressing* personal development than fostering it. By contrast, what the schools seemed to do best was precisely to produce the 'good citizen' — its integrative function.

Why this pattern of success and failure? Is it to be found in the educational system itself or in the articulation of the school system with the social structures within which the schools are located? We concluded the latter. Dewey, in *Democracy and Education*, argued that a prerequisite for education's fulfilment of its egalitarian, developmental, and integrative requirements of the citizenry are the abilities to relate to one another equally and reciprocally in controlling their common affairs. Schools that prepare students for this task of life will be necessarily egalitarian. Moreover, full personal development involves precisely the development of those cognitive and other social powers that allow individuals effectively to participate in democratically constituted collectivities and thereby to control their lives.

The critical problem in the articulation of schooling with advanced capitalism, we suggested, lies in its undemocratic structure of control over the process of production. The capitalist enterprise is not characterized by civil liberties, due process, democratic participation, or guaranteed rights. Rather, it is characterized by rights vested in property rather than persons and the control of the production process by capitalists and managerial personnel, giving rise to a class structure quite inimical to democratic principles.

A main proposition in *Schooling in Capitalist America* held that a major objective of capital, in its interventions into the formation and evolution of the educational system, was precisely the preparation of students to be future workers on the various levels in the hierarchy of capitalist production. Given the quite significant success of capital directly and indirectly structuring schools and in the face of the undemocratic nature of economic life, schools could not fulfill their egalitarian and developmental objectives. We concluded that the only means toward the achievement of progressive educational reform is the democratization of economic life, allowing for a democratic and emancipatory school system which does not conflict with the formation of adults capable of effective participation in the system of production.

We also argued specifically that the current relationship between education and economy is ensured not through the *content* of education but its *form*: the social relations of the educational encounter. Education prepares students to be workers through a *correspondence* between the social relations of production and the social relations of education. Like the division of labor in the capitalist enterprise, the educational system is a finely graded hierarchy of authority and control in which competition rather than co-operation governs the relations among participants, and an external reward system — wages in the case of the economy and grades in the case of schools — holds sway. This correspondence principle explains why the schools cannot at the same time promote full personal development and social equality, while integrating students into society. The hierarchical order of the school system, admirably geared towards preparing students for their future positions in the hierarchy of production, limits the development of those personal capacities involving the exercise of reciprocal and mutual democratic participation and reinforces social inequality by legitimating the assignment of students to inherently unequal 'slots' in the social hierarchy.

The correspondence principle, we believe, makes four positive contributions to progressive educational strategy. First, its explanatory value is great. Despite the considerable skepticism which greeted publication of our book, critics have made little headway in overturning our major empirical conclusions. Indeed the one major subsequent statistical investigation of sources of educational and economic success — Christopher Jencks *et al.'s Who Gets Ahead?* — dramatically confirms our own findings.[4] Second, in an era where the failures of liberal school reform have become increasingly evident to policy-makers and the public, the correspondence principle shows a positive alternative. Egalitarian and humanistic education are not unattainable due to some inherent defect in human nature or advanced industrial society, but to the undemocratic nature of participation in economic life. Educational reform requires at the same time economic transformation towards democratic socialism. Third, our formulation rectifies an earlier preoccupation of both liberal and Marxian analysis with the overt content of schooling. By focussing upon the experience of schooling, the correspondence principle provides a consistent analytical framework for understanding the school as an arena of structured social interaction. Fourth, our formulation of the correspondence principle contributes to a more positive understanding of the goals of socialist transition. In older critiques of capitalist society, almost unique stress was laid on the private ownership of means of production. At least as far as educational reform is concerned, we have been able to show that not *ownership*, but *control* is central to social inequities. Merely passing from private to social ownership without challenging in any substantial way the social relations of economic life, can have no impact on the egalitarian and humanistic goals of progressive educational reform. The correspondence principle then represents a powerful antidote to the authoritarian tendencies all too often found in an otherwise progressive socialist movement.

The correspondence principle is, however, not without its problems. The most critical is simply this: by standing, in our approach, as the *only* structural link between education and economy, and by its character as an inherently *harmonious* link between the two, the correspondence principle forced us to adopt a narrow and inadequate appreciation of the *contradictions* involved in the articulation of the educational system within the social totality. Yet as we have stressed, no political strategy can be developed without due attention to the systemic contradictions that can be exploited towards effective and progressive intervention. It is perhaps for this reason that our approach has been variously termed as 'radically functionalist' and imbued with 'missionary pessimism'.

This is not to say that our educational theory has been devoid of principles of contradiction. Indeed, we went to great lengths to demonstrate the 'lack of fit' between education and society at large.[5] Our major contribution in this respect was what we termed the contradiction between *reproduction* and *accumulation* in advanced capitalism. The educational system, we suggested, contributes to the reproduction and legitimation of the social relations of capitalist production. Yet at the same time the tendency of capitalist production is accumulation — the expansion of the wage labor system and the eclipse of older forms of production. This movement leads inevitably to a re-structuring of the social relations of production and a consequent change in the requirements for their reproduction. The contradiction between reproduction and accumulation thus takes the form of the educational system periodically falling *out of harmony* with the evolving structure of capitalist production relations. We do not think the contradiction between reproduction and accumulation is incorrect. Indeed, it is capable of aiding our understanding of both the striking periodicity of educational reform and of the major periods of educational change — such as the Common School Movement, the Progressive Education movement, and most recent the movement for the reform of higher education in the United States. Let us take the latter case as an example.

Many have wondered why such intense opposition to dominant social institutions in the decade of the 1960s occurred predominantly among students in higher education. Our answer, which we still believe correct, ran as follows. The social relations of higher education were laid down in the United States early in the twentieth century to train a professional, managerial, and propertied elite capable of controlling their own lives as well as the lives of others. With the vast increase in the economy's demand for skilled white collar labor after World War II and popular demand for access to higher education, however, higher education had to fill the gap in training students who, far from constituting a quasi-independent élite, were destined to staff the relatively powerless middle levels of the capitalist hierarchy of production. The norms of liberal education, critical thought, and free space for personal expression, all fostered by higher education, clearly failed to provide an adequate affective, normative, or even cognitive preparation for students *en route* to the fragmented, routinized and closely supervised work life of the salaried worker. Whence the material basis for their revolt: a discrepancy between the social relation of education and social relations of production. Indeed, our analysis of the contradictions of higher education has been substantiated by subsequent events. In the United States the response to the student movement in the decade of the 1970s was the move towards the *vocationalization* of higher education: raising tuitions, promoting two-year vocational as opposed to four-year liberal arts schools, redesigning the curriculum to eliminate 'critical thought' in favor of 'occupational skills', and stressing the commuter campus in contrast to the resident university where an oppositional 'youth culture' might develop.[6]

So-called 'back to basics', while having little rationale in terms of either pedagogical or technological reason, may be understood in part as a response to the failure of correspondence between schools and capitalist production brought about by the dynamics of the accumulation process confronting the inertia of the educational structures. This principle of contradiction, however, is clearly insufficient for effective political intervention. For it is purely inertial and passive: education merely *lags behind* a developing economic system. Such a mode of analysis provides no reasons why anything other than a periodic lagging-followed-by-catching-up dynamic might be present in the educational system. This dynamic is hardly absent: indeed it provides a compelling basis for identifying the quite distinct major epochs of educational reform in the United States. Yet it fails to elucidate the dynamic of change internal to the school system. For this reason it provides no clear-cut method for political intervention in the process we have theoretically isolated.

The task of searching for an adequate principle of contradiction between education and economy to supplement the correspondence principle is hampered, we now believe, by the very methodological stance we adopted in analyzing social life. We found ourselves much impressed with the classical Marxian paradigm of base/superstructure, according to which the economic system forms a base of material relations defining the essence of social life, with respect to which such institutions as the family, the state, the educational system, the communications media, and cultural relations in general, appear as mere superstructural reflections. According to this approach contradictions in the economic system can have reverberations in other spheres of social life, but the latter cannot impart any autonomous contradictory effects to the reproduction process as a whole save the inertial non-correspondence which then formed the basis of our reasoning.

It is hardly surprising, then, that we failed to locate a central contradiction in the education/economy relationship.

Sites and Practices

If a social formation is not to be viewed as an economic 'base' with a series of social levels successively stacked on top, how should it be conceived? We suggest that society be treated as an ensemble of structurally articulated *sites of social practice*. By a *site* we mean a cohesive area of social life characterized by a specified set of characteristic social relations or structures. These distinct 'rules of the game' regulate the manifold social practices at each site. Thus the state, the family system, and capitalist production are all sites in a capitalist social formation. Briefly speaking, the site of capitalist production is characterized by private property in the means of production, market exchange, wage labor and capitalist control of production and investment. The state is characterized by the institutions of liberal democracy, and the family site by the structure of power and kinship known as patriarchy.

These three sites — state, family, and site of capitalist production — we take as fundamental to the dynamics of advanced capitalist social formations. In the first instance, they define the three major relations individuals have *vis-à-vis* their society; each person has at the same time a specific citizenship, gender, and class status, and none of these can be understood as flowing simply from the others. Again, each of these sites is independently capable of supporting relations of dominance and subordinacy. Indeed, we would characterize the site of capitalist production as the site of dominance of capital over labor and the family as the site of dominance of men over women. By contrast, the state in its liberal democratic form, while required to reproduce the conditions of domination and subordinacy in family and economy, is not itself necessarily a site of domination. This observation will be important for our analysis of contradictions in the educational system.

The dynamics of a site cannot be deduced from its structure — its characteristic social relations — either alone or in relation to the structure of other sites. Rather, we must view sites as merely *structuring the practices occuring within them*. Practices, in turn, must be seen as neither the effects nor the reflection of structures, but fundamental and irreducible elements of social dynamics. The relation of a site to practices occuring with it is analogous to the relation between a language and a conversation: the language *structures* the conversation in terms of syntax and grammar, while exercising only partial control over the content of communicative exchange. But we must be more precise concerning our use of the term 'practice'. By a *practice* in general we mean a social intervention on the part of an individual, group, or class, whose *object* is some aspect of social reality, and whose *project* is the transformation (or stabilization) of that object. We will lay stress on four basic types of practice — appropriative, political, cultural, and distributive. By an *appropriative practice* we mean labor in its usual sense of transforming nature; its object is the natural world and its project is the creation of useful products. By a *political practice* we mean a social intervention geared to changing the social relations of a site — the 'rules of the game'. The object of a political practice, then, is the structure of a site or its articulation with other sites, and its project is the transformation of these social relationships. By *culture* we mean the ensemble of tools of discourse that a group employs towards exchanging information, expressing states of consciousness, forming bonds of solidarity, and forging common strategies of action. A *cultural practice*, then, is one whose object is culture and whose project is the transformation of the tools of discourse on the basis of which the formation and co-ordination of all group practices can be undertaken. Finally, the object of a *distributive practice* is the distribution of power, income and other desirable social prerogatives, and whose object is effecting a change in this distribution.

In summation, then, a social formation is a structural articulation of sites, and a site is a structure articulating the appropriative, political, cultural, and distributive practices occuring within it.

Our next goal will be to argue that in view of the particular nature of state, family, and economy in an advanced capitalist social formation, these sites articulate as a *contradictory totality*, and that the dynamics of the whole derive from the contradictory nature of this totality.

We may characterize the interaction of sites in general in terms of two dynamic principles: *structural delimitation* and the *transportation of practices across sites*. By delimitation we refer to the constraints placed on the development of a site by the very nature of its articulation with environing sites. By the transportation of practices we refer to the fact that groups, in their struggle and confrontations, do not always limit themselves to practices characteristic of the site in which these struggles occur but will under specific circumstances, attempt to 'transport' practices characteristic of other sites. These two processes, we suggest, account for the possibility of sites articulating as a contradictory totality. An example from the education/economy interaction will serve to clarify these two dynamics. First, it is well known that funding for the educational system and willingness of students to participate depend significantly on its ability to enhance the economic status of its graduates. Thus the requirements for economic success, determined within the site of capitalist production, *structurally delimit* the forms of change open to the educational system, whatever the desires of educational reformers. Indeed, this in part accounts for the very existence of the correspondence principle in education. Conversely, educators intent on improving support for educational expansion, have consciously *transported political practices* from the site of capitalist production to restructure the social relations of education.

These two mechanisms account for the structure of education. We have not characterized the educational system as a site, because rather than exhibiting a uniform set of social relations, schools participate both in the state site and the private economy. By and large, however, the educational system is a sub-site of the state but with radically different principles of internal organization and participation. While the state in general is organized according to the principle of majority rule, the schools are organized according to that of top-down control. The mechanism of structural delimitation penalizes forms of educational change which expose students to political relations not compatible with their future positions as workers by ensuring a limited range of job opportunities for these students. In addition, as Raymond Callahan has shown in *Education and the Cult of Efficiency*[7] educators have not merely passively followed the dictates of structural delimitation, but have actively undertaken the transportation of capitalist practices: they have drawn on the literature and philosophy of business organization to mold the schools into forms favorable to the needs of capital accumulation and reproduction of the subservient position of workers at the site of capitalist production.

These examples, however, take the form of *reproductive* delimitation and transportation. We may equally validly speak of these mechanisms as *contradictory*. In terms of delimitation, contradiction takes the form of distinct sites, developing according to their own internal principles, changing so as to *undermine* the reproduction of the social processes of other sites. Contradictory delimitation in the educational system accounts for many of the concrete ways in which the schools fail to conform to the dictates of the capitalist economy. Let us cite three examples. Two of these relate to the critical location of education as *within* the state yet *serving* the site of capitalist production. First, the formally equal status of women as citizens, gained early in the Twentieth Century, virtually ensures that the state political mechanism will come to supply relatively equal education to men and women. Yet the reproduction of hierarchical relations in the capitalist enterprise has depended on the subordination of women to men. The outcome of this discrepancy is either a delegitimation of the educational system or a delegitimation of the economic subordination of women to men in the economy. Second, a parallel development with respect to blacks and minorities has occurred over the past two decades: their relatively equal position as citizens has produced a great deal more educational equality than the capitalist economy, whose hierarchical relations depend in part on the maintenance of the inferior position of blacks, is capable of matching. Once again, delimitation acts *contrary* to the requisites for reproducing the social relations of capitalist production. A third example of contradictory delimitation has been previously mentioned. The expansion of higher education in the post-World War II period, while serving the needs of the site of capitalist production for white collar wage-labor, has still taken the *form* of traditional liberal arts, quite incompatible with the social relations of the capitalist enterprise. This mechanism, which we previously thought of as simply an inertial dynamic of the educational system, now can be more comprehensively described as a form of contradictory delimitation.

The transportation of practices can also take a contradictory form, through their possible effect of the superposition of practices within a site. In terms of education, as we shall stress in the next section of this paper, contradictory transportation often takes the form of imposing forms of democratic participation in education which have been lifted from the state site, of which the educational system is a sub-site with a distinct structure of social relations.

Before returning to a direct treatment of education, we shall elucidate the two principles of contradictory delimitation and contradictory transportation in terms of the notion of the rights characteristic of the three major sites of advanced capitalist social formation.

Political practices at the site of capitalist production are characterized by *rights vested in property*, the rights being exercised by individuals only insofar as they own property or represent those who do. By contrast, political practices in the liberal democratic state are characterized by *rights vested in persons*, according to which all individuals, as citizens, participate equally (though indirectly through representatives) in the determination of state decisions. Again by contrast, the family site is characterized by *rights vested in adult males* to control the labor and reproduction of women.

The articulation of sites in advanced capitalism as a contradictory totality flows, we maintain, from the discrepancies among these forms of vesting of rights of political participation. This is most evident in the case of the transportation of practices. For instance women, having gained the status of full citizenship in the state site, have struggled in recent years to *extend* rights vested in persons to the family site — in the form of the demand for full equality in family life — where they come into direct confrontation with the principles of patriarchal domination.

Another important instance of the transportation of practices has taken the form of workers demanding, and often succeeding in attaining, the precedence of person rights over property rights at the site of capitalist production. We may cite several types of demands that illustrate this process in the history of the workers' movement from the nineteenth century when even full citizenship rights were only extended to the propertied, to the present. The first is the clear and insistent demands of workers for suffrage: full political participation on the basis of person rather than property or estate. The second is the right of workers to associate and organize common representation *vis-à-vis* employers, superseding the market-mediated confrontation of capital and labor. Third, and manifestly unrealizable under capitalism, is the right to employment, negating the market-determination of rates of unemployment. Fourth, and increasingly important since World War II, has been the demand that the civil rights of equal treatment and due process apply to, and hence dominate, market transactions. Thus the Civil Rights Movement in the United States in the 1960s demanded the equal treatment of blacks and whites by merchants and employers, limiting thereby their powers of unrestricted use and free contract. Similarly, the women's movement in the United States and Europe has demanded equal treatment in the capitalist economy in an attempt to weaken the free exercise of property rights on the part of discriminatory employers. Even workers' struggles for decent occupational safety and health conditions have taken the form not primarily of agreement through collective bargaining but of state regulations governing and restricting all contractual relations. Finally, the increasingly popular social goal of equality of opportunity is simply the application of the liberal concept of equality before the law, but now applied to the capitalist economy itself, where it is manifestly unrealizable within the context of the capitalist class structure.

The positive rights to full participation on the basis of person rather than property has involved as well the demand for *the extension of the spheres of social life governed by formally democratic procedures*. The possibility of popular participation in politics in nineteenth century Europe and the United States rested upon the *laissez-faire* state — the state whose concrete practices and interventions were strictly limited to a restricted range of social decision-making. Indeed, for the 'late developers' in Europe — such as Germany, Italy, and Russia — the reliance on a state actively intervening in the process of capital accumulation increased the stakes involved in the granting of democratic forms tremendously — a fact amply reflected in their twentieth century histories. Yet the *laissez-faire* state could not be contained. In part, of course, capitalists themselves demanded extensions towards economic stabilization and the building of the social infrastructure of capital accumulation. But equally important, citizens have demanded extensions of state practices to cover what were traditionally market-governed determinations.

Three dominant trends have been evident in recent decades. While these recent trends are virtual extensions of the historical logic of transportation of practices, their substance is qualitatively distinct. The first involves the transportation of civil equality to the economic sphere. Equality before the law has been a bourgeois demand since the French Revolution but the right to equal treatment in economic relationships directly expresses the dominance of person over property rights. Yet such have been the explicit demands of women, racial and religious minorities, and immigrant workers. Equally potent, but quite unrealizable under capitalism have been the demands for substantive equality of economic opportunity. A second dominant trend has involved the extension of the concepts of positive right from suffrage and association, won by women and the working class through struggle, to a comprehensive set of minimum rights due an individual by the very fact of citizenship. These demands, which may be called an Economic Bill of Rights, include state-provided services, such as health, education and social security, as well as interventions into private economic transactions, as in the case of occupational health and safety regulations, consumer protective laws, and life-line utility guarantees. Finally, demands for the extension of democracy have taken the form of struggles over the transportation of parliamentary democratic practices to those most sacrosanct arenas of capital control — the production and investment processes. While support for due process and constitutional guarantees have always formed part of twentieth century worker demands, rebellion against 'checking your civil rights at the factory gate' has in recent years blossomed into increasingly self-conscious demands for full workplace democracy and control of investment.

Capitalist social formations, then, are inherently contradictory systems, faced with the difficulty of maintaining the reproductive boundaries between the spheres of application of property rights, person rights, and male prerogatives. Nor has it done an acceptable job of maintaining these boundaries. If our analysis of social struggles presented above is correct, an Achilles heel of the capitalist system lies in its characteristic articulation of the state, economy, family totality. The liberal democratic state is at once the citadel of private property and the instrument of incursions upon this venerable institution. What E.P. Thompson has called the 'logic of the process' of social struggles has taken in part the form of the demand for the dominance of person rights over property and male privilege.[8] These struggles have complemented direct confrontation in family and production sites and can be expected to form an integral element in any effective socialist movement of coming years.

Before turning to the implication of this analysis for education, we must stress one aspect of this dynamic of social struggle: its occurrance wholly *within* the liberal discourse of natural rights. Workers have opposed the domination of capital not by moving outside liberal discourse, but by turning one of its internal principles against another. Socialists have often lamented this tendency of the workers' movement, seeing in it a lack of workers' consciousness of their class condition. Were workers adequately attuned to the true nature of their social condition and aware of their objective interests, it is argued, they would reject liberal discourse in favor of a Marxian analysis of social life. Workers would then demand an end to exploitation and alienated labor and strive for a classless society.

This interpretation of liberal discourse is, however, quite inappropriate, and indeed idealistic. Liberal discourse is not a coherent political philosophy or a set of ideas. Nor was it the creation of the leading classes in society bent on the legitimation of the exploitation of labor.[9] Liberal discourse is the structure of cultural practices in advanced capitalist social formations. As a real ensemble of social relations, it is no more capable of being 'false' or 'true' than is a political or appropriative structure. Rather than reflecting or embodying ideas, it is simply a medium of communication. Like other structures, it in no way determines the acts of communication which occur through it, though it may delimit the range of communicative forms capable of expression within it. Finally, while liberal discourse may be criticized, it can only be transformed *internally*, through the conscious cultural practices of contesting groups. Indeed, this is exactly the way in which liberal discourse has developed through time. To view this fact in proper perspective, we must reject the notion that terms of discourse have 'meanings' in favor of the more operational notion of their having concrete *social uses* and specific *ranges of application* determined by modifiable social conventions.[10]

After a certain point in the industrial revolution, workers ceased operating outside the structure of liberal discourse, and rather began to contest the *use* and *range of application* of its fundamental terms. The conditions surrounding this transformation of discourse varied from country to country, but they generally coincided with workers' receiving concrete gains in the form of political rights and rights of association in return for their acquiescence to the employment of the liberal tools of communicative discourse. They did not, however, leave these tools intact in their bourgeois form. Thus contemporary liberalism, far from being a unified expression of a political philosophy, is itself an internally contradictory system incapable of reproducing the boundaries between the major sites of the advanced capitalist social formation — state, family, and site of capitalist production. In particular, the essence of the demands for democratic socialism are partly expressible through the tools of liberal discourse. Socialism is in part the application of the principle of rights vested in persons to the major institutions of economic life. Its fulfilment involves two major elements. First, the replacement of the political structure of the production process by a fully democratic system of participation and control. Second, in place of capitalist control of investment and growth, a democratic decision process controlled by the groups and communities affected by investment decisions. Similarly, the essence of the demands for women's liberation are easily expressible through the tools of liberal discourse. The subordinate economic position of women can be overturned by applying the principle of the equal rights of citizens to the area of hiring and promotion, in place of the property norms of free contract and hierarchical authority. Similarly the principle of democracy and reciprocity in personal relations is quite adequate to express the basis for a non-patriarchal reorganization of family life.

What then are the limitations of operating within liberal discourse? By couching its fundamental concepts in terms of *person* rights, liberal discourse has difficulty in expressing issues of solidarity and co-operation as goals of political practices. The only generalizable form of bonding recognized in liberal discourse is that of nationality based on common citizenship and culture. Similarly, by relying on concepts of rights, whose use is virtually restricted to procedural issues, any assessment of the *substance* of democracy and participation lies outside its purview. For this reason appeals for solidarity and co-operation must and do transcend liberal discourse, drawing on the discourse of co-operative, family, brotherhood, and community. The actual discourse of socialism is thus an amalgam of liberal discourse and these expressions of bonding normally banished to the hinterlands of the political idiom.

Education and the Contradictions of Social Life

The central contradiction in the educational systems of advanced capitalist society derives from two aspects of its location in the social totality. First, it forms in general a subsystem of the state site, and therefore is directly subject to the principle of rights vested in persons. Second, education plays a central role in reproducing the political structure of the capitalist production process, which in turn is legitimated in terms of rights vested in property. Thus education is directly involved in the contradictory articulation of sites in advanced capitalism and is expressed in terms of the property/person dichotomy: education reproduces rights vested in property while itself organized in terms of rights vested in persons.

We have emphasized that it is the *form* of the educational encounter — the social relations of education — that accounts for both its capacity to reproduce capitalist relations of production and its inability to promote domination and healthy personal development. The actual *content* of the curriculum has little role to play in this process. The contradictory location of the educational system can also be described in terms of its characteristic *form* of discourse, as opposed to the actual *content* of the curriculum. The form is that of the cultural structure of liberal discourse.

That liberal discourse has become the predominant cultural-structural form for the constitution of class and gender demands can certainly not be attributed to the educational system alone. Indeed, we have elsewhere argued that the hegemony of liberal discourse in class and gender struggles depended on an historically specific 'accord', arriving at different times in different countries. By an accord, we mean a mutually accepted joint redefinition and consequent reconstitution of political reality by antagonistic classes or class fragments. Through an accord, class interests are redefined. Class identities are respecified so as to produce a novel logic of social action. An accord is a reorganization of society on two levels: institutions and communicative tools of political discourse. On the institutional level, the accord results in the admission of a new set of organizational forms (associations, unions, commission, electoral laws and practices, etc.) and corresponding to these a new specification of organizational legitimacy. On the communicative level, the accord results in the creation of new communicative tools which (a) provide a common framework for political discourse across contending groups, (b) express the moral legitimacy of the newly created institutional nexuses, (c) are admitted by speakers and hearers as intelligible and worthy of affirmation, and (d) are affirmed in all the major formal institutions of daily life (media, political speeches, educational institutions, churches, law). In short, it is the coming into being of a new set of 'rules of the game' of political discourse and struggle.

An accord is likely to set into motion a totally new logic of social action and class struggle. On the institutional level, the existence of new organizations implies a redefined distribution of political power and a consequently redefined constellation of viable political strategies available to social groups. The new set of tools of communicative discourse, endowed with a new effectiveness by the very institutional forms they express and legitimate, will tend to force out of the political arena older forms of discourse (in the case of the capital/labor accord, for instance, theological and socialist forms) and the organizations that support them. These new tools will in turn represent the only available means of political communication and, thus, will be the basis for any future expression and organization of political demands (until, of course, the accord is destroyed).

The accords giving rise to the current logic of class struggle in advanced capitalist countries occurred in the first decades of the twentieth century, and took distinct forms in each social formation concerned. in nearly all cases the working class was granted suffrage and the right to form workers' associations; in turn, elites have isolated and eliminated revolutionary socialist alternatives. The results were as varied as the conditions giving rise to the heightening of class confrontation. In Northern Europe, the smooth transition to social democracy resulted; in Germany, Italy, and Eastern Europe, the result was the total rupture of political life and the rise of fascism. In the United States, the Progressive Era witnessed the transition from *laissez-faire* to monopoly capitalism, the rise of 'safe' unionism and the squelching of hitherto growing socialist and populist movements.

Thus while the educational system cannot be cited as the source of the near universality of liberal discourse, it certainly has played a central role in its reproduction. Whatever the actual content of the political philosophy and social theory presented in schools, the educational system in the twentieth century surely has provided students with little facility in any but modes of discourse based on natural rights. This contradictory position of education explains its dual progressive/reproductive role (promoting equality, democracy, toleration, rationality, inalienable rights, on the one hand, while legitimating inequality, authoritarianism, fragmentation, prejudice, and submission on the other) and is, in part, a reflection of the stress in liberal discourse on procedure over substance. But it provides as well the tools by means of which it can be transformed into an instrument in the transition to socialism: the exploitation of the contradictions that have come to inhere in the tools of liberal discourse. The goals of progressive educational reform must be framed within the structural boundaries of liberal discourse, and can be simply expressed as the full democratization of education. These goals can be divided into two complementary projects: the democratization of the social relations of education, and the reformulation of the issue of democracy in the curriculum.

We have stressed in *Schooling in Capitalist America* that the transformation of the schools cannot proceed without parallel developments at the site of capitalist production. Demands for the democratization of the social relations of education therefore are likely to be effective only in the context of workers' demands for the democratization of the production process — in short, for the full development of workers' control. The first step in the democratization of education is a similar move toward teachers' and parents' control of the educational process. For teachers, as workers, will surely be involved in the movement for the democratization of economic life and parents, as community members, will similarly be involved in the extension of the powers of local community decision-making.

Beyond this, the philosophy of education must develop in the direction that personal development through schooling be geared toward rendering students capable of controlling their lives as citizens, family members, workers, and community members. In particular, the educational process must be structured so that students gradually come to control increasingly substantial spheres of their education as they move from early to later levels of schooling. Current theories of progressive education stress that students be given free rein to develop their individual personalities, to be self-motivated and self-actualizing. While the substance of such educational reforms must be conserved, they can be criticized in general for their failure to recognize the inherently *social* character of educational formation. As we emphasized in our book, there is no 'true self' to emerge prior to the concrete social interactions that individuals experience. This is not to say that individuals are infinitely malleable or that they should be subjected to rigidly conformist schooling. Rather, it is to say that the ineluctibly social impact of education cannot be ignored.

The admirable quality of the self-development philosophy of education lies in the power it draws from embracing a central category of the discourse of rights: the right to freedom from unwarranted interference, of which John Stuart Mill was the most eloquent exponent. Its drawback, of being incurably a-social, is easily remedied by recourse to the communitarian emphasis on joint democratic control of conditions of social life by affected groups and individuals. No doubt there are formidable obstacles in the development of such a philosophy of educational structure and we are not personally equipped to meet this task. But it remains central to the growth of an effective movement toward socialist education.

Finally, progressive educators must exploit the internal contradictions of liberal discourse by developing curricula which dramatize the major oppositions inherent in the joint advocacy of rights vested in persons and property. Moreover, it must emphasize the subordination of property and gender rights to person rights in a just society. This of course does not preclude some emphasis on the proper role for property and gender rights as adjuncts and supports for rights vested in persons — for instance a woman's right to choose when to conceive and bear a child independent of the preference of the natural father, or an individual's rights to personal (not productive) property free from social interference.

Liberalism puts forth a promise it cannot make good. The promise it extends is that of democracy, equality, liberty, and personal fulfilment for all, within the context of capitalism. Unlike traditional theology's balm of beatific after-life, this promise is in the here and now and it is the codification of two centuries of struggles, ideals, and aspirations by oppressed groups in capitalist society. The emptiness of its promise must be exposed and this, indeed, has been the project of socialists over the years. Socialism, should it come to pass in the adanced capitalist countries, will however have little to do with the inevitable process of advancing forces of production bursting asunder their capitalist shackles. Rather, it will be the real fulfilment of the liberal promise, and with it the transformation of tools of communicative discourse of capitalism. Our arguments in this paper are no doubt sitting ducks for misinterpretation and calumny. Are we not justifying liberalism? Are we not advocating socialism as its logical culmination? No. We are arguing that liberal discourse is a fact not a defeat. It is a site of intervention and it embodies the emancipatory achievements of the popular classes. The logical culmination, if it have any, is its own demise. In what way depends on conscious choices of political actors. 'As soon as democracy shows a disposition . . . to become an instrument of the real interests of the people', as Rosa Luxembourg has noted, 'the democratic forms themselves are sacrificed by the bourgeoisie and their representatives'. Yet for all that, socialism remains the extension of democratic freedoms from civil and political life to economic life itself.

Notes

1 Bowles, S. and Gintis, H. (1976) *Schooling in Capitalist America*, London, Routledge and Kegan Paul.
2 *Ibid.* chapter 11.
3 Dewey, J. (1966) *Democracy and Education*, New York, The Free Press.
4 Jencks, C., Bartlett, S., Corcoran, M., Crouse, J., Eaglesfield, D., Jackson, G., McLelland, K., Mueser, P., Olneck, M., Schwartz, J., Ward, S. and Williams, J. (1980) *Who Gets Ahead*? New York, Basic Books.
5 See especially Bowles, S. and Gintis, H. (1976) *op. cit.*, chapters 9 and 11.
6 The Carnegie Commission on Higher Education, (1973) *Priorities for Action*, New York, McGraw-Hill Book Company; Keniston, K. and the Carnegie

COUNCIL ON CHILDREN, (1977) *All Our Children*, New York, Harcourt, Brace, Jovanovich.

7 CALLAHAN, R. (1962) *Education and the Cult of Efficiency*, Chicago, University of Chicago Press.

8 THOMPSON, E.P. (1979) *The Poverty of Theory and Other Essays*, London, Merlin Press.

9 The analysis of liberal discourse as the outcome of class struggles in the early stages of capitalist development is made in GINTIS, H. (1980) 'Theory, practice, and the tools of communicative discourse', *Socialist Review*, spring.

10 This type of analysis of social discourse was first developed by the philosopher Ludwig Wittgenstein, and has never been adequately developed in social theory. See GINTIS, H. (1980) *op. cit.*

3 *Contradictions in the Educational Theory of Gintis and Bowles**

Since its publication in 1976, Bowles and Gintis's *Schooling in Capitalist America* (hereinafter referred to as *Schooling*) has received a considerable amount of attention mostly from those sympathetic to its commitment, but critical of its economistic base/super-structure analysis. In 'Contradiction and reproduction in educational theory' Gintis and Bowles reply to the criticism of *Schooling* but limit their reply to a single question — their handling of contradictions within education and contradictions in the capitalist social formation resulting from the specific nature of the educational system. The article begins with a defence of 'the correspondence principle', continues with a formulation of sites and practices and concludes with an evaluation of the potential of liberal discourse.

In this paper, I will attempt to analyze some of the claims made by Gintis and Bowles in their article.

My main arguments are that their theory of sites and practices, though weakly formulated, is a considerable improvement on their earlier economism and that such an analysis has important progressive potential for future theoretical development but that their continued defence of the correspondence principle is misguided and, in fact, the principle *can* have reactionary rather than progressive implications and that their (pluralist) theory of the state and idealist exaltation of liberal discourse *does* have reactionary implications. I will sugest that liberal discourse, far from having liberating potential, is reformist and that, in fact, discourse must be made socialist, feminist and anti-racist in order for it to have implications for progressive change. I am aware that Bowles and Gintis and Gintis and Bowles need to be situated. They are writing specifically *about* the United States and also in the United States. Is it the case, therefore, that the American educational apparatus *is* more functionally subservient to capital on the one hand and is it the case, on the other, that there are more constraints on socialist writing in the USA? In answer to the first question, it

*Extract from *The Sociological Review*, 31. 3, August 1983, pp. 471–88.

would seem to me that struggles within the American educational system have been well documented so as to make a 'European Marxist' analysis a worthwhile challenge. (Indeed, this is currently being attempted by, for example, Henry Giroux.) Secondly, although there are indeed more constraints on advocating socialism in the United States, Bowles and Gintis, as declared revolutionary socialists (in *Schooling*), have little need or reason to tread warily.

In this paper I have tended to examine the implications of their arguments for analyzing educational systems in capitalist societies in general. While there have been different class histories in different social formations, educational systems in capitalist societies have enough in common to encourage an attempt to formulate a general theory which can then be applied to *specific* capitalist social formations. Since Britain and the United States are the countries with which I am most familiar, it is these countries to which I tend to test the applicability of their theory.

Contradictions in the Educational Theory of Gintis and Bowles

The best reviews of Bowles and Gintis's *Schooling in Capitalist America*[1] have recognized the importance of the work and the great contribution it made to the development of economic and sociological understanding.[2]

These reviews also noted a number of weaknesses in the analysis. In 'Contradiction and reproduction in educational theory,'[3] Gintis and Bowles attempt to deal with what they describe as *Schooling's* 'inadequate treatment of the systematic contradictions of advanced capitalism', 'one of the weaker aspects of our book', (page 16 of this volume).

They begin by a brief summary of *Schooling*, in particular the 'correspondence principle', and argue that it makes four positive contributions to progressive educational strategy. These are: (i) its explanatory power is great; (ii) it implies that educational reform requires at the same time economic transformation towards democratic socialism; (iii) it rectifies earlier preoccupations with content and provides a framework for an analysis of structural social interaction; (iv) it stresses control as well as ownership.

In order to begin to evaluate the claims, it is necessary to define the 'correspondence principle'. According to Bowles and Gintis, 'the educational system helps integrate youth into the economic system . . . through a structural correspondence between its social relations and those of production.[4] The description of the correspondence, they acknowledge, 'has been documented many times', but they maintain that attempts at statistical verification are recent. I would agree, in fact, that this is probably the most interesting feature of the book, notwithstanding certain criticisms of specific statistical techniques and claims.[5] I would now like to look, one by one, at their claims that 'the principle' has inherent potential for 'progressive' strategy. First of all, its explanatory power: while it may be true that it does attempt to explain, in a deterministic way, that there is a relationship between schooling and production, this in itself does not necessarily lead to any progressive interpretation or action. Indeed, Madan Sarup has picked out a quote from *Schooling* which epitomizes their structural-functionalist view of people's passivity. 'To reproduce the labour force, the schools are *destined* to legitimate inequality, limit personal development for forms compatible with *submission to arbitrary authority and aid in the process whereby youth are resigned to their fate*' (my emphasis).[6] It is true that Bowles and Gintis do advocate progressive action but this suggestion is tacked on concluding sections of the book and is certainly not an integral part of their discussion of the 'correspondence principle'; yet it is, of course, in production and (to a lesser extent) in education where real struggles are taking place.

Their second point is that the 'correspondence principle' implies the need for democratic socialism. This it certainly does not, except perhaps in the sense that it implies the futility of transforming education from within. In itself it does not imply democratic socialism. Much has to be applied to infer this need. In fact it is again only the concluding chapters of the book which take up this issue. Moreover, an unquestioning acceptance of the 'correspondence principle' can produce a reactionary rather than progressive response. Some of my student teachers have even looked upon the principle as reassuring in its promise of stability and the maintenance of the status quo, while others, with a more radical mind, have despaired at the seeming lack of space for individual and collective action. Thirdly, Gintis and Bowles claim, the principle rectifies preoccupations with content and provides a framework for an analysis of structured social interaction. By 'rectifying preoccupations with content', presumably they mean that by emphasizing form (for example, hierarchical relations) they are spurring on demands for democratization. However, as I argue later, *their* preoccupation with *form* has some reactionary connotations. Their claim that 'the principle' provides a framework for an analysis of structured social interaction is even more difficult to substantiate. It is, in fact, their obsession with the macro level which precludes a useful analysis at the level of interaction and makes it difficult for teachers to relate their work in the classrooms to the functions which Bowles and Gintis say the education system is performing.[7]

Finally, 'the correspondence principle', they argue, is progressive because it stresses control as well as ownership. While I would agree with their view of the importance of stressing 'control' and their condemnation of 'authoritarian tendencies in [the] socialist movement' I fear that the notion of control inherent in the 'correspondence principle' is not, in itself, progressive. In fact, probably one of the weakest aspects of the book (and the 'Contradictions' paper) is Bowles and Gintis's stubborn refusal to enter into forms of neo-Marxism which have emphasized control. As has been widely remarked, a serious application, of, for example, Gramsci's concept of hegemony, i.e. the fusion of economic, political, intellectual and moral leadership which is brought about by one fundamental group, and groups allied to it, through ideology (a considerable enrichment of crude notions of class control), would have greatly enhanced their work.[8] Not only would an awareness of hegemony have extended understanding of the nature of control in capitalist society (its constant tensions and ensuing struggles) it would have also revealed space in which counter-hegemonic practices by teachers and others could be enacted. To sum up then, while the 'correspondence principle' has progressive implications in contributing to the demystification of the relationships between capitalism and schooling, its radical promise is not realized because of contradictions within the principle itself. Thus, while it undermines both liberal and conservative analyses of that relationship its inherent functionalist presuppositions inhibit purposeful progressive action.

One of the most telling critiques of the principle is provided by Paul Willis.[9] (Although his research was conducted in Britain, similar conclusions may well be applicable to capitalist countries in general.) Willis, in fact, turns the correspondence principle on its head. Schooling delivers 'the lads' as compliant factory workers by *failing*. By stressing cultural patterns which, given the dialectic between penetrations and limitations, end in stabilization, Willis advances us considerably from crude mechanistic economism. Here neo-Marxism of the European variety is at its best, with its emphasis on culture and hegemony on lived experience and struggle. However, even the process outlined by Willis is only partially successful for capital. As Simon Frith argues, the Manpower Services Commission (MSC) in Britain, while ostensibly existing to teach specific skills to young people, in fact exists to create a more disciplined, flexible and accepting workforce, needed by capitalism in crisis and at this stage of its development.[10] Here is one way in which the state intervenes in a very direct and forceful manner. Simple correspondence is not apparent. Having attempted to defend 'the correspondence principle' Gintis and Bowles then address themselves to the specific criticism of functionalism which has been levelled at them. They begin by rejecting their espousal in *Schooling* of a simplistic base/superstructure model where the base has a 'series of social levels stacked on top'. However, it is pertinent to ask why they ever had such a model in the first place. As Althusser has argued such economism is a mere inversion of Hegel: 'While for Hegel, the politico-ideological was the essence of the economic', a reading of Marx which reduces the dialectic of history to the 'dialectic generating the successive modes of production' is to simply make 'the economic . . . the essence of the politico-ideological'.[11] They go on to search for a conception of the social formation which can reveal 'a central contradiction in the education/economy relationship'. This sounds promising. Have they discovered European neo-Marxism at last? Have they realized that levels do not simply correspond but are complex, uneven and contradictory? The answer is 'yes and no'. 'Yes' because their attempt to locate this contradiction in order to open up space for struggles does draw on an (albeit weak) formulation of society as 'an ensemble of structurally articulated sites of social practice'; 'no' because no debt is paid, no reference made to the theoretical work of any Marxist on which their own work is based (notwithstanding a rhetorical quote from Rosa Luxemburg at the end). This is surprising since their formulation is reminiscent of 'relative autonomy' and their definition of 'practice' (which is structured, but not determined by sites), as 'a social intervention on the part of an individual, group, or class whose *object* is some aspect of social reality and whose *project* is the transformation (or stabilization) of that object' recalls Althusser's discussion of Generalities I, II and III.[12] What, then, we are forced to ask, is the source of *their* tradition? There is, of course, an American tradition and I do not wish to deny the important contributions made by American Marxism, represented in the influential work of Baran and Sweezy and, more recently, Braverman. Even Braverman, however, underestimates worker resistance to the capitalist labour process and his work needs to be supplemented by theories which stress struggle, for example, the theory of hegemony. In reformulating basic European neo-Marxist categories, Gintis and Bowles are clearly aware of this theoretical weakness, but why don't they spell it out? Are they trying to build an American neo-Marxism by default?

Gintis and Bowles locate three major sites; capitalist production, the family and the state system. Why three, and not four, five or six; why these and not others they do not say. The definition of the first rightly asserts that it is characterized by private property in the means of production, market exchange, wage labour, and capitalist control of production and investment. However, it would have been useful to have stressed and explained the extraction of the surplus, this being the source of exploitation — what they refer to as the 'dominance of capital over labour'. They then differentiate it from the family which they describe as the site of dominance of men over women.

In so arguing, they fail to realize that production is also the site of dominance of men over women (women do more menial jobs, earn less money, are almost invariably dominated by men by their subordinate positions and greater propensity for being removed to the 'reserve army').[13] Interestingly Gintis and Bowles show awareness, further on in the paper, of the importance to capital of women's subordination; 'the reproduction of hierarchical relations in the capitalist enterprise has depended on the subordination of women to men, (page 23 of this volume). Why, then, do they not incorporate this in their definition? Furthermore, in describing the family as (only) the dominance of men over women they seem to ignore the fact that the family, when thought of as a second site of the labour process, is also the site of dominance of capital over labour.[14]

Finally, I would question the use of the term 'family', since it implies the conventional nuclear form. 'Household' might be a more appropriate term, since this can encompass the varied living patterns apparent in contemporary capitalist societies. It can include couples of the same sex or opposite sex living together, it can include group forms and it can include one-parent families. The arguments pertaining to the dominance of men over women would still apply in the majority of cases although in some cases, for example one-parent (i.e. mother!) families the dominance may be seen as equally (or more) apparent but perhaps less direct and of a different form. In other words the father is still directing the upbringing of the children, is still making this the responsibility of the woman but from a distance. (This is not, of course, to deny the fact that a number of women bring up children without male influence.)

The state, they claim, in its liberal democratic form, 'while required to reproduce the condition of domination and subordinancy in family and economy is not itself necessarily a site of domination' (p. 21). Whether the state retains its 'liberal democratic' form is problematic. Many neo-Marxist writers argue that we are witnessing the move, especially in Britain and the United States, towards a new form of the state, a more authoritarian, law-and-order populist state (see, for example, the recent contributions in the journal *Marxism Today*). Moreover, this assertion contains a contradiction. If the state is reproducing the conditions of domination in family and economy, how can it be 'not itself necessarily a site of domination'? As I will show their theory of the state is pluralist. This allows for the assertion of its 'possible neutrality' but doesn't resolve the contradiction. Pluralism is, of course, rejected by all Marxist theorists of the state.[15] Also contested by Marxist theorists is the idea that the state is synonomous with government,[16] which seems to be Gintis and Bowles's contention since they claim that it is 'organized according to the principle of majority rule', unlike the schools which are 'organized according to . . . top down control'. Modern Marxist concepts of the capitalist state have incorporated a complex of institutions including, for example, the higher echelons of the civil service, the judiciary, the military, the welfare (as well as the political). Such institutions, of course, do not exhibit democracy, do not have 'radically different principles of internal organization and participation' (p. 23) to the educational system.

Even if we work within Gintis and Bowles's narrow conception of the state as government, 'majority rule' is still far from a reality. Apart from the simple observation that 'majority rule', is, in fact, rarely that — the government in power is not often elected on account of the support of *the majority* of the population of a given country — there are strong grounds to contest conceptions of 'democracy' which stress a severely limited five-yearly choice of electing a representative (who does not usually fulfil her/his promises anyway!). Democracy thus defined points to the limitations of liberal discourse which, as we shall shortly see, Gintis and Bowles put so much trust in. What seems to have happened, in fact, in 'Contradiction and reproduction in educational theory' is that the tendency in *Schooling* towards a worrying 'faith' in the liberal democratic state has become a fully fledged pluralism. In contrast to the '*rights vested in property*' (p. 24) at the site of production, we are told that 'political practices in the liberal democratic state are characterized by rights vested in persons, according to which all individuals, as citizens, participate equally (though indirectly through representatives) in the determination of state decisions'. Their unquestioned acceptance of the state as truly democratic extends beyond white males. Blacks, we are told, have a 'relatively equal position as citizens' (p. 23) while women have 'gained the status of full citizenship in the state' (p. 24). There are two problems with these assertions. The first is semantic; to differentiate between 'blacks' and 'women' is problematic since half of the former category are of course 'women' and many of the latter are, of course, 'black'. As I have argued elsewhere, to refer to 'blacks' in one category and 'women' in another allows our 'conditioned' minds to read 'black male' for 'black' and 'white women' for women, thereby denying black women an identity.[17] It exemplifies the inherent sexist (and racist) nature of liberal discourse and is a further indication of its limitations.

The second problem is that it is simply not true that black and white women and black men have acquired equality as citizens (or indeed the implicit corollary that white men had it already). Gintis and Bowles do distinguish substantive from formal democracy, but only in passing — this is not developed. Even if we leave aside the top of the civil service, the judiciary and the military, (where in the USA black and white women and black men are very poorly represented) and again work within Gintis and Bowles's narrow conception of the state as 'government', here also the number of black and white women and black men is extremely low.[18] Furthermore, in terms of everyday experience, the *rights* of black and white women and black men on the one hand and white men on the other are not equal; for example, women can't walk into a bar alone or even, at times, along the street without being hassled. Black women and men, of course, suffer the limitations imposed by a racist society, unlike white men.

Nevertheless, a theory of the social formation which stresses sites and practices is certainly useful if still underdeveloped and imprecise. As the Education Group of the Centre for Contemporary Cultural Studies argue, 'site' indicates a particular social space but also has the useful connotation of institutional or material hardness.[19] Paradoxically, I would maintain that the theory of sites and practices has potential in the analysis of *struggle*. Characteristically, Gintis and Bowles use it to emphasise domination (and passivity) at the sites of the family and production and even assimilation and concomitant 'race' and gender equality at the site of the state. If, however, we tease out the implications of the Gintis and Bowles' definition of 'practice' (a conception which, I suggested, may have been appropriated, albeit usefully, from Althusser) which is concerned with 'a social intervention on the part of an individual, group or class whose *object* is some aspect of social reality and whose *project* is the transformation (or stabilization) of that object', we are better able to formulate analyses of struggle rather than domination/passivity. Intervention by groups is an important feature of contemporary capitalist society. This is particularly apparent between certain groups and the state. I would like to briefly mention several relevant instances. Women's groups in Britain, for example, are intensifying struggle, are transforming social practice across and between sites. Increasingly, the site where the state, defined in a Marxist sense, meets women's groups is the street (a central site in both Britain and the United States but unmentioned by Gintis and Bowles). Women in Britain responded to the state's 'institutional hardness' witnessed, for example, by a recent judicial verdict on a rape case, which implied that women who hitchhike at night are in a sense 'asking for it' and (since the offender was merely fined) that there is a small price (literally) for men to pay for rape, by a number of successful 'Reclaim the night' street protests. More recently, the very impressive women's peace camp at Greenham Common and subsequent mass women's demonstrations in support has had a major impact on thinking about CND. Here women were seen to transform social practice from the household site to that of the street site. Many brought photographs of loved ones and items of personal significance and attached them to the fence of the base where the cruise missiles are intended to be situated. The very act of 'embracing the base' may also be viewed as transforming of social practice from household to street. The street site is also the site where confrontations between the state and young black females and males is most apparent. Recent statements by leading police authorities have warned black youths to stay off the streets and, although not specifically naming black youths, have stressed the necessity of harassing a minority of inner-city dwellers 'not fit to salvage'. Such statements, *even* if not directed at blacks, could be used to justify their harassment, a form of policing which now seems a regular feature of the inner city.

The response of black (and white) youth in Britain is exemplified by 'the riots' of 1980 and 1981. (Such 'riots' are not, of course, confined to Britain. Forty-eight hours of street struggle between blacks and the police in Miami has just been announced, at the time of writing.) Gintis and Bowles then begin a discussion of one of the main planks of their argument, namely that the dynamic of social struggle occurs 'wholly *within* the liberal discourse of natural rights'. Earlier they had noted that sites structured the practices occurring within them but that practices were not determined by sites. Practices they defined as 'a social intervention on the part of an individual, group, or class, whose *object* is some aspect of social reality, and whose *project* is the transformation (or stabilization) of that object.' A 'cultural practice' they went on to define as a practice 'whose object is culture and whose project is the transformation of the tools of discourse on the basis of which the formation and co-ordination of all group practices can be undertaken' (p. 22).

What then of the potential for transforming liberal discourse? Rightly they stress that while it can be criticized, it can only be transformed *internally*, through the conscious cultural practices of contesting groups. However, it is clear that Gintis and Bowles do not favour the transformation of liberal discourse, certainly not into socialist discourse. Socialist attempts to argue for its replacement by a Marxist analysis are described as 'idealistic' (p. 26). Liberal discourse is not, they claim, an embodiment of ideas, simply a medium of communication (pp. 26–7). This, however, contradicts their final description of it as a 'site of intervention embodying the emancipatory achievements of the popular classes' (p. 31). In fact, I would argue, it is both a medium of communication with 'concrete social uses and specific ranges of application' (p. 27) and the embodiment of ideas. While agreeing with Gintis and Bowles that we need to change its *use* we also need to change its content, i.e. make it socialist. Gramsci, for one, insisted on this: 'the content of language must be changed even if it is difficult to have an exact consciousness of the change in immediate terms'[20]. In fact, Gintis and Bowles's discussion of 'accords' as 'mutually accepted joint redefinition(s) and consequent reconstruction(s) of political reality by antagonistic classes or class fragments' (p. 28) would indicate that they agree with the importance of content. Socialists, they later argue, must expose 'the emptiness of its promise' (p. 31). This all seems very contradictory until we remember that Gintis and Bowles's theory of the state is pluralist. Equality, for them, has already been achieved for all in civil life. Liberal discourse can almost move us towards equality in economic life. One thing is missing. To them, 'the actual discourse of socialism is . . . an amalgam of liberal discourse and . . . expressions of bonding normally banished to the hinterlands of the political idiom' (p. 28). 'Rights vested in person's equal rights of citizens' (p. 27) need only to be coupled with basic psychological drives (for example, familial) and we are in the realm of revolutionary discourse. The struggle for socialism is to be waged on the terrain of juridico-political ideology and informed by a reductionist geneticism.

If this were the case, there would be no need for Marx's *Capital* (or even for Bowles and Gintis's *Schooling*). If commodities could be defetishised with the application of genetics to liberal discourse, if profit revealed itself relatively openly as surplus value, who would need a labour theory of value? Poulantzas has expressed well the ideological content of liberal discourse:[21]

> the unity of the ideological is not derived from some kind of genetic relation to a class-subject and its class consciousness. It is derived fundamentally from the relation between ideology and human

> experience in a formation, and to the imaginary form which this relation takes on. As opposed to science ideology has the precise function of hiding the real contradictions and of *reconstituting* on an imaginary level *a relatively coherent discourse which serves as the horizon of agents' experience . . . In other words, the structures of ideological and scientific discourse are fundamentally different* . . . (my emphasis).

In total opposition to Gintis and Bowles, Poulantzas sees concepts like 'equality', 'rights', 'individuals/persons' as not in need of amalgamation with 'bonding discourse' to create socialist discourse but as 'the catchwords under which bourgeois class exploitation entered and ruled in history'.[22] He stresses the derivation of such concepts from juridico-political ideology which he sees as the most appropriate ideology to the capitalist mode of production in that it 'separates and unties', sets up 'individuals/persons' 'subjects of law' who are 'free' and 'equal', one to the other[23]. It is, I would suggest, this ideology and its attendant discourse to which Gintis and Bowles have fallen victim.

Far from liberal discourse being liberating, it, in fact, 'conceals class exploitation in a specific manner *to the extent that all trace of class domination is systematically absent from its language'*[24].

Our counter-hegemonic role as socialists must surely be to demystify slogans, like 'a fair day's work for a fair day's pay',[26] 'ladies first', 'preferring your own kind is only natural'. Liberal discourse must give way to a discourse which makes *socialism* 'common sense', a discourse which is Marxist/feminist, anti-racist in form and content as well as progressive in potential. As Lenin reminded us, 'the *interests* of some class or other are behind all moral, religious, political and social phrases, declarations and promises.' With Larrain, I would agree that crucial qualifications need to be made with respect to 'religion'[26] but, bearing this in mind, I would maintain that this dictum must be carefully borne in mind when formulating struggle at various levels in capitalist society. It is a very different interpretation of liberal discourse to Gintis and Bowles's notion of an 'ensemble of social relations . . . [not] capable of being 'false' or 'true' [and which] *in no way* determines the acts of communication which occur through it' (pp. 26–7) (my emphasis).

We need therefore to develop *our own discourse, discourse in the interests* of the people in general and which is specifically anti-sexist and anti-racist. The thrust of my argument should not be taken to imply that no concepts within liberal discourse can be applicable to socialist, feminist and anti-racist discourse. The point is that many need to be demystified and/or qualified. Many nineteenth-century bourgeois conceptions have already been successfully challenged, and have taken on socialist connotations, for example,

liberty — liberation

democracy	—	democratic socialism
upper class	—	ruling class
lower class	—	working class

Significant strides have of course been made in feminist and anti-racist discourse. For example, in the first case the way in which language is couched in male-related terms is being constantly undermined. Just as the interests of the ruling class are behind liberal discourse, so too are the interests of the male sex.

As Dale Spender points out, language is primarily the property of the male. Women remain 'outsiders', 'borrowers' of language.[27]

> So, although it is readily demonstrable that both sexes use the language, this cannot be taken as sufficient evidence that both sexes stand in the same relationship to that language . . . historically and currently — men have held greater 'rights' to language . . . This monopoly over language is one of the means by which males have ensured their own primacy, and consequently have ensured the invisibility or 'other' nature of females, and this primacy is perpetuated while women continue to use, unchanged, the language which [they] have inherited.

We need, she says, to 'unmask some of the mechanisms whereby the male supremacist society is maintained through language'.

It is not, she argues, just that women do not see themselves as encompassed in the he/man symbol, men do not see them either. The effect that 'man' includes puts women on the defensive and allows men to treat women as 'unreasonable' if they enquire of a speaker as to whether they are included in 'mankind' or 'man'. Frequently the replies tend to be patronising: '*Everyone knows* that *man embraces women*'.[28] Some women have, in fact, so rejected 'man-made language' that they are attempting to purge of sexism all words which have become semantically misappropriated. Thus, for example, they are using the spelling 'wimmin' rather than 'women' to describe themselves.[29] Spender is hopeful about the future.[30]

> Women-centred meanings will multiply as the pattern of women's existence begins to emerge, women will gain confidence from this emerging reality and will make greater efforts in shaping it. As they do so, they will make a contribution towards changing society and its rules for making sense of the world . . . Male-defined meanings are so pervasive in patriarchal order and alternative women-centred meanings are so few that the effort to encode and preserve the women-centred meanings must be constant.

The development of an anti-racist discourse is also crucial. Young people of African and Asian descent refer to themselves (proudly) as they are ('black' as opposed to 'white'), rather than using the cautiously ambiguous term, the derogatory term, 'coloureds' so long prominent in liberal discourse. The Rastafarian movement is of considerable importance. As Gilroy has argued[31]

> It is often forgotten that blacks arrived here bearing traditions of anti-colonial struggle wherever they set out from. Older West Indians have encountered the discourse of Rasta before, and though sometimes critical of it, many . . . were happy to recount tales of their contact with the Garveyites 'at home' . . . the solidarity [the movement] provides the whole community appears to offer a refuge from the new pressures of *popular* racism.

Rasta discourse, he argues, is communalist and able to convey commitment in a selective or intermittent manner. It invites speakers, furthermore, to appropriate the ideas which appeal to them without being pigeonholed by the oppressor. The operation of a shared language 'far more than the colours and vestimentary codes of dread style, marks the frontiers of a discursive community in which deep disagreement is possible without condemnation or schism'.

Marxist analyses of race are directed at understanding historically and materially specific ideologies of racism within the context of the uneven development of capitalism, rather than with 'understanding discrimination'. They are concerned with 'fighting racism' rather than with the liberal concern with 'improving race relations'.

Socialist practice then does not completely transform language but rather, as Gramsci has said, 'purifies it of all its metaphysical apparatus and brings it on to the concrete terrain of history.'[32] Gintis and Bowles's reluctance to advocate change of content in liberal discourse corresponds with their reluctance to advocate change of content in education. Ignoring well-argued criticisms of this reluctance they reiterate what they consider to be the overriding importance of form over content in education. What they actually say is that the form of the educational encounter 'accounts for both its capacity to reproduce capitalist relations of production and its inability to promote domination and healthy personal development'. We have to assume that this is a misprint and what should have been written is 'accounts for both its capacity to reproduce capitalist relations of production and domination and its inability to promote healthy personal development'. 'The actual *content* of the curriculum,' they note, 'has little role to play in this process.' This is quite extraordinary. What about the emphasis in history on 'white ruling class men', the well-documented sexist and racist content of textbooks, the way in which British imperialism is taught or the American Civil War? Of course, this must contribute massively to the reproduction of capitalist relations of production, to the domination of capitalist over worker, white over black, male over female. Again it is their pluralist theory of the state which allows such assertions. They claim, accordingly, that the 'formally equal status of women as citizens . . . *virtually ensures* that the state political mechanism will come to supply relatively equal education to men and women and, for parallel reasons, blacks and minorities have a great deal more equality than the capitalist economy is capable of matching' (my emphasis) (p. 23). They conclude that socialism, should it come to pass, will be the real fulfilment of liberal promise', a mere 'extension of democratic freedoms' already apparent in civil and political life to the economy (p. 31). This is idealism. The need is not to perfect liberal discourse but to generate 'ideas, aspirations and objectives that, by their content, transcend the established universe of discourse and action'. We must counter the tendency for these 'ideas, aspirations and objectives' to be 'repelled or reduced in terms of this [established] universe'.[33] We must undermine the one-dimensional throught exemplified by liberal discourse. As I have argued in this paper, it is the interpretations of Gintis and Bowles (rather than that of the socialists they lament on p. 26) which are idealistic. This idealism has political effects, namely reformism.

In this paper, I have attempted to enter into an important and controversial debate within Marxist sociology of education. I have been concerned primarily with a critique of two of sociology of education's major figures. I would like to reiterate that I have great respect for the way in which they were able to intervene in the discipline and were responsible, with others, for changing its direction.

However, since they *are* such major figures, it is important that their work continues to be subjected to comradely criticism. There have been many criticisms of *Schooling* but none, to my knowledge, of their major published reply to these criticisms. It is for this reason that I have not specifically paid attention to *Schooling* and have concentrated on a critique of their reply. Thus the criticisms I have made should be read with an awareness of their larger arguments in *Schooling* in mind.

I began by questioning the political worthiness of retaining the notion of 'correspondence' except at the very general level of maintaining that there is a link between schooling and production and that, therefore, it is futile to attempt to change education from within. I then briefly noted some empirical research in Britain which tends to undermine the coherence of the correspondence principle.

Next, I went on to examine Gintis and Bowles's theory of sites and practices, suggested its European neo-Marxist origin and attempted to outline ways in which this undeveloped theory (itself a considerable improvement on correspondence theory) might be reformulated.

I concluded by considering Gintis and Bowles's theory of liberal discourse and socialism. This I found to be the weakest part of their overall project. In fact, an implicit critique of this approach, I demonstrated, is to be found in both humanist (for example, Gramsci) and structuralist (for example, Poulantzas) neo-Marxist thought, as well as in traditional Marxist discourse (for example, Lenin) and in feminist and anti-racist practice and theory.

Returning to the reality of the classroom situation, I concluded that their rejection of content in education has serious consequences for any attempt at socialist/anti-sexist/anti-racist intervention.

Acknowledgements

I would like to thank Madan Sarup for his helpful comments on an earlier draft of this paper and for his encouragement. I would like to thank Joan McFarland and especially Peter MacDonald for their comments on a later draft. Finally, my thanks to the anonymous referees for *Sociological Review*. All will recognize the extent to which I am indebted to them for their comments.

Notes

1 Bowles, S. and Gintis, H. (1976), *Schooling in Capitalist America*, London, Routledge and Kegan Paul. This is subsequently referred to as *Schooling*.
2 See, for example, Hall, S. (1977), *Review of the Course*, Unit 32 of the Open University course, Schooling and Society (E202); Sarup, M. (1978), *Marxism and Education*, London, Routledge and Kegan Paul; Hogan, D. (1981), 'Capitalism, liberalism and schooling' in Dale, R. *et al.*, (Eds) *Education and the State Vol. 1: Schooling and the National Interest*, Lewes, Falmer Press; MacDonald, M. (1980) 'Sociocultural reproduction and women's education', in Deem, R. (Ed.), *Schooling for Women's Work*, London, Routledge and Kegan Paul. I would agree that the publication of *Schooling* was a major socialist intervention and what follows should be taken as comradely criticism.
3 Gintis, H. and Bowles, S. (1980), 'Contradiction and reproduction in educational theory', in Barton, L. *et al.*, (Eds) *Schooling Ideology and the Curriculum* Lewes, Falmer Press. The paper also appears in Dale R. *et al.* (1981), *op. cit.* and as Chapter 2 of this volume. The page references refer to this volume.
4 Bowles, S. and Gintis, H. (1976) *op. cit.*, p. 131.
5 See, for example, Sarup, M. (1978) *op. cit.*, pp. 173–5.
6 Bowles, S. and Gintis, H. (1976). *op. cit.*, p. 266, quoted in Sarup, M. (1978) *op. cit.*, pp. 178–9.
7 Sarup, M. (1978) *op cit.*, p. 179.
8 See, for example, Hall, S. (1977) *op. cit* and Sarup, M. (1978) *op. cit.*
9 Willis, P. (1977) *Learning to Labour: How Working-Class Kids get Working-Class Jobs*, Farnborough, Saxon House.
10 Frith, S. (1980) 'Education, training and the labour process', in Cole, M. and Skelton, B. (Eds), *Blind Alley: Youth in a Crisis of Capital*, Ormskirk, Hesketh.
11 Althusser, L. (1979) *For Marx*, London, Verso, p. 108.
12 *Ibid*, p. 185. Although, as we shall see, Gintis and Bowles lack awareness of structures of dominance across sites, they do acknowledge the possibility of 'transportation of practices across sites'.
13 See Cole, M, 'Racism, sexism and capital accumulation' in Cole, M. (Ed), *Dimensions of Oppression: Race, Sex and Class* (unpublished). See also MacDonald, M. (1980) *op. cit.*, for a similar criticism pertaining to *Schooling*.
14 The implications of considering the household as a second site of the labour process

are discussed in SECCOMBE, W. (1980) 'Domestic labour and the working-class household', in FOX, B. (Ed.) *Hidden in the Household*, London, The Women's Press, and in COLE, M. (unpublished), *op. cit.*

15 For a summary of Marxist theories of the state, see, for example, JESSOP, B. (1977) 'Recent theories of the capitalist state', *Cambridge Journal of Economics*; HOLLOWAY, S. and PICCIOTTO, S. (Eds) (1978) *State and Capital*, London, Arnold and COLE, M. and SKELTON, B. (1980), 'Capital, the state and youth', in COLE, M. and SKELTON, B. (Eds), *op. cit.*

16 In fact, most neo-Marxist theories of the state *begin* with the assumption that the state is *more* than government.

17 COLE, M. *op. cit.*

18 'Whereas women form over 50 per cent and "non-whites" between 10 and 20 per cent [depending on whether you accept official or non-official sources] of the total population of the U.S.A., in the last two years, the highest representation in the House of Representatives for both women and blacks has been a meagre 4 per cent (while "non-whites other than blacks" failed to even reach 1 per cent) and in the Senate both women and blacks have ranged from a low of 0 per cent to a high [sic] of 1 per cent . . . at State level, the female membership of the State Executive and Judiciary was a mere 207 (3 per cent) in 1977 while black members of U.S. and State legislatures numbered 316 in the same year. ("State Executive and Judiciary" is similar but not identical to "U.S. and State legislatures".) Separate figures for black and non-white women were not available.' (COLE, M. *ibid.*) It is thus only in the extremely narrow sense of 'being allowed to vote' (for white middle-class men) every five years that black and white women and black men have equality as citizens.

19 CCCS Education Group (1981), *Unpopular Education*, London, Hutchinson, p. 24. Interestingly, unlike Gintis and Bowles, they stress the sites of family, school and waged labour (the state is out and school in). Like Gintis and Bowles they don't say why three and not more sites, nor why these sites in particular.

20 GRAMSCI, A. (1978) *Selections from Prison Notebooks*, London, Lawrence & Wishart, p. 453.

21 POULANTZAS, N. (1978) *Political Power and Social Classes*, London, Verso, pp. 207 and 208.

22 *Ibid.*, p. 211

23 *Ibid.*, pp. 213–4.

24 *Ibid.*, p. 214.

25 As Braverman points out, 'a fair day's work' as defined by F.W. TAYLOR, the founder of 'scientific management', means 'all the work a worker can do without injury to his [sic] health, at a pace that can be sustained throughout a working lifetime'; in other words, a physiological maximum. As Braverman explains, this, in practice, is a pace only few can maintain and then only under strain (BRAVERMAN, H. (1974) *Labour and Monopoly Capital*, London, Monthly Review Press).

26 LARRAIN, J. (1979) *The Concept of Ideology*, London, Hutchinson), p. 216. Essentially Larrain argues that only in a socialist society can we be sure whether religion is ideology pure and simple or whether it is something more. My own view is that religion in essence is not ideology, but that ideologies have arisen under the guise of religion. I differ from many other Marxists and neo-Marxists in that I see no contradiction in being a Marxist and believing in the concept of God. It depends very much on the nature of that concept. Larrain also points out that religion has often served the historical role of unmasking and revealing social contradictions. This seems to me to be true and the work of certain Catholic priests in South America may serve as a current example of 'demystifying work', as might the Rastafarian movement, and even the response of the Church of England to the

Falklands War. Social contradictions have also, of course, been masked and justified in the name of religion.

27 Spender, D. (1980) *Man Made Language*, London, Routledge and Kegan Paul, p. 12.

28 *Ibid.*, pp. 154–5.

29 For a report on the Wimmins' Fire Brigade, — an organization to combat pornography in Vancouver, see *Toronto Globe and Mail*, 23 November 1982.

30 Spender, D. (1980) (op. cit.), pp. 74–5.

31 Gilroy, P, 'Steppin' out of Babylon — race, class and autonomy', in CCCS, *The Empire Strikes Back*, London, Hutchinson, pp. 292–3.

32 Gramsci, A. (1978) *op. cit.*, p. 450.

33 Marcuse, H. 'The new forms of control', in DALE, R. *et al.*, *Schooling and Capitalism*, London, Routledge and Kegan Paul, pp. 214–15.

Part II

A Re-evaluation of Reproduction Theory in Education

4 *The Correspondence Principle and the Marxist Sociology of Education*

Robert Moore

The purpose here is to examine the impact of *Schooling in Capitalist America* upon the Marxist sociology of education and the subsequent development of the field as it has been shaped by the various strategies which have evolved in order to repair, extend and supplement the original formulations of that seminal work. The analysis presented here will differ from those more usually encountered in this area in that it will propose an underlying *continuity* in the development which has taken place over the decade since the publication of *Schooling*. Rather than seeing that process as involving fundamental breaks and reformulations which have left 'simple correspondence' theory far behind, it will be argued that those developments have simply increased the *complexity of the model of the system of social relationships* within which the correspondence principle operates rather than address the problematics of the principle as such.

It is being proposed that the correspondence principle constitutes the major domain assumption of the Marxist sociology of education as it is currently constituted and that this assumption takes its effective form from a particular understanding of the concept *capitalist social relations of production* and of the character of the *relationship* of the educational system to the social relations of production. It will be argued that this view is fundamentally in error. This error has critical implications for our understanding of schooling both at the macro level and in terms of our orientation towards educational processes and classroom interaction.

The manner in which the correspondence principle could address the problem of the relationship between the macro and micro levels significantly influenced the original impact of *Schooling* upon the radical sociology of education in Britain. At that time, writers associated with the 'New Sociology of Education' (NSE) were preoccupied with the problem of the relationship between three areas: social structure; situational (or classroom) analysis; and the possibilities of radical change. The manner in which these areas were seen as problematical reflected the fundamental ambiguity of the NSE's relationship to phenomenological sociology. It will be argued that the correspondence principle supplied an *apparent* resolution of some of the tensions within these three critical areas but that the developments which have occurred within the field since that time reflect the actual instability of that resolution. These issues remain the critical foci of the field and developments within the field represent not so much fundamental revisions of correspondence theory as movements within the theoretical matrix which they construct.

Phenomenology and the New Sociology of Education

The impact of *Schooling* has to be seen, initially, within the context of the condition of the radical sociology of education at the time of its publication. In Britain, the sociology of education was, for a variety of reasons, in a particularly innovative and controversial state. Indeed, the New Sociology of Education was often defined as constituting a *paradigm change* within the sub-discipline. To a large degree this reflected the more general condition of sociology as such and in particular the preoccupation with so-called 'positivism' and the impact of phenomenological sociology. Although there was (and still is) a widespread tendency to discuss the NSE *simply* in terms of phenomenology, the relationship between the two was in reality much more ambiguous. The reception accorded to *Schooling* by NSE radicals reflected the manner in which the correspondence principle apparently provided a solution to the problems associated with their reservations concerning phenomenology.

The NSE writers were attracted by the radicalism of phenomenology. But it is important to realize that that radicalism was a radicalism of the *discipline* rather than a thoroughgoing social and political radicalism. In fact the very character of phenomenology's sociological radicalism actually negated the *politically* radical aspirations of the NSE. This conflict between *sociological* and *political* radicalism occurred at two interrelated levels. The first was phenomenology's *cultural relativism* with its morally nihilistic implications which removed any possible grounds for political commitment and action, and the second was its fundamental theoretical rejection of the concept of *social structure*.

The wider political objectives shared by the NSE writers demanded not only that they be able to retain grounds for *acting* but also that they be able to maintain a *strong concept* of social structure. Fundamental to the phenomenological perspective was the rejection of the view that concepts such as 'social structure' and 'class' refer to *ontologically effective categories*, i.e. that they exist in some form that is not simply reducible to individual subjectivity and that, as such, they have determinant effects at the level of social meaning and action. This view provided the basis of phenomenological sociology's most distinctive feature — the (in principle) infinite regress of 'accounts'.

Because, according to the phenomenologists, social situations comprise nothing but accounts, all accounts are equal and the number of possible accounts of any situation (or accounts of accounts) is infinite. This is something those in the NSE did not accept. Although the approach was centrally concerned with actors' meanings in social situations (in the classroom especially), and although it advocated the suspension of taken-for-granted assumptions concerning meaning (and value judgments in particular) it did not accept that all accounts were *equal*. In fact the major preoccupation of these writers was with the granting of a privileged status to a particular category of 'accounts', namely those which revealed the manner in which the construction of meaning in the classroom reflected class interest and power. The purpose of such understandings of educational processes was to aid and encourage radical educational and social change. The objective was not to produce *any* possible accounts but to produce accounts of a *given* type. Although such language was not used, what this implies is that some accounts are 'right' and others 'wrong' and that part of what being 'right' means is that such understandings can help bring about effective action for predetermined ends.

Whitty (1977) described the difference between phenomenologists and the NSE in terms of a distinction between '*analytic*' and '*possibilitarian*' approaches respectively. Whereas the former were merely concerned with 'exposing the constitutive features of lived reality', the latter were concerned to 'actually challenge the mundane experience of that everyday world' (p. 31). In using the same distinction, Sarup says of the 'analytic' approach that, 'The 'new' sociology of education has no sympathy with this type of apolitical theorizing. It is felt that that more is needed than merely 'showing' the form of life . . . it should be challenged' (Sarup, 1978, p 48).

The relationship between meaning and social structure was central to a 'sociology of knowledge' approach to classroom interaction as advocated by the NSE. The problem, however, for an action approach which focused upon classroom processes, was how to translate that theoretical presupposition into a methodological procedure. Phenomenology provided certain key *predispositional* rules such as 'making rather than taking' problems, suspending taken-of-granted assumptions, etc., but these things did not help either the radical sociologist or the radical teacher in explicating, controlling and transforming the actual processes within the classroom which were active in the reproduction of class relationships and social inequalities. As Young (1971) put it in *Knowledge and Control*:

> We can make this more explicit by starting with the assumption that those in positions of power will attempt to define what is to be taken as knowledge, how accessible to different groups any knowledge is, and what are the accepted relationships between different knowledge areas and between those who have access to them and make them available. It is thus the exploration of how

> these processes happen ... that should form the focus of a sociology of education. *Our understanding of the process is so rudimentary at present, that it is doubtful if we can postulate any clear links between the organization of knowledge at the level of social structure and the process as it involves teachers in the classroom.* (p 32, my emphasis)

It is the last sentence that is particularly significant here because it states quite clearly and unambiguously where *the problem* is seen to lie. Although a phenomenological perspective underpinned the ethnographic approach to the analysis of educational processes which the NSE advocated, a detailed explication of the link with the social structure was necessary in order to guarantee the ideologically preferred interpretations. It was not the case that NSE writers *rejected* the concept of social structure in the fashion of phenomenologists, rather they were brought up against the problem of tracing the effects of social structure within the very specific context of classroom practices.

There were three fundamental problems for the NSE:

(i) how to achieve a non-positivistic conceptualization of social structure which preserved the radical humanism of the phenomenological critique but which did not entail its rejection of social structure (and *class* in particular) as an ontologically effective category;
(ii) how to construct a methodological procedure whereby the class form of social structural relationships could be revealed within the power relationships of the educational system and classroom interaction;
(iii) how to retain the possibility of radical action and change, both within education and in society at large, within a theoretical framework in which the principle for analyzing social interaction was derived from an assumption of the determining power of social structure.

Between the publication of *Knowledge and Control* in 1971 and *Schooling in Capitalist America* in 1976 these issues came increasingly to the forefront of discussion within the radical sociology of education. A number of key texts published around the later data reveal this process. The Open University Reader, *The Process of Schooling*, (Hammersley and Woods, 1976) for instance, records in its introduction that 'there has been a swing back towards an emphasis on the determining effects of social systems, particularly of the capitalist system' (p 62). Reporting on the OU 'Schooling and Society' conference at Cranfield in 1975, the same two writers refer to the polarization between interactionists and phenomenologists and 'those who favour more structural, materialistic and historical explanations' (Woods and Hammersley, 1977, pp 14–15). Significantly they present the argument that without a sense of structural context, subjectivists have 'the ironic effect of reproducing the alienative, reified relations which they themselves denounce.'. The structural perspective was now being seen as revealing the essentially *conservative* character of the 'analytic' approach.

As these texts show, the swing back to structure was nevertheless seen as problematical, especially in relation to the active model of the subject which had been a central feature of the NSE's original association with phenomenology. The particular problem which this posed was how far a structural approach, by defining the material limitations of situations, restricted the possibilities of *action*. Ironically this reinstated, in a different form, the original problem of phenomenology: whereas phenomenological nihilism denied any *grounds* for action, the structural approach could deny the *possibility* of action.

The link between the *conceptualization of social structure, situational analysis, and the possibilities of action* constitutes the basic matrix of issues and concerns within which the development of the Marxist sociology of education has taken place. This development has been concerned almost entirely with increasing the level of complexity *within* that network rather than with examining its theoretical foundation.

The Correspondence Principle

The correspondence principle propounded by Bowles and Gintis in their study of schooling in capitalist America precisely met the requirements of the NSE's commitment to the concept of social structure in its strong form. Not only was the general theoretical approach of the 'political economy' perspective one towards which the NSE would be sympathetic but the idea of a correspondence between the social relationships of schooling and those of work provided the key to the problem of the interpretation of classroom interaction. The social relationships of work and the general structuring of the occupational system, provided a *paradigm* for the analysis of the classroom and the school system. Hence correspondence was not just satisfying *theoretically*, it also served as a *rule of method*. It constituted a guideline for the description and interpretation of what was going on in classrooms. It defined the form to be taken by radical 'accounts' of classroom organization and interaction and effectively closed down the regression of accounts characteristic of phenomenology.

Bowles and Gintis themselves have summarized their specific proposition as follows:

> We also argued specifically that the current relationship between education and economy is ensured not through the *content* of education but its *form*: the social relations of the education encounter. Education pepares students to be workers through a

> *correspondence* between the social relations of production and the social relations of education. Like the division of labour in the capitalist enterprise, the educational system is a finely graded hierarchy of authority and control in which competition rather than cooperation governs the relations among participants, and an external reward system — wages in the case of the economy and grades in the case of schools — holds sway. (p 18 of this volume)

The correspondence principle and the general approach of *Schooling* both responded to a specific need and resonated with a developing trend within the radical sociology of education. The declining influence of phenomenology in general was associated with the rise of interest in humanist and praxis Marxism which revealed that the anti-positivist concerns with meaning and action could be approached from within a tradition which had always treated social structure seriously (indeed, for some phenomenologists Marxism was simply another form of positivism). That the impact of *Schooling* should be understood in terms of the condition of the intellectual field of the radical sociology of education at that time rather than in terms of some Romanticist mysticism of the essential power of the work in itself (which in no sense detracts from its intrinsic qualities) is indicated by the parallel and (as was generally perceived at the time) complementary effects of Althusser's essay on 'Ideology and the Ideological State Apparatuses'[1].

Between them *Schooling in Capitalist America* and 'Ideology and the ideological state apparatus' redefined the central focus of radical sociology of education, *not* by reconstructing its basic ground, but by giving a specific articulation to its underlying premise. The correspondence principle gave a substantive form to what Young (1971) termed the *metatheoretical position* of the NSE:

> . . . the meta-theoretical position being proposed here is that the sociology of education (or any other sociology for that matter) must take into account the historical and situationally specific character of both its phenomena and its explanations. Thus in order to explore situationally defined meanings in taken for granted contexts such as schools, very detailed case studies are necessary which treat as problematic the curricular, pedagogic and assessment categories held by school personnel. However, *such studies on their own*, which give accounts of the realities which emerge from the interaction of members, cannot help avoiding the sociohistorical contexts in which such realities become available . . . these interactional studies *must be complemented* by attempts to conceptualize the links between interactions and changing social structures . . . (p. 4, my emphasis)

The relationship between the social relations of education and those of production defined that 'link' which Michael Young (in the earlier quote) postulated as existing between 'the organization of knowledge at the level of social structure and the process as it involves teachers in the classroom', but which at the time of his writing was seen to be obscure.

The similarity between *Schooling* and *Ideology* lies in the manner in which both focus in a specific way upon the relationship between the social relations of education and the social relations of production. This particular issue will be returned to later, but it should be noted here that the major difference between them resided in the fact that whereas Bowles and Gintis were operating with a 'classic' base/superstructure model (see this volume, p 20) Althusser's project was to produce a critique of that approach. Hence from within two very different theoretical forms of Marxism an essentially similar account of education in capitalist society emerged (or was constructed).

This similarity persists between two very different models of the social totality, models which vary in terms of the theorization of its *complexity*, and where the form of one is grounded in a critique of the form of the other[2]. The comparison between Bowles and Gintis and Althusser reveals the feature that is characteristic of the development of the Marxist sociology of education over the past decade — the view of the relationship between the social relations of education and those of production being translated into increasingly complex models of the social totality.

What both Bowles and Gintis and Althusser provided were powerful articulations of a principle already implicit within a field dominated by the requirement to conceptualize the notion of social structure relative to particular concerns with the issues of situational analysis and radical intervention. The correspondence principle linked classroom processes with social structure and by defining social structure specifically as *capitalist social relations of production*, contextualized that linkage within a system of Marxist theoretical categories. However, because of the pre-eminence of the concern with *action*, with the phenomenologically inspired active model of the subject and the political concern with radical intervention and transformation, the problem of *conceptualizing social structure* has dominated the development of the field. Underpinning this is the classic macro/micro, determinist/voluntarist problem in sociology.

Developments

The interpretation of developments over the past decade which is being offered here stresses an underlying *continuity* of themes and concerns, i.e. it is seen as the development *within* a particular intellectual field rather than as a series of radical breaks or retheorizations of basic principles. In this respect the interpretation differs from some recent commentaries on the state of the Marxist sociology of education which portray revisions as more fundamental in character. Nash (1984), for instance, in his discussion of Hickox's (1983) critique of the Marxist sociology of education argues that Hickox 'attacks a Marxism which most of its former proponents have abandoned through a process of internal theoretical and political self-criticism' (p 29). This 'abandoned Marxism' he identifies as the 'structural, economistic determimism so evident in Bowles and Gintis (1976)' (p 20), and with the influence, 'for a short but heady period' (*loc cit*), of Althusser and Poulantzas.

However, Nash gives no systematic account of this process of internal theoretical self-criticism whereby it is possible to judge how far it is actually fundamental in character or merely a set of ad hoc revisions of fairly obvious simplifications in the original Bowles and Gintis formulations. He is typical, however, in attributing particular significance to the introduction of concepts such as *relative autonomy, resistance, transformation* and *hegemony* into the discourse of the Marxist sociology of education. The unexamined question is how far these concepts reconstruct or simply repair the original model. And this in turn depends upon how far they are seen as addressing the 'real' problems of correspondence theory.

In another review of the recent condition of the field, Arnot and Whitty (1982) describe the development of radical perspectives from 'reproduction' to 'transformation' in terms 'rapid shifts in fashion' (p 93) and 'transformations at the theoretical level' (*loc cit*). Undoubtedly fashion plays its part in these things, but what is again unclear is how far the 'theoretical transformations' which they describe in fact *transform*.

They define three phases over the period with which they are concerned: the phenomenological orientation of the early seventies, the 'rather economistic Marxism' of the midseventies, and a concern with social and cultural reproduction in the late seventies. They go on to argue that there is developing in the eighties a new 'critical' approach in the US and Canada which is represented in the work of writers such as Apple, Giroux and Anyon. This work, they say, is notable for its increased theoretical sophistication, but also, especially in relation to British work of the seventies, for its capacity to produce substantive studies in conjunction with its theory. Though differing in emphases, Arnot and Whitty argue, these writers share 'a commitment to developing a critical approach to curriculum analysis and to using their work to foster radical educational and social change' (*ibid*, p 94).

The article describes the accumulation of problems around correspondence theory and the range of responses to those problems.

> By and large, it failed to describe and explain classroom life, the conflicts and contradictions *within* the school and the distance and conflict between the school and the economy. Further, it could not account for the variety of responses of teachers and pupils to the structures of the school — some of which were liable to threaten the successful socialization of the new generation . . . (The 'critical'

> writers) recognized the effects of class culture on the ways pupils made sense of and responded to the ideologies and culture of the school. They further argued that the hidden curriculum of schooling was not merely the terrain of social control but also the ground on which ideological and political struggles were fought and hence a potential site of interventions for change. (*ibid*, p 98)

The authors argue that these arguments seemed to point towards a form of 'complex correspondence theory' (*loc cit*), but, they suggest, Giroux's work indicates that it is necessary to go even further and that the way to do this is by developing conceptions of *consciousness* and *culture*. All this should be an effective aid to radical teachers in their oppositional, transformative activities in the classroom. Where do these theoretical transformations of radical theory lead?

> What this work certainly does recognize is that the precise relationship between the political economy of schooling, the form and content of the curriculum and the social relations of the classroom cannot be resolved at a purely theoretical level. Thus the theoretical exploration of the broader dynamics of capitalist societies and the historical and situational analysis of curricular practice need to be brought together. (*ibid*, p 99)

What is remarkable about this statement is how precisely it simply restates what Michael Young was saying in *Knowledge and Control* in 1971!

Certainly Arnot and Whitty are correct in their strictures concerning the lack of substantive work accompanying the changes of theoretical fashion in Britain and their argument that the rapidity of these changes contributed to this failure makes good sense. But the view that it is desirable for theory to be complemented by substantive analysis is hardly a profound insight and the idea that our North American colleagues should be so heartily congratulated simply for doing what we all should be doing anyway reflects more the derelictions of us in Britain than any special virtues in those across the Atlantic. This certainly does not amount to a major advance[3].

Essentially the criticisms of correspondence theory referred to by Arnot and Whitty are concerned with the *complexities* of the relationships between education and production which Bowels and Gintis' original formulations are seen as ignoring. Specifically these complexities reside in three areas:

(i) the relationship between the educational system and production;
(ii) within the educational system itself;
(iii) in the relationship between education and pupils/students.

It is in terms of these relationships that much of the criticism of *Schooling* has developed, essentially by increasing their *complexity*. Bowles and

Gintis themselves contribute significantly to this type of critique in their own retrospective examination of their early work (chapter 2 of this book). It is important to note that they still maintain a strong commitment to the basic principle of correspondence and define what they see as its four major positive contributions to 'progressive educational strategy' (p 17 above). They describe its major defect as follows:

> The correspondence principle is, however, not without its problems. The most critical is simply this: by standing, in our approach, as the *only* structural link between education and the economy, and by its character as an inherently *harmonious* link between the two, the correspondence princple forced us to adopt a narrow and inadequate appreciation of the *contradictions* involved in the articulation of the educational system within the social totality. (see p 19 in this volume)

Hence the problem, in their view, was not simply that they underestimated the complexities of the education/production relationship but that they failed to take into account *additional and equally significant links* between education the economy and between education and other sites and forms of oppression, not all of which (for example, patriarchy) are necessarily reducible to class interest. These factors lead to a major restructuring of the model of the social totality with a significant expansion in the recognition of possible sites of contradiction and opposition.

The original limitation upon their notion of *contradiction* in *Schooling in Capitalist America* they attribute to the effects of the 'classical' base/superstructure model which informed their analysis. This model effectively reduces all areas outside of direct production to mere reflections of the social relations in production. The one access they did have to a principle of contradiction between education and production (that between reproduction and accumulation) presented education as simply lagging behind production and failed to acknowledge any dynamic internal to it. They emphasize the failures of the early approach to provide any adequate basis for 'effective political intervention' (p 20.).

The principle features of the authors' own criticism of their early formulations encompass the basic types of response from other writers. They can be listed as follows:

- (i) *complexity*, the early formulation fails to take account of discontinuities and breaks in the system of relationships between production, education, and pupils' backgrounds;
- (ii) *omissions*, the correspondence principle itself is class-based and fails to acknowledge other systems of oppression with which education is involved and which also find specific expressions within the economy;
- (iii) *contradictions*, largely as a result of the first two, the original

model had an extremely restricted potential for defining contradictions;

(iv) *interventions*, the cumulative effect of the above is to eclipse potential sites for effective change.

Together they are grounded in a set of basic theoretical limitations such as 'economism', 'reflectionism' a deterministic top-down view of ideological imposition and a passive model of the subject all of which relate to the base/superstructure model.

It is possible to identify in the broad body of literature which has developed around the issues raised by *Schooling* a number of strategies which identify and attempt to correct these various problems. Obviously in any individual case, the issue taken and the solution offered reflects the particular concerns of the writer, but in total it is possible to discern what might be treated as the outline of a general programme within the radical sociology of education which has moved on through the matrix of possibilities within its theoretical field. Although collectively these various tendencies have constructed an approach which is both complex and coherent, it is noticeable that the concern has been virtually exclusively concerned with *developing the complexity of the model* within which the correspondence principle is seen to operate rather than investigate the principle *as such*. Revisions occur *within* the paradigm, as it were, rather than transcend it.

The range of strategies within the literature can be summarized as follows:

(i) the first type of response is concerned with developing the complexity of the model by identifying a number of breaks and discontinuities in the education/production relationship;
(a) the 'needs of capital' are not automatically given. They require formulation and translation into an education policy at the level of the state. This process reflects not only the condition of class struggle but also competition between fragments of capital itself as well as the general political state of society;
(b) even when the needs of capital have been translated into a policy, that policy cannot be unilaterally imposed upon the education system. The system, reflecting its own autonomy, has its own interests and capacity to resist or renegotiate policy at various levels;
(c) a further translation occurs at the level of the classroom itself within the pragmatics of classroom control and the capacities of both pupils and teachers to resist imposition from above;

(ii) the second type of response has to do with repairing the omissions of the original model. Primarily these are to do with gender and race, though in particular circumstances they could also involve religion or other dimensions. Essentially the argument is that the correspondence principle was exclusively classbased and ignored the role of education in reproducing other types of oppression. As such it reflected a predominantly white male point of view. These arguments might be seen as either complementing or superceding class analysis depending upon the particular theoretical perspective;

(iii) the third type of response has to do with developing the concept of resistence by moving away from a simple ideological imposition view through the concept of *hegemony* towards more complex conceptualizations of consciousness and culture.

This development from 'simple' to 'complex' correspondence theory is represented in figures 1 and 2.

Bowles and Gintis themselves include a number of these responses in their own revision of the early model and it is significant that they see this as perfectly compatible with the correspondence principle. Essentially these transformations of the model of totality mediate the *determinism/voluntarism* problem. At each level of complexity, increasingly sophisticated models of the social totality aspire to reconcile the strong concept of social structure (necessary for situational analysis) with the active model of the subject (necessary for intervention and transformation). It is for this reason that the concept of *contradiction* comes to be so important. Contradictions represent both *complexity* and *sites for oppositional action*[4].

Figure 1 Simple Correspondence

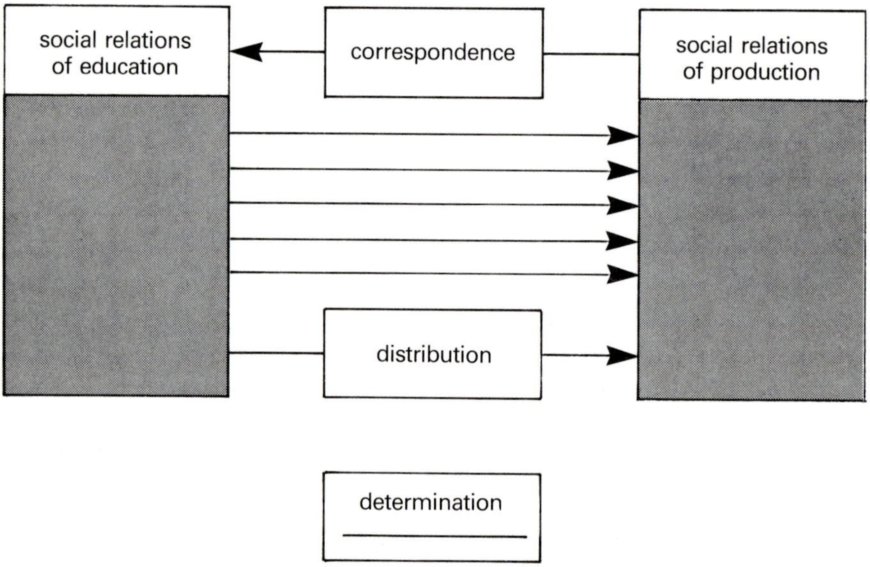

Figure 2 Complex Correspondence

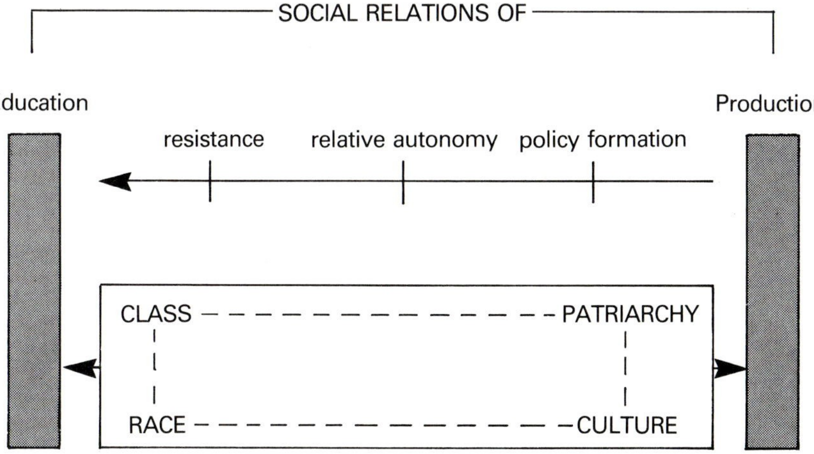

The relations between education and production are interrupted by resistance, relative autonomy and the politics of policy formation and mediated by class, patriarchy and race both at the level of social relations and culture. Education is involved in the reproduction of each of those systems of oppression.

The most striking feature of the development of the radical sociology of education since the publication of *Knowledge and Control* is the regularity with which the *same problems* resurface. They are the classic dilemmas of the macro/micro, objectivist/subjectivist, determinist/voluntarist dichotomies and the problems posed by determinist pessimism and relativist nihilism for action within the classroom[5].

The phases between the NSE and the 'critical' approach reflect not so much theoretical transformations as the movement between the opposite poles of a single theoretical field. Certainly at each point there is an increase in sophistication and complexity, a deepening of understanding and texture. Yet it is difficult to see how any of this *fundamentally* restructures the basic principle which *Schooling in Capitalist America* constructed when the correspondence principle provided the substantive form of the link between social structure and educational processes which the NSE sought. Indeed, when we read Arnot and Whitty (1982) saying of the most recent phase of this development that the 'critical' approach, 'Despite an apparent commitment to a broader transformation of society ... remains overly school-centred in its analysis of the politics of the curriculum and tends to assume that educational interventions will necessarily have radical effects' (p 102), the strong sense of déjà vu suggests that the most developed characteristic of the radical sociology of education is our capacity to forget nothing and remember nothing.

The Basis for the Critique of the Correspondence Principle

The correspondence principle addresses three interrelated aspects of the education/production relationship. First, there is the argument that the form of social relations in education correspond to those in production, secondly that these forms develop attributes required in production, and thirdly that this process determines and legitimates the allocation of workers to production. The various responses to the problems of 'simple' correspondence, outlined above, disrupt and interrupt these sets of relationships, for example, by challenging the assumption of the effectivity of educational processes, by making the requirements of production problematical, by pointing out that education is subject to other influences and is doing other things as well. As has been pointed out, these objections develop the complexity of the system of relationships within which correspondence is seen to operate rather than challenge the principle as such.

Such an increase in complexity in no way automatically undermines the veracity of the principle. Gintis and Bowles are perfectly well able to both reaffirm their commitment to correspondence *and* develop a much more sophisticated model of the social totality within which it is seen to operate. Whilst they developed their original version from within a base/superstructure perspective, Althusser reached substantively the same conclusions within the framework of a theoretical programme aimed precisely at overthrowing that approach.

A full critique of the correspondence principle would involve three dimensions:

(i) *Substantive*
Is it *in fact* the case that the educational system relates to production in the ways specified by the theory? Quite rightly, much has been made of Bowles and Gintis' willingness to approach issues at this concrete level and when they argue now that one of the principles' four positive contributions is that 'its explanatory value is great' (p 18 of this volume) and invoke Jenck's work in support, one assumes that it is to the empirical level that they refer. It is not my intention here to address this level. My own view is that the grounds for their optimism are questionable — the implications for *radical* theory of Randall Collins' work on the education/production relationship are especially significant[6]. However, the area of substantive relevance is both wide and complex and problems of interpretation notoriously difficult. These difficulties have in fact been added to by the development of more sophisticated models within which to locate correspondence because any of the strategies outlined above can be invoked in an ad hoc way to cover apparent anomolies or disconfirmations.

(ii) *Formal*
Is it in *principle* possible for the educational system to relate to production

in the ways specified? The most significant work applying to this aspect of the problem is that of Raymond Boudon[7]. The condition for correspondence is the possibility of an articulated sysnchronization between education and production over time. Although *Schooling* itself offered the possibility of contradiction in the relationship between the imperatives of reproduction and accumulation, and Gintis and Bowles have significantly increased the range of contradictions in the later work, the assumption of the *possibility of correspondence in the first instance* is taken for granted. Indeed, it is implicitly assumed in all the strategies described earlier. They extend its form or delimit its range, but do not question its *possibility*. It is in this sense that the correspondence principle remains the major domain assumption of the Marxist sociology of education. The logical simulation models developed by Boudon demonstrate that the condition for correspondence to be possible is non-obtainable *in the first instance*.

(iii) *Theoretical*

The Marxist theoretical status of the correspondence principle is significant in two respects. First, *explicitly* Bowles and Gintis' work *is* within the Marxist tradition, is perceived as such and has played a paramount and exemplary role in constructing the field of the Marxist sociology of education. This is the *use* which has been made of their work by those who share their interest and commitment. For the past decade the Marxist sociology of education (in the Anglo-Saxon world at least) has been essentially a dialogue with Bowles and Gintis. Secondly, *implicitly*, the force of the correspondence principle as such resides in the manner of its conceptual formulation: 'Education prepares students to be workers through a *correspondence* between the social relations of production and the social relations of education'. It is the term 'social relations of production' which is significant here by virtue of its centrality within the Marxist theoretical system. From a theoretical point of view the key question is, how should we understand the term 'social relations of production'? It is this issue that I wish to explore.

The Social Relations of Production

The factor which remains constant between the various models based on the correspondence principle is the central identification of the *social relations of production* with the *system of social relationships in production*. It is this identification or conflating of terms which constructs the effective theoretical foundation of the Marxist sociology of education in its current form. I have already mentioned how more or less contemporaneously (within the field) both Bowles and Gintis and Althusser provided *substantively* similar models of the education/production relationship from within very different models of the social totality. That this should be possible reflects the fact that in both cases the same identification of the *social relations of production* with *social relationships in production* occurs. And it is this which provides the dimension of continuity within the development from simple to complex correspondence models and why the various responses to and strategies for developing correspondence only develop the complexity of the model within which the principle operates rather than transform the theory. What we see over the past decade is the progression of this basic equation through base/superstructure, Althusserian/Poulantzian and post-Althusserian type models of the social totality.

The preoccupations referred to above have led to a concern with issues such as ideology and hegemony, relative autonomy and the state and an almost complete neglect of the fundamental concept of *the social relations of production* itself. It is in Althusser's essay on the ideological state apparatuses that the theoretical issues are most clearly revealed and this is a useful starting point for approaching the problem of identifying the social relations of production with social relationships *in* production.

Althusser takes as his starting point the general problem of the *reproduction of the conditions of production*, i.e. perpetuating the productive forces in society so as to secure its existence over time. The forces of production are always set to work within definite *social relations of production*. So, to reproduce itself a society must reproduce both its productive forces and its social relations of production. The key question that Althusser is addressing is that of the reproduction of the social relations of production, but in order to answer the question of *how* they are reproduced, he needs to develop an extended analysis of the *forces of production*. The argument unfolds as follows.

It is necessary, first of all, he argues, to distinguish between the *means of production* and the *forces of production*. The distinctive feature of the latter is that they include *labour power*. The question now taken up is, how is the reproduction of labour power ensured? This is where the argument becomes significant for education. Althusser argues that in considering the reproduction of labour power we have to take account of two things: (a) the reproduction of its material conditions of existence; and (b) the reproduction of its *competence*.

(a) The reproduction of the material existence of labour power involves:
   (i) a basic means of subsistence sufficient to keep the worker alive and in 'working order';
   (ii) a means of raising and educating children, i.e. new generations of workers;
   (iii) an historical factor reflecting the general condition of life in a society and the fruits of the victories of class struggle in raising the workers' standard of living.

   This list is clearly identifiable as that which Marx himself gives in chapter 6 of Volume 1 of *Capital* (see Marx, 1976, pp 274–6).

(b) By the competence of labour power Althusser (1972) means that it is 'suitable to be set to work in the complex system of the process of production' (p 245). He goes on to say:

> The development of the productive forces and the type of unity historically constitutive of the productive forces at a given moment produce the result that the labour power has be (diversely) skilled and therefore reproduced as such. Diversely: according to the requirements of the socio-technical division of labour, its different 'jobs' and 'posts'. (p 245)

Althusser argues that the reproduction of labour power as *competent* in this fashion entails the reproduction of skills and knowledge *and* of its 'submission to the ruling ideology' (*ibid*). However, these two things always occur *simultaneously* — 'it is in the forms and under the forms of ideological subjection that provision is made for the reproduction of the skills of labour power.' (p 246). It is this process which is achieved by the capitalist education system, within the *educational ideological apparatus*.

Education is concerned with developing the *competence of labour power* and this competence is defined by the diverse requirements of the socio-technical division of labour. In a much quoted section (p 260) of the essay, Althusser describes how portions of 'scholastically adapted youth' are ejected at various stages into the appropriate sectors of production — 'Each mass ejected *en route* is practically provided with the ideology which suits the role it has to fulfil in class society'.

The educational ISA is specifically concerned with the crucial task of reproducing the competence of labour power. But what are ISAs as such *doing*?

> All ideological state apparatuses, whatever they are, contribute to the same result: the reproduction of the relations of production, i.e. of capitalist relations of exploitation. (*ibid*, p 259)

It is through the reproduction of the *competence* of labour power by the education ISA, in forms determined by the diverse requirements of the socio-technical division of labour, that the *social relations of production* are reproduced.

> But it is by an apprenticeship in a variety of know-how wrapped up in the massive inculcation of the ideology of the ruling class that the *relations of production* in a capitalist social formation, the relations of exploited to exploiters, and exploiters to exploited, are largely reproduced. (*ibid*, p 261)

Hence Althusser answers the question of how the social relations of production are reproduced by defining that reproduction as identical with the reproduction of relations *in* production and that being achieved by the reproduction of the diverse competencies of labour power required in production.

Of specific interest here is not particular Althusserian formulations, or theories of ideology or the state, but the underlying logic which resulted in this identification of the social relations of production with the system of social relationships in production. In order to explicate the key moment in this logic it is necessary to return to the general issue of the *reproduction of labour power*.

Althusser distinguishes between the reproduction of its conditions of material existence and the reproduction of its competence. It is the latter which he goes on to develop at length. However, it is in his treatment of the former that the key lies.

At first glance, the list that Althusser provides for reproduction of the material conditions of existence of labour power is unexceptionable — furthermore, we can clearly see its source in Marx. But what Marx is actually talking about here is *the determination of the value of labour power* (see Marx 1976, p 274). What is being presupposed here (and without this presupposition the factors listed would be no more than universal abstractions) is that labour power already has the form of a *commodity with an exchange value*. The conditions for the material existence of labour power cannot be posed abstractly, they can only be defined relative to a mode of production.

What is distinctive about the existence of labour power under capitalism is that it acquires the form of a commodity with an exchange value. Hence the material conditions for the existence of labour power under capitalism are the general conditions which bestow this form and which construct wage labour as a *category*. It is these conditions which constitute capitalist *social relations of production*, and they are prior to and are the precondition for wage labour within the process of *direct production*. Capitalist relations of production are *general conditions* and *prior* to the system of social relationships *in* production.

Marx defines labour power as follows:

> We mean by labour power, or labour capacity, the aggregate of those mental and physical capabilities existing in the physical form, the living personality, of a human being, capabilities which he sets in motion whenever he produces a use value of any kind. (*ibid*, p 270)

Obviously this definition in itself is abstract and universal. Marx goes on to provide it with a concrete form specific to the capitalist mode of production: 'But in order that the owner of money may find labour power on the market as a commodity, various conditions must first be fulfilled' (*loc cit*). These conditions are:

(i) That the worker be the *owner* of his or her own labour power and free to offer it for sale on the market. The worker must be a legally free individual.

(ii) The worker is formally separated from both the means of production and the products of his or her own labour. They are neither consumed nor sold by those who produce them. The means of life are accessible to the worker only through the wage, through the sale of labour power.

(iii) The principle of production is *exchange* rather than direct consumption.

(iv) These conditions coincide with a certain level of the historical development of the money economy.

> The historical conditions of (capital's) existence are by no means given with the mere circulation of money and commodities. It arises only when the owner of the means of production and subsistence finds the free worker available on the market, as the seller of his own labour power. And this one historical precondition comprises a world's history. (*ibid*, p 274)

These are the *social relations of production* under capitalism. They construct wage labour as a social category. Existentially they constitute a condition of total dispossession from which follows the *compulsion* upon the 'free' worker to enter direct production as a wage-labourer in order to gain the means of life.

In concrete terms 'the means of life' are expressed in those items defined by Althusser as reproducing the material existence of labour power and which Marx goes on, from the point above, to elucidate as giving the *value* of labour power. It is important to note that the value of labour power is given *prior to* the worker's actual entry into the process of direct production. It cannot be deduced from the *concrete form of labour* (which is not to be confused with *labour power*) the worker performs — indeed, it is not even necessary that the worker works at all![8] Nor can it be deduced from either the *wage* the worker receives (which can be above or below the *value* of labour power) or the *price* of what is produced (which can also be sold above or below its *value*). Value theory entails a set of quite fundamental theoretical distinctions which decisively separate capitalist *social relations of production* from the *system of social relationships in (the immediate process of direct) production.*

These distinctions are expressed in that between the 'process of capitalist production as a whole' and the 'immediate production of commodities'.

> Thus when we look at the process of capitalist production as a *whole* and not merely at the immediate production of commodities, we find that although the *sale and purchase of labour power* (which itself conditions the transformation of a part of the capital into variable capital) is entirely separate from the immediate production process, and indeed precedes it, it yet forms the *absolute*

> *foundation* of capitalist production and is an integral *moment* within it. Material wealth transforms itself into capital simply and solely because the worker sells his labour power in order to live. The *articles* which are the material conditions of labour, i.e. the *means of production*, and the articles which are the precondition for the survival of the worker himself, i.e. the *means of subsistence*, both become *capital* only because of the phenomenon of *wage labour*. Capital is not a *thing*, anymore than money is a *thing*. In capital, as in money, certain *specific social relations of production between people* appear as relations of *things to people*, or else certain social relations appear as the *natural properties of things in society*. Without a *class dependent on wages*, the moment individuals confront each other as free persons, there can be no production of surplus value; without the production of surplus value there can be no capitalist production, and hence no capital and no capitalist. (*ibid*, p 1005)

The distinction between the social relations of production and the system of social relationships in production corresponds to that between the 'process of capitalist production as a whole' and 'the immediate production of commodities'. The assumption of correspondence theory is that the immediate form of the capital relation as it is expressed in the direct process of production is *sufficient* to serve as the foundation for the form of the educational system and as the *principle* for explicating its processes. But as Simon Clarke (1980) has oberved:

> If we look only at the immediate forms of existence of the relation between capital and labour we cannot find a class relation. Within circulation capitalists and workers enter as individuals engaged in a free and equal exchange of commodities. Thus there is no class relation here. Within production again we find only individual relationships between individual capitalists and the group of workers under their command. Certainly workers have a common interest against their own capitalists, and workers have a common interest against capitalists as a whole. But a common interest is not sufficient to define an especially privileged class relation ... A class relation is not defined subjectively by the existence of a common interest, it is an objective social relation that exists independently of, and prior to, any particular interests. (p. 10)

The basic problem with correspondence theory is that it assigns to the immediate forms of the capital relation a privileged status which they cannot in fact bear and which are insufficient to ground something as immensely complex as the historical emergence of, the form taken by, and the character of the processes within the educational system. Hence the weight and authority which the correspondence principle apparently acquires by linking the social relations of education to those of production are undeserved for as long as *the social relations of production* are identified as the social relationships *within* the system of immediate production.

Underpinning the development of correspondence theory is a particular view about the way in which the base/superstructure model is a problem. The real problem of this approach is *not* in its treatment of the *superstructure* relative to the base, but in the treatment of the *base* itself and its continuing identification with relationships *in* immediate production. The solution to the base/superstructure problem lies not in rearranging the relationship of the superstructure to the base, by moving away from simple reflectionism to more subtle forms of articulation, but by reformulating the concept of *economic base* as such through a different understanding of the concept of *social relations of production*.

Implications

The immediate implication of distinguishing between *social relations of production* and *the system of social relationships in production* is that both the educational and occupational systems can be approached *as* systems. A major problem for theories which approach education from the point of view of immediate production alone is the possibility of seeing the educational system as *a field in its own right*, i.e. as the site of the social relations of the material production of knowledge. This is ultimately more significant than its role in the cultural reproduction of any particular ruling class membership group or in its servicing of the occupational system. The autonomy and specificity of the educational field lies in the *first place* in the speciality of its distinctive discourse — knowledge. Although there is not space here to develop these points, it must be noted that:

(i) *education* (as opposed simply to *schooling*) is not limited (formally or informally) to *the* educational system;

(ii) *knowledge production* in the full sense of the term occurs only in limited areas of the educational system and in certain areas *outside* of formal education;

(iii) *schooling* as such is not a site of *knowledge* production. The question is how far its social relationships are *structured* by principles derived from the site of knowledge production or from elsewhere;

(iv) in the case of knowledge production itself, it is necessary to distinguish (as Berstein (1982) puts it) between the *speciality of discourse* (i.e. knowledge qua *knowledge* — a material force of production in its own right) and the social relations of its *production* and of its *transmission*.

The realist theory of knowledge enables us to see the educational system, as the site of *knowledge production*, as an autonomous, constitutive site of social practice. The *regulation* of these practices (through the regulation of the *autonomy* of the system) is a key concern. In Bowles and Gintis' terms, this has to do with the *transportation* of principles and practices between sites, i.e. between the site of knowledge production and schooling, between the educational system and other parts of the social formation (especially areas of the state and the media [sites of cultural reproduction and control]), and between the site of *direct material production* and education. In the UK at the moment, schooling can be seen as a contested area where practices developed within a relatively autonomous educational system (in a traditional liberal humanist form) are being systematically replaced by forms derived from a particular ideology of production[9].

When seen as a site of production in its own right rather than simply as an agency of social control in the service of immediate production, questions can be raised concerning *the regulation of the educational field itself* and of its *agents*. Vocationalist rhetoric within educational ideologies serves not only (or even primarily) 'the needs of industry' it legitimates also particular modes of control over education.

This failure to acknowledge the significance of the educational system as a *site of production* in its own right, as a consequence of the persistence of the identification of the concept of *social relations of production* with the system of social relationships within the occupational system, is reflected in Gintis and Bowles' characterization of education as simply a 'sub-site of the state' (p 23 of this volume). They define its 'critical location' as being '*within* the state yet serving the site of capitalist production' (*loc cit*). They see this as constituting a contradictory position because the liberal-democratic state is grounded in formally egalitarian notions of the rights of the person, whilst capitalist production is expressed through rights vested in *property*[10]:

> The central contradiction in the educational systems of advanced capitalist society derives from two aspects of its location in the social totality. First, it forms in general a sub-system of the state site, and therefore is directly subject to the principle of rights vested in persons. Second, education plays a central role in reproducing the political structure of the capitalist production process, which in turn is legitimated in terms of rights vested in property. Thus education is directly involved in the contradictory articulation of sites in advanced capitalism and is expressed in terms of the property/person dichotomy: education reproduces rights vested in property while organized in terms of rights vested in persons. (*ibid*, p 28)

The major problem with this model is that it provides no constitutive base for the educational system itself apart from an implicityl functionalist 'need' of capitalist production for an agency for the inculcation of those attributes of consciousness and skill required in the production process. Education remains as 'epiphenomonal' as it ever was in simple base/superstructure models. What is crucially missing from the entire analysis is precisely that element which is the intrinsically distinctive property of the educational system: namely *knowledge*. Behind this is the more general absence from the Marxist sociology of education of a materialist (realist) theory of knowledge as such and an accompanying model of the educational system as the site of material production of knowledge[11].

The manner in which Gintis and Bowles appear to define the *specificity of sites* is indicative of the problematical nature of the model. The three sites of *the family*, *the state*, and *capitalist production* define the 'three major relations individuals have *vis-a-vis* their society' (*ibid*, p 21): gender, citizenship and class. These relationships and their associated sets of practices are independent in the sense that 'none of these can be understood as flowing simply from the others' (*loc cit*) (although, they argue, practices can be *transported* across sites). Class and the family are 'characterized' as sites of dominance: of capital over labour and of men over women. The state functions mainly to reproduce those conditions of domination rather than being a site of domination in its own right.

I take this as implying that these relations of domination are *constitutive* of the sites (especially as patriarchy cannot simply be reduced to a requirement of capital). Underpinning this would seem to be a theory of *interests*, i.e. the interest of capitalists against those of workers and of men against women, and, consequently, that social relationships *express rather than construct* interests. Hence the capital relation is (with the exception of the secondary phenomenon of *transported practices*) restricted to its immediate form within the production process and the relationships of conflicting interests between capitalist and workers.

A critical consequence of the continued conflation of *social relations of production* with the *system of social relationships in production* is that the specificity of sites cannot be defined except in terms of *interests* or (implicitly) of functions. The origins of 'interests' themselves remain mysterious or contingent — *why* is it in the interests of men to dominate women or whites, blacks — is it in their 'nature' or has it just always happened to be that way?

Alternatives

I now want to examine some of the implications of exploring the relationship between the educational and occupational systems from the perspective which *does* differentiate the social relations of production in the manner described above.

From this point of view, four basic sets of problems emerge concerning the relationship between the educational and occupational systems:

(i) the determination of their *forms*;
(ii) the relationship between the two *systems* in society;
(iii) the characteristics of the systems of relationships *within* each;
(iv) the relationship *between* the two systems of relationships.

The basic model is represented in figure 3.

Figure 3 Education, Occupation and Production

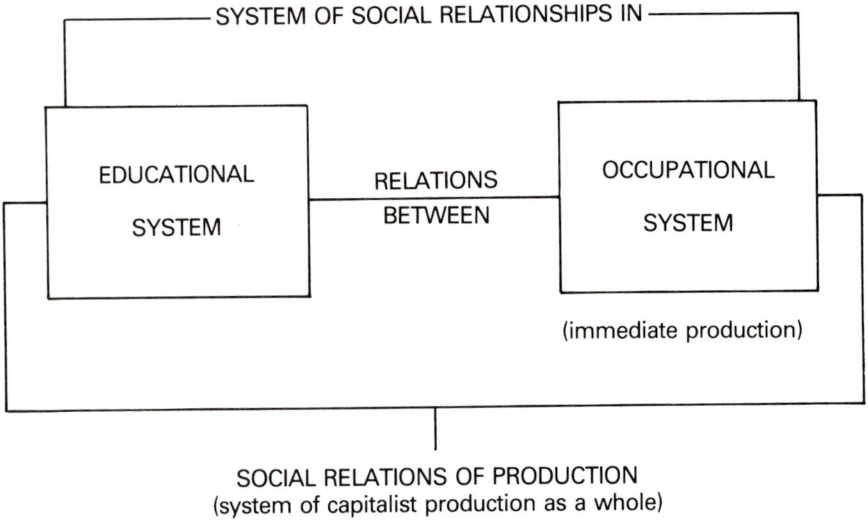

Although it is question (i) which relates most directly to the concept of *social relations of production* (in that both the form and principle of education in society will derive from and, consequently, vary according to the mode of production), it is the others which will be dealt with here in that they address the kinds of issue usually associated with correspondence theory. It should be pointed out that the argument being advanced here is not that education is *not* concerned with reproducing the social relations of production, but rather that that proposition needs to be radically reformulated.

Once the theoretical separation (both conceptual and ontological) is made between the *social relations of production* and the *system of social relationships wihin the process of immediate production* (or simply 'the occupational system'), then both the educational and occupational systems can be approached as distinctive sites of production (under the social relations of production) with their own intrinsic principles and possibilities. As such they provide the material, social and cultural bases for those individuals who are their 'agents'. Hence the relationship between the two systems and their degree of distinctiveness or separation is reflected within the relationship between social groups (most specifically, between fragments of the middle class).

The control of education and the regulation of its relations of production and relationships of transmission is crucial for the control of those groups not subjected to the class discipline of the immediate production of commodities. This problem of control is not restricted to those immediately employed within education. The post-war expansion of education itself and, beyond that, of the social democratic welfare state, extended the possibilities of a cultural field which derived its form not from a material base located within immediate production, but from within knowledge production. This very expansion facilitated the development not of the traditional conservative, or orthodox, position within the field, but of its radical, heterodox pole (associated with the middle class cultural radicalism of the sixties).

Symptomatically, the broad sweep of Thatcherite reform (from privatization to the attacks upon the health service, local government, the civil service, the BBC and education itself) has been concerned with imposing modes of control derived from relationships within immediate production in the industrial and commercial spheres ('the discipline of the market') upon those areas outside of immediate production and those who work within them. In Bowles and Gintis terms this can be seen as an instance of the transportation of practices between sites. I want to see this in terms of the regulation of the autonomy of the educational system and the forms of knowledge transmission.

Applications

Correspondence theory derives the form of education from the system of relationships in immediate production. The basic question which follows from this approach is the manner in which that relationship, and the associated system of distribution of people back into production, is interrupted, distorted and delimited by other factors and forces. The approach being advocated here, from an alternative analysis of the concept of *social relations of production*, sees the educational system as an independent field with its own internal constitutive principles. These principles are the basis of the field's autonomy. The question which follows from this is the manner in which that autonomy is regulated. This general condition of the relationship of education to society is referred to by Bourdieu and Passeron (1977) as the 'dual objective truth of a system defined by its capacity to employ the *internal logic* of its functioning in the service of its *external function of social conservation*' (p 177). It is the recognition of this '*dual* objective truth' which enables a definition of the *specificity* of the educational field, though precisely how it is defined will depend to a significant degree upon epistemological assumptions, for example, as to whether it is seen as essentially *arbitrary*, as with Bourdieu, or as with Bernstein as grounded in the 'speciality of discourse', i.e. in a *realist* view of knowledge.

It is interesting that alongside the powerful influence of correspondence theory within the sociology of education, the areas' three major theorists, Bourdieu, Boudon and Bernstein each operates with what could be termed a 'dual systems' model of the relationship between education and production which acknowledges the specificity of education and attempts to explicate the resulting complexities of its internal and external relations. It is within Berstein's work that this approach has its most systematic development.

In the essay 'Aspects of the relations between education and production' (Bernstein, 1977, pp 174–200) Bernstein indicates his reservations concerning *Schooling*. He argues that only a 'small fraction of the output of education bears a *direct* relation' to the requirements of production (*ibid*, p 187). The dispositions appropriate to different locations in production are mainly acquired in the home. In order to understand the relationship between the educational and occupational systems, it is necessary to distinguish between the *systemic relations* and the strength of the *classification* between the categories of education and production.

In general terms the *systemic relations* refer to the relationship between the systems of relationships *within* education and production whereas *classification* refers to the relationship *between* the categories of education and production as such.

More specifically, *the systemic relations* can be seen in terms of:

(a) the relationship between the *distribution of categories* in each system; for instance: is it the case that the categories *a, b, c etc* in education correspond to the categories *a, b, c, etc* in production and is it the case that *a is to b* in education as *a is to b* in production? And;

(b) the *realizations* of those categories in terms of the mutuality of expectations concerning knowledge, skill, attitudes and dispositions etc between the two systems; for instance: do educators and employers have a common model of what it is to be 'an engineer'?

Together, these things could be illustrated as follows: is it the case that the categories of 'science' and 'engineering' in education correspond with those categories within the occupational system (for example, in terms of the credentialization of recruitment or 'supply and demand'), and is it the case that their relative status in the educational system matches that within industry. Futhermore, do educators' ideas about what a 'good' scientist or engineer should be like coincide with those of employers?

The *classification* of the relationship *between* the *categories* of education and production has to do with the strength of the boundary between the two — the degree of insulation between the 'principles, contexts and possibilities' (*ibid*, p 188) of the two systems. This is particularly significant at the level of educational ideologies. Where classification is *strong*, the principles, contexts and possibilities of education will be highly distinctive relative to production. Educational ideologies will emphasize the *intrinsic* significance of education as opposed to its *instrumental* implications. There will be a concern with objectives such as 'developing individual potential' or 'the whole person' or 'rational autonomy' or 'the logic of the discipline'. Within the English tradition there is a strong cultural division between the broader liberal-humanist culture in which education has participated and the world of industry and commerce.[12] Education, indeed, has been seen as hostile to industry and commerce and to its materialistic values. Rather than preparing people *for* production, education has often been seen as providing the antidote to its dehumanizing and vulgarizing effects (the Leavisite movement is a major example).

Although it is the case that both dimensions can vary independently, they are, of course, interrelated. This interrelationship will be particularly evident in the crucial area of the *realization* of educational categories. For instance, it could be the case that as a result of manpower planning policies the categories *within* education and production are brought into close alignment but, because of the persistence of *strong classification between* the two systems, educationalists retain control over the realizations of the categories, for example, what it *means* to be an engineer. Consequently, the regulation of the educational field involves *control* over both the systemic relations between education and production *and* over the classification between the two categories. Hence the capacity to determine and legitimate what counts as educational knowledge is crucial and this resolves into questions of *power*. It involves the ability of groups (class fragments) to construct educational mandates[13] which articulate (or construct) the supposed interests of constituencies within the wider society. An extended model is now possible in which Bernstein's dimensions are included (see figure 4).

In the essay, Bernstein summarizes part of his argument as follows:

> We shall argue that, where there is a strong classification between education and production, this creates the condition for the relative autonomy of education, and thus a division of labour between those who are located in production and those who are located in cultural reproduction (education): that is, between power and control. We

Figure 4 Regulation of the Relationship Between the Educational and the Occupational Systems (systemic relations and classification)

SYSTEM OF SOCIAL RELATIONSHIPS IN

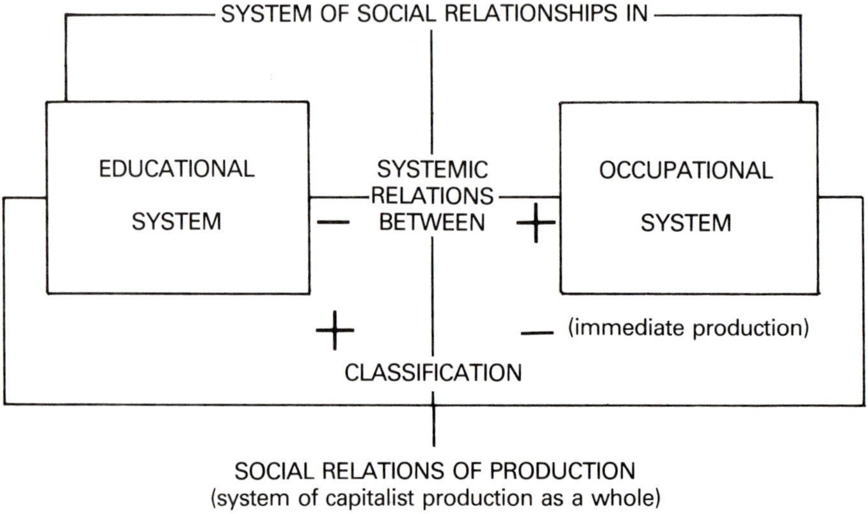

> shall argue that a fraction of the middle class has become the producers and disseminators of theories of social control which are institutionalized in agencies of cultural reproduction and which are incorporated at different historical periods into the social relationships of production. We shall be concerned to examine the relationship between the relative autonomy of education and the formation and reproduction of the consciousness of the middle class. (*ibid*, p 175)

Against this background, I now want to take this model and indicate how Bernstein's explication of the relationship between education and production can be used to generate models of educational ideologies which would correlate with the basic forms of relationship between the systemic relationships and the strength of classification. The degree of alignment between the systemic relations will be denoted by SR+/SR−, and the strength of classification by C+/C−. This gives four basic positions[14]:
C+, SR−: This represents the highest degree of educational *autonomy*. The *categories* of education and production are strongly insulated and, therefore, strongly differentiated within educational ideologies. Although the most obvious example of this type is traditional, academic elitism, there are also progressive/critical forms. The educational field as such (its

'principles, contexts and possibilities', *and* the social and cultural fields of its agents) will assume a distinctive and separate form relative to the industrial and commercial sphere. The issue of the 'transportation' of its practices to other sites is particularly contentious and problematical — especially in a period of welfare state expansionism.

C+ *SR*+: The strengthening of the systemic relationships in this case represents the introduction of knowledge from and about production into the educational sphere. In this sense it represents a weakening of the boundary between (traditional) educational and non-educational knowledge. However, because of the strong classification, that knowledge is incorporated, interpreted and evaluated according to *educationalist* criteria and within an autonomous educational paradigm. A category such as 'the world of work' might be introduced into the curriculum under the heading of 'relevance' within a programme of radical innovation. This is teaching about the 'world of work' in the *interests of pupils* rather than teaching *for* the 'world of work' in the interests of *employers*. Such an approach could be associated with *social education* in the early seventies in English secondary education[15]. Such an approach is particularly problematical because it subjects this material to the direct scrutiny of a possibly hostile educational perspective.

C−, *SR*+ In this case education has its *least* degree of autonomy and is most directly under the control of agencies (purporting) to represent the requirements of production. The *form* of relationships within education will be regulated by principles, contexts and possibilities derived from production. Its *practices* will be modelled upon practices transported from the site of immediate production. The educational field and the social and cultural fields of its agents will be integrated with those of production. This can be seen in terms of the Manpower Services Commission's influence upon education in the UK. A number of devices have been developed in order to achieve this new integration: the idea of deriving a 'curriculum' from an occupational skills inventory or matrix, of organizing educational programmes under the headings of so-called 'occupational training families', of integrating educational credentials into the system of vocational credentialization through the National Council for Vocational Qualifications (NCVQ). The traditional distinctiveness of education is being undermined by forcing educational institutions (especially within the further education sector) to compete within non-professional, commercial training agencies.

C−, *SR*− In this case education incorporates categories of production in various ways but does so without direct control by agencies formally representing 'the needs of industry'. This situation is most clearly represented where the educational qualification functions as a *professional qualification* in a traditionally legitimated form, for example, as in medicine and law. Beyond that, in the UK context, it could be seen as occurring where certain sectors of industry (specialist engineering or pharmaceutical concerns) have an established, mutually supportive association with certain educational institutions or even specific departments. It might be speculated that within a comparative perspective this situation is the norm in societies (for example, Sweden) where there is a broad consensual hegemony within the middle class and where the strong, antithetical division between liberal professional and industrial commecial fragments, which exists in Britain (or perhaps more correctly, England), is absent.

It is important to note that the category 'production', here, is always an *ideologically constructed* category. Ideologies of production (in negative, culturally conservative, or more positive social democratic or technicist forms) regulate, in different ways, the discourse of education and structure and legitimate its relationships and practices. As a site of production in its own right, education has the potential to generate its own, distinctive forms of social relations. The greater its autonomy, the more distinctive both the relations of knowledge production and the social relationships of knowledge transmission can become. Consequently, the more strongly differentiated the social and cultural fields of its agents. The strong classification between education and production is reproduced in educational ideologies and practices, *but also* (in both conservative and radical forms) in the social and cultural fields of those involved in education (as workers).

The key question now becomes the possibility of the transportation of these forms of social relationships, their principles and practices, beyond the immediate site of the educational system into the broader area of the welfare state and the ideological state apparatus. The critical problem which arises is the possibilities of the reproduction within these other areas of the *principle of strong classification* in relation to the system of the immediate production of material commodities (especially where there is an existing anti-commercial professional ethic). This is particularly crucial because of the role of these agencies in social control — viz the new-right Tory obsession with the BBC.

As far as the form of social relationships in education is concerned, it is necessary to distinguish between the social relations of the site as such (derived from the speciality of the discourse of knowledge) and the specific relationships of educational transmission. It is the former which are most significant by virtue of their capacity to structure the social relations of other areas. How far the social relationships of knowledge transmission, through their effects upon *pupils*, affect the site of immediate production will be largely contingent and, in most cases, relatively inconsequential given the essentially arbitrary relationship between their social forms at any point in time.

Although the examples used to illustrate the positions generated by Bernstein's principles are derived from the British educational context, obviously his theory has general application. The critical issue is that of the specific conditions under which various possibilities are realized and their form and social distribution within a society. The situation in Britain at the moment is particularly interesting because there is a clearly defined struggle in progress to bring about a radical restructuring of education which involves a movement from a +C−SR/+C+SR situation (ie one which combines traditionalist and progressive forms within a relatively autonomous system) to a −C+SR situation in which 'education' is strongly defined in terms of an occupational vocationalist model. This move is associated with the emergence of the Manpower Services Commission and its powerful and distinctive capacity to intervene within the educational system and is more widely associated with the restructuring of British politics following the collapse of the post-war social democratic consensus and the emergence of the Thatcherite new-right.[16]

Conclusion

The argument developed in this chapter is as follows:

(i) The radical sociology of education in the early seventies was constructed around three interrelated concerns: (a) how to preserve a phenomenologically inspired *active model of the subject* whilst (b) retaining a *strong concept of social structure* in which to ground the ethnographic analsysis of educational processes; and (c) maintaining the *possibility of radical action and social transformation*.

(ii) The correspondence principle, that the form of the social relations of education correspond to the form of the social relations of capitalist production, articulated the relationship between *social structure* and *educational processes*. However, whilst apparently providing a solution to the structure/process problem, the principle in its original formulation violated the conditions for action and transformation. Much of the following revision of correspondence theory traces and retraces the movement between the subjectivist/voluntarist, structural/determined poles of the theoretical field.

(iii) The subsequent development of the field involves a number of strategies which in various ways repair, extend and supplement the original model (a) by *interrupting* the relationship between education and production by addressing the issues of *policy formation*, *relative autonomy*, and *resistance*; (b) by including the dimensions of gender and race; and (c) by shifting from the concept of *ideology* to that of *hegemony* and the analysis of class culture.

(iv) Taken together these strategies considerably develop the *complexity* of the model of the social totality within which the correspondence principle operates — in particular by defining areas of *contradiction*. But whatever their virtues in raising and focussing *issues*, these developments *do not*, contrary to the claims of certain commentators, fundamentally develop the *theory*.

(v) Essentially the field has been developed through *issues* rather than by *theory*. This is most critically reflected in the neglect of the central concept in the correspondence thesis, namely *capitalist social relations of production*. The foundation of the field and the basis of its essential continuity lies in the identification of the concept *social relations of production* with *the system of social relationships in production*.

(vi) By failing to distinguish between the *immediate production of commodities* and the *process of capitalist production as a whole* and by identifying the social relations of production with the immediate form of the capital relation as it is structured in direct production, the correspondence principle grounds education in a category which is insufficient to support its thesis.

(vii) A major consequence of this is an inability to acknowledge the distinctiveness and specificity of education *as a field (or 'site') in its own right* based in the social relations of *knowledge production*. This, in turn, relates to the lack within the current Marxist sociology of education of a materialist (realist) *theory of knowledge*.

(viii) Some of the implications and possibilities of approaching the Marxist sociology of education from the alternative perspective outlined were explored in relation to the work of Bernstein.

The alternative approach suggested neither abolishes nor automatically solves any of the major issues or problems raised within the development of correspondence theory. It advocates their theoretical *relocation* in terms of the division between the systems of education, production and the social relations of production. It is suggested that it is (a) theoretically more consistent with the basic categories of Marxist theory (though it should be noted that the capacity to differentiate the educational and occupational systems is not an exclusive property of Marxism); (b) that a model which acknowledges the independence of the educational system from production is *more successful* (*pace* Bowles and Gintis) than correspondence theory in accomodating the *relevant body of substantive* data; (c) provides a crucial addition by raising the issue of the *specificity* of education in terms of the social relations of knowledge production and the subsequent requirement for an appropriate theory of knowledge; and (d) is able to accomodate its *complexities* within a *systematic theoretical form* (viz Bernstein) as opposed to the essentially ad hoc manner in which the (issues led) development of correspondence theory has proceeded.

Ten years on from the publication of *Schooling in Capitalist America* the Marxist sociology of education must consolidate its gains and cease retracing its own footsteps between the class structure and the classroom. Perhaps the reason that there have been so many departures and so few arrivals is that too much time has been spent returning home to collect things we forgot.

Acknowledgement

The development of the views expressed here owes a great deal to the time I was fortunate to spend teaching on the education branch of the MSc Sociology degree course at the Polytechnic of the South Bank between 1979 and 1986. I would like to express my thanks to my colleagues and friends, Mike Hickox, Eva Stina Lyon, Jean Seaton and Paul Hebden and to all those who were our students in that period. I would also like to thank Basil Bernstein for the characteristic generosity in time and attention that he gave to the first draft of this chapter and Mike Cole and Gerald Grace for their comments on revised versions.

Notes

1 See, for instance, MacDonald (1977).
2 E S Lyon stressed, at the time of its publication, the degree to which *Schooling* can be located within a distinctively American radical tradition of sociological work (she refers to C. Wright Mills and Veblen). She refers to the book's *Marxism* as a 'perspective' rather than a deeply theorized position (Lyon, 1977). The contrast with Althusser and *his* tradition is obvious.
3 For a critical discussion of this article see Hargreaves, 1982.
4 On the concept of *contradiction* see, for instance, Keat and Urry, 1975, pp 114–8.
5 These preoccupations are very much evident in the book which can be seen as the successor to *Knowledge and Control Society, State and Schooling* edited by Michael Young and Geoff Whitty (Young, and Whitty, 1977).
6 See, for instance, Collins, 1981 and Tyler, 1977.
7 See Boudon, 1974.
8 In the *Grundrisse* Marx (1973) writes: 'If the capitalist were to content himself with merely the capacity of disposing (of labour power), without actually making the worker work, e.g., in order to have his labour as a reserve . . . then the exchange has taken place in full' (p 282).
9 See Moore, 1987.
10 For a recent example of a somewhat similar argument which well represents a clear commitment to the correspondence principle see Carnoy and Levin, 1985; and Review Symposium, British Journal of Sociology of Education, 7, 3, 1986.
11 For a notable exception to this see Matthews, 1980. On 'realism' see in particular the work of R. Bhaskar and, within the wider context of sociological theory, Benton, 1977.
12 For various aspects of this see Wiener, 1981; and Hickox, 1986.
13 See Dale *et al*, 1986.
14 I am grateful to E.S. Lyon for her comments on an earlier version of this application of Bernstein's ideas.

15 See MOORE, 1983 and 1984.
16 See DALE *et al*, 1986; and MOORE, in press.

References

ALTHUSSER, L. (1972) 'Ideology and the ideological state apparatuses' in COSIN B. (Ed) *Education: Structure and Society*, Harmondsworth, Penguin Books.

ARNOT, M.and WHITTY, G. (1982) 'From reproduction to transformation ...', *British Journal of Sociology of Education*, 3.

BERNSTEIN, B. (1977) *Class, Codes and Control*, Vol 3, London, Routledge and Kegan Paul.

BERNSTEIN, B. (1982) 'Codes, modalities and the process of cultural reproduction: A model', in APPLE M. (Ed) *Cultural and Economic Reproduction in Education*, London, Routledge and Kegan Paul.

BENTON, T. (1977) *The Philosophical foundations of the Three Sociologies*, London, Routledge and Kegan Paul.

BHASKAR, R. (1975) *A Realist Theory of Science*, Leeds, Leeds Books.

BOUDON, R. (1974) *Education, Opportunity and Social Inequality*, New York, John Wiley.

BOWLES, S and GINTIS, H. (1976) *Schooling in Capitalist America*, London, Routledge and Kegan Paul.

CARNOY, M. and LEVIN, H. (1985) *Schooling and Work in the Democratic State*, Stanford, Stanford University Press.

CLARKE, S. (1980) 'The value of value: Rereading capital', *Capital and Class* 10.

COLLINS, R. (1981) *The Credential Society*, New York, Academic Press.

DALE R. *et al* (1986) *TVEI: A Policy Hybrid*, unpublished paper, Open University.

GINTIS, H. and BOWLES, S. 'Contradiction and Reproduction in Education', this volume.

HAMMERSLEY, M. and WOODS, P. (Eds) (1976) *The Process of Schooling*, London, Routledge and Kegan Paul.

HARGREAVES, A. (1982) 'Resistance and relative autonomy theories.', *British Journal of Sociology of Education* 3.

HICKOX, M. (1982) 'The Marxist sociology of education: A critique', *British Journal of Sociology*, 33.

HICKOX, M. (1984) 'A reply to Roy Nash', *British Journal of Sociology of Education*, 5.

HICKOX, M. (1986) 'Has there been a British intelligensia?', *British Journal of Sociology*, 37.

KEAT, R. and URRY, J. (1975) *Social Theory as Science*, London, Routledge and Kegan Paul.

LYON, E. S. (1977) 'The sociology of capitalist education', *Sociologisk Forskning*, 2 March.

MACDONALD, M. (now ARNOT, M.) (1977) *Culture, Class and the Curriculum*, Open University Schooling and Society Course, Block III, unit 16, Milton Keynes, Open University Press.

MARX, K. (1973) *Grundrisse*, Harmondsworth, Penguin Books.

MARX, K. (1976) *Capital*, vol 1, Harmondsworth, Penguin Books.

MATTHEWS, M. R. (1980) *The Marxist Theory of Schooling: A Study of Epistemology and Education*, Brighton, Harvester Press.

MOORE, R. (1983) 'Pedagogy, production, and further education', in GLEESON D. (Ed) *Youth Training and the Search For Work*, London, Routledge and Kegan Paul.

MOORE, R. (1984) 'Schooling and the world of work', in BATES I. *et al*, *Schooling For The Dole*?, Basingstoke, Macmillan.

Moore, R. (1987) 'Education and the ideology of production', *British Journal of Sociology of Education*, 8, 2.

Nash, R. (1984) 'On two critiques of the Marxist sociology of education', *British Journal of Sociology of Education*, 5.

Purvis, J. and Moore, R. (1986) '"Schooling and work in the democratic state", M. Carnoy and H. Levin' *Review Symposium, British Journal of Sociology of Education* 7, 1986.

Sarup, M. (1978) *Marxism and Education*, London, Routledge and Kegan Paul.

Tyler W. (1977) *The Sociology of Educational Inequality*, London, Methuen.

Whitty, G. (1977) 'Sociology and the problem of radical educational change' in Young M. F. D. and Whitty G. (Eds) *Society, State and Schooling*, Lewes, Falmer Press.

Wiener, M. (1981) *English Culture and the Decline of the Industrial Spirit, 1850–1980*, London, Cambridge University Press.

Woods, P. and Hammersley, M. (Eds) (1977) *School Experience*, London, Croom Helm.

Young, M. F. D. (Ed) (1971) *Knowledge and Control*, London, Collier MacMillan.

Young, M. F. D. and Whitty, G. (Eds) (1977) *Society, State and Schooling*, Lewes, Falmer Press.

5 *Historical School Reform and the Correspondence Principle*

Peter MacDonald

Introduction

Perhaps the most important characteristic of contemporary systems of education is that they are public — both sponsored and secured by the state. As such, contemporary education expresses within its existence the culmination of an historical process that had its origin (in North America at least) in the common school movement. To genuinely comprehend modern education, then, is to equally comprehend the genesis of the common school; it was at this historical moment that the state commenced its appropriation of that particular space within civil society.

The above is not likely to be controversial. However, an implication emerges from this perspective: a theory purporting to interpret contemporary systems of education must equally be able to interpret the origins of the common school. Indeed, its capacity to do so may be considered a test of its validity.

This, then, is one criterion according to which theories of education may be evaluated. And this is the criterion to be employed here where the specific theory of education to be assessed is the correspondence principle set forth by Bowles and Gintis in their classic *Schooling in Capitalist America*. [1]

History is important. Bowles and Gintis are well aware of this; fully four of the eleven chapters of *Schooling in Capitalist America* are devoted to it. Thus. the utilization of this criterion has the value that Bowles and Gintis are likely to find it acceptable. They themselves place great weight on the relevance and significance of historical interpretation. They point out, for instance, that an

> . . . understanding of US education, however, requires that we know more than the dominant economic effects of schooling and the structural mechanisms which produce these effects. We must discover how the school system changes.[2]

To discover how the school system changes requires a theory capable of comprehending the patterns of historical development. Further, such a theory, argues Bowles and Gintis, must cope with each of the moments in that pattern, each of the historical periods of school reform. Finally, Bowles and Gintis follow their own advice, isolating and interpreting in part III three great historical moments of school reform, the first of which was the origins of mass public education.

Moreover, in their self-criticism 'Contradictions and reproduction in educational theory', Bowles and Gintis reiterate the validity of history as a test of the correspondence principle:

> The contradiction between reproduction and accumulation thus takes the form of the educational system periodically falling out of harmony with the evolving structure of capitalist production relations. We do not think the contradiction between reproduction and accumulation is incorrect. Indeed it is capable of aiding our understanding of both the striking periodicity of educational reform and of the major periods of educational change — such as the Common School Movement . . .[3]

Though other mistakes were made, this was not one of them.

In light of the above, it is reasonable to assess the validity of the correspondence principle in terms of how it copes with the intepretation of the common school movement. That is the point of this chapter, firstly by presenting an overview of Bowles and Gintis' analysis, secondly by critiquing that analysis, and finally by offering a few suggestions toward an alternative explanation. This will be done in the concrete, comparative historical context of nineteenth-century Ontario and New England.

Correspondence in History

The correspondence principle is the theoretical heart of *Schooling in Capitalist America*. Its particular contribution, identified by Bowles and Gintis in *Schooling in Capitalist America* and reiterated in their self-critique, is that it derives its explanatory power from its emphasis on the underlying structure of social relations shaping the site of schooling. As a consequence, analytic attention is directed to the primacy of form or structure over the actual content (for example, curriculum) of schooling.[4]

The fundamental structural element which specifies the correspondence principle is the contradiction between the accumulation of capital and the reproduction of its requisites. It is this contradiction that shapes, through correspondence, the particular role of education. For it is the system of education that vitiates this contradiction by means of its structural correspondence with the social relations of production. Moreover, as the rhythms of capital accumulation ebb and flow in defining the history of a given social formation, the nature and the extent of this contradiction itself proceeds and recedes, thereby providing the theoretical probability of the absence of correspondence between education and production relations. It is in precisely these historical moments that educational reform movements appear, their particular natures being formed by the historical content of the fundamental contradiction. The consequence of reform is the re-establishment of correspondence. This is the foundation for the interpretation of educational transformations.

Moving from the abstract to the specific, Bowles and Gintis argue that the '... educational system reproduces the capitalist social division of labour ... through a correspondence between its own internal social relationships and those of the workplace'.[5] In matters of authority relations (between teachers and students), alienated labour (assignments, tests, and grading), and fragmentation (of the curriculum), the experience of schooling presages the experience of labour; simply, the labour process of schooling corresponds with the labour process of production.[6] Moreover, the variety of levels of schooling (themselves characterized by different social relations) feed students *qua* workers into the variety of levels of the occupational structure.[7] It is these structural details of correspondence that provide for the vitiation of the contradiction between accumulation and reproduction while simultaneously providing for the formative features of educational systems.

Having established the theoretical bona fides, the concern at hand can now be addressed — applying the correspondence principle to the genesis of the common school. Rather reminiscent of Dreeben,[8] Bowles and Gintis argue that as the social patterns characterizing families become increasingly unlike the social patterns of production, the structural space for mass, public education is created.[9] The problematic of correspondence is thus established, providing a general context for the interpretation of schooling. Specifically, the pattern of capital accumulation undermined the combination of production and reproduction within the household unit of production in the years 1820–1860, thereby resulting in the ever increasing bifurcation of the social relations of production from those of reproduction.[10] Bowles and Gintis cite many instances indicative of this more general, underlying process: these include the creation of a powerful capitalist class, the concomitant appearance of wage labour, changes in the skill requirements structured by the labour process thereby rendering family education useless and apprenticeship redundant, the appearance of worker mobility both geographical (labour migrations and immigration) and social (in and out of the reserve army of labour), and increases in inequality.[11] From this constellation of factors Bowles and Gintis give pride of place to the rise of the factory as the dominant unit of production.[12] In light of this analysis of New England society in the first half of the nineteenth century, Bowles and Gintis conclude that the family's role in

> ... reproduction was increasingly out of touch with economic reality. A permanent proletariat and an impoverished and, for the most part, ethnically distinct, reserve army of the unemployed had been created. Economic inequality had increased. Small manufacturing towns had become urban areas almost overnight. The expansion of capitalist production had at once greatly enhanced the power of the capitalist class and had inexorably generated a condition which challenged their continued domination.[13]

This was the historical conjuncture which saw the origins of the common school.

The disjunction between production and reproduction, created by the replacement of the household unit of production with the factory system, defines the lack of correspondence which mandated the historical arrival of the common school. This is a critically significant event for it symbolizes the appropriation by the state (in the form of an ideological state apparatus) of a site in civil society. As noted earlier, common schools were, above all, state schools. It was under the aegis of the state that correspondence was established between production and reproduction. By means of the common school the reproductive requisites for capital accumulation were institutionalized. To use Bowles and Gintis' words, the '... expansion of mass education ... has been a central element in resolving — at least temporarily — the contradiction between accumulation and reproduction'.[14]

It is on this foundation that educational transformations in general, the common school in particular, are to be understood. As a result of their historical analysis, Bowles and Gintis conclude that the

> ... changes in the structure of education are associated with changes in the social organization of production. The fact that changes in the structure of production have preceded parallel changes in schooling establishes a strong *prima facie* case for the causal importance of economic structure as a major determinant of educational structure.[15]

The dynamics of capital accumulation incessantly alter the organization of production and, with it, the appropriateness of the social relations of reproduction. The gulf is bridged, correspondence re-established, via educational transformation. Given the boundaries of the correspondence principle, the genesis of the common school is thus interpreted.

In conclusion, capitalism in general, the pulse of capital accumulation in particular, was responsible for structuring the conjuncture of the common school. The expansion of the forces of production together with the transformation of the social relations of production by the factory system (in terms of both ownership and the labour process) created the fundamental contradiction between accumulation and reproduction. This contradiction provided the foundation for the origin of mass, public education. As Bowles and Gintis themselves conclude:

> We have argued that the expansion of the industrial capitalist system was a major force promoting educational reform and expansion in the ante bellum period.[16]

This is the analysis to be considered below.

Correspondence and Periodization

With the emphasis of the correspondence principle on the replication of the labour process within the social relations of education, the question of the periodization of history becomes absolutely crucial. To determine if the structure of education indeed replicates production relations as posited by this principle demands very careful historical specification of the development of those production relations. And this, of course, is the question of the periodization of history.

Dividing history into periods appears simple, but this is deceptive. The very act of periodization conceptually constitutes historical moments of stability and transformation, thus providing the point of reference for the determination of correspondence. To assert that education corresponds within the social relations of production is to assert that both are within the boundaries of a given moment. To assert that education is not in correspondence with the social relations of production is to assert that education has 'fallen behind', thereby providing the conjuncture for reform. The correspondence principle can only make sense by presupposing periodization; periodization is a prerequisite to the application of the correspondence principle. The significance of this question cannot be overestimated. The theoretical act of periodization takes primacy over all other theoretical endeavours; indeed, correspondence acquires its theoretical significance only in the context of appropriate periodication.

The above suggests that the application of the correspondence principle is a two-stage affair. One must firstly determine the period of the historical moment in question and secondly ascertain whether the system of education does replicate the essential structural nature of that period. It is to the former question that concern is now directed, with primary concern being directed to the criteria according to which periodization is to be accomplished.

Marxist historiography must have as its primary focus the reproduction of the capital-labour relationship.[17] This focus itself points the way to periodization. The capital-labour relation presupposes primitive accumulation (the onset of proletarianization). At the core of this relationship is the production of surplus value. The manner in which it is produced and later transformed into capital determines the organization of the labour process. Here one is referring to the nature of the subordination of labour to capital (formal or real) and the corresponding sort of production unit (manufactory or factory). Transition from one to the other defines the meaning of the concept of capital accumulation.

It is perhaps too simple to say that the concept of capital accumulation provides the framework for the historical exercise of periodization.Only when one realizes that this grasps primitive accumulation, the production of absolute surplus value, and finally the production of relative surplus value (and the corresponding types of production relations) can one realistically construct the periodization of history. Only when one carefully specifies such terms as capitalism and industrialization in terms of their concomitant articulation of the forces of production with the social relations of production can one commence periodization. And only when one conceptualizes this changed articulation of forces and relations of production that specify the rhythms of capital accumulation can one complete the periodization exercise. Yet this is precisely what must be done as a prerequisite to the application of the correspondence principle.

The question which now arises is whether this is the procedure actually employed by Bowles and Gintis. To deal with this question is the real point of this chapter. For now it is important to make one observation on Bowles' and Gintis' approach.

In an essay on the historiography of educational transformation, Curtis points out that much of the recent work on historical educational reform has been situated within what he refers to as the social control paradigm.[18] This paradigm sees educational reform as the product of the response of elites or the bourgeoisie to the problems of social unrest endemic to early industrial capitalism.[19] Factors constituting this unrest identified by the paradigm range from urban poverty and crime to the formation of a class conscious proletariat.

Within the confines of the social control paradigm, Curtis identifies two principal variations — revisionism and reproduction theory.[20] The former tends to the concepts of industrialization, urbanization, and poverty, while the latter emphasizes capitalism and class conflict. However, these differences are subsumed within membership of the larger social control paradigm.

Curtis notes that the outstanding exponent of revisionism is Michael Katz. Having made this point, he then proceeds to argue that reproduction theory, the second variant, has

> ... largely been conducted within the same social control paradigm, with a few changes of a largely terminological nature. Bowles and Gintis, for instance, take Katz's study as the basis of their examination of educational reform in the United States in the middle of the nineteenth century.[21]

This observation is not unwarranted for Bowles and Gintis themselves acknowledge their debt to revisionism in general and Katz in particular.[22] They do, however, specify where they depart from the revisionists, which they see primarily in their utilization of the Marxist model of capital accumulation.

This is partially correct. At the theoretical level, Bowles and Gintis do operate within the Marxist model of capital accumulation. Indeed, the very essence of the correspondence principle is defined by this model. But at the level of empirical analysis, Bowles and Gintis rely heavily on the studies done by Katz and the revisionists (which is not surprising given the broad aims of *Schooling in Capitalist America*). The effect of this procedure is to rest their reproduction theory on the empirical foundation of revisionism. Thus, the empirical validity of the correspondence principle is evaluated according to the concrete history produced by the revisionist lens.

The consequences of this strategy will be discussed in some detail below. For now, recall that the very concept of correspondence is bound inextricably with the theory according to which history is periodized. It is reasonable, then, to examine both the manner in which the revisionists have gone about the periodization process and the difficulties they have faced. Because of this, what follows is as much about the substance of revisionist historical interpretation as it is about the theory of the correspondence principle. When this has been done, it will be possible to ascertain whether the reliance by Bowles and Gintis on revisionist history has undermined their historical application of the correspondence principle and, with it, its theoretical validity.

Revisionism and Periodization

Consider the quotation below, taken from Michael Katz:

> Within the lifetime of one man a new society was born, a society that smashed old expectations with the force of steam, that ripped apart and restitched the web of relationships comprising the experiences of men.[23]

Now consider the following quotation, taken from Marvin Lazerson:

> Assuming that New England society had once been homogeneous, its institutions balanced and sharing in the education of all individuals, . . . nineteenth century reformers believed that a prior social harmony had been rudely shattered.[24]

A rather curious point emerges from the comparison of these quotations. While each is dealing with the phenomenon of educational transformation in nineteenth century Massachusetts, they are analyzing periods of history separated by three decades (the ellipsis in the second quotation replaces the word 'late'). Indeed, the statement in the second quotation describing a previously homogeneous and balanced society is speaking of precisely the same society depicted as ripped apart in the first.

One might suppose that such anomalies as this in periodization are to be explained with reference to the different factors being utilized in each case as the basis for the periodization exercise. But this is not so for, as both authors work within the revisionist paradigm, both periodize educational history on the basis of identical factors. As their foundation for historical periodization is industrialization and urbanization, to point to anomalies in periodization is simultaneously to question the formative role of industrialization and urbanization on educational reform.

With the publication of the expanded edition of *Class, Bureaucracy, and Schools*, Katz took the opportunity to argue in the epilogue that while Schultz was too early in his identification of the origins of the common school, Lazerson was too late.[25] But while acknowledging these difficulties of periodization, he did not deny its foundation. Instead, he argued that the problem was more a question of the use of urbanization to specify unique historical eras. Nineteenth century schooling, Katz notes, functioned to discipline the work force by '... teaching an essentially rural and non-industrial population the norms of modern urban life ...'[26]. Thus the relevance of both industrialization and urbanization to the historical conjuncture of the common school is reiterated.

Thus, within the revisionist position itself there is a dispute over appropriate periodization. It is not that different structural features are being utilized to accomplish periodization; the problem appears to lie more in the manner in which these factors are conceptualized and applied to concrete history. Moreover, to the extent to which Bowles and Gintis rest their theory of the correspondence principle on the empirical studies of revisionism, they equally import the revisionist problems of periodization into their analysis. Not only do they rest the theory of the correspondence principle on an empirical history constituted by revisionist theoretical categories, they also depend on an ambiguous, problematically constructed history. In depending upon the work of the revisionists, Bowles and Gintis unwittingly appropriate serious difficulties in periodization. Resting reproduction theory on revisionist evidence may be a questionable procedure; when the evidence itself is problematic, the procedure appears even more questionable.

These difficulties are indicative and symptomatic of the problems associated with the factors used by the revisionists in doing their periodization. Simply by their presence, the urban-industrial (and capitalist) model of educational transformation is open to question. In light of this, a closer examination of the way in which the revisionists conceptualize these factors should prove useful.

The revisionists conceive of urbanization primarily in terms of the geographical concentration of population, constituted by immigrants and dispossessed agrarians, resulting in a marked increase in the size of the working class.[27] Revisionist work in Canada in particular makes much of this class of urban poor, stressing the consequences of delinquency, crime, and vagrancy.[28] Abetting this process was industrialization understood primarily in such terms as the growth in manufacturing and the number employed by industry.[29] Katz extends this analysis to the case of shoemakers, discussing how the organization of their work was transformed by industrialization.[30] Bowles and Gintis, operating within the model of capital accumulation, speak more of capitalism than industrialization, tending to highlight the development of the factory system and the creation of a proletariat. But although they use the theory of capital accumulation, they also use the empirical findings of the revisionists, themselves the product of urban-industrial model.

Now despite the use of such terminology as the changing organization of work, the appearance of a proletariat, the norms of modern urban life, and the like, neither industrialization nor urbanization are explicitly defined. Moreover, the connection of these concepts with the social relations of production is left unspecified. Precisely because of their interpretive burden, and because of the disputes over periodization, it is vital to do so.

Neither the revisionists nor the reproduction theorists have done this. Thus, this is the task at hand. The concepts to which history is to be periodized must be carefully constructed. And they must be conceptualized with a view to their effects on the structuring of the labour process. As Bowles and Gintis employ the Marxist model of capital accumulation, it is to Marx that one must turn. Once this model of periodization has been devloped, it will become possible to reanalyze revisionist history. One will then be in a position to determine the effects of Bowles and Gintis' utilization of revisionism to empirically document their correspondence principle.

Theory of Periodization

In one of the prefaces to *Capital*, Engels argues that conventional political economy was content to take the everyday terms of commercial and industrial life thereby distorting the analyses so produced. This was especially true of the term industry (and consequently of industrialization) the usage of which denied the distinction between

> . two great and essentially different periods of economic history: the period of manufacture proper, based on the division of manual labour, and the period of modern industry based on machinery.[31]

The theoretical significance of this distinction was highlighted by Stedman Jones when he pointed out that Marx's analysis in *Capital* of the industrial revolution was concerned not so much with a change in the ownership of the means of production but rather with changes in the organization of the labour process (from division of manual labour to machinery).[32] Balibar makes much the same point in his proposed distinction between the formal and real subsumption of labour by capital. He argues that capitalism as a social relation of production existed prior to the real subsumption of labour, that its inception corresponded with the formal subsumption of labour.[33] Finally, Hogan notes that it is only subsequent to the appearance of capitalism that the labour process is reconstituted '. . . upon a new social and technical basis which gave capital control of the labour process'.[34] The transition from formal to real subordination of the labour process occurred within the framework of capitalist social relations; it did not occur at the level of capitalist social relations but rather at the level of the labour process once it had initially been structured by capital.[35]

The point of the foregoing is that, as these types of subsumption correspond with the historical periods of manufacture and modern industry, their distinction must be founded on the manner in which the labour process is constituted. To speak, as do the revisionists, in terms of industrialization or even of capitalism is to miss this distinction for it cannot be apprehended on the level of the ownership of the means of production alone. This becomes all the more critical for Marx defined industrialization as the transition from manufacture to modern industry.[38] Thus, to use this concept without the correlative concepts of manufacture and modern industry is to miss the notion of period and transformation. Without the concepts of manufacture and machinofacture, there can be no analysis of the labour processes embodied in each — which, of course, is crucial to the documentation of the correspondence principle. All of these concepts must be specified to provide for the periodization exercise.

As both these historical periods are characterized by constancy in the social relations of production, this discussion will be focussed around the variability in the productive forces, in the organization of the labour process.

Marx defined manufacture as '. . . the assemblage, in one workshop under the control of a single capitalist, of labourers belonging to the various independent handicrafts . . .'[37]. The earliest stages of manufacture, however, are '. . . hardly to be distinguished . . . from the handicraft trades of guilds, otherwise than by the greater number of workmen simultaneously employed by one and the same individual capital'.[38]This handicraft mode of the existence of capital defined by Marx as simple cooperation is characterized by the absence of fundamental alteration in the labour process relative to its predecessor, independent commodity production.[39]

Though cooperation is the first form of capital and thus its necessary condition, it is not a stage of production in its own right.[40] Since '. . . the sway of capital develops into a requisite for carrying on the labour process itself, into a real requisite of production'[41] simple cooperation inevitably leads to the reorganization of work into a systematic division of labour. Marx referred to this phase of manufacture as the detail division of labour characterized by '. . . the decomposition of the process of production into its various successive steps ... with the resolution of a handicraft into its successive manual operations'.[42] This detail labourer is constituted by the transformed labour process in the manner indicated below:

> While simple cooperation leaves the mode of working by the individual for the most part unchanged, manufacture thoroughly revolutionizes it, and seizes labour power by its very roots. It converts the labourer into a crippled monstrosity, by forcing his detained dexterity at the expense of a world of productive capabilities and instincts . . .[43]

Manufacture, then, is characterized by the reconstitution of the labour process from the inception of the phase of simple cooperation to the phase of the detail division of labour.

The stage subsequent to manufacture is modern industry. Here the transformation is not so much with labour as it is with the instruments of labour, with the means of production. Modern industry is founded on the introduction of machinery:

> The starting point of modern industry is ... the revolution in the instruments of labour ... which attains its most highly developed form in the organized system of machinery in a factory. The revolution in the mode of production ... begins with the instruments of labour being converted from tools into machines.[44]

The conversion of the means of labour from tools into machines acquires its significance from its effects on the labour process. Again, quoting Marx:

> In manufacture, the workman makes use of a tool, in the factory, the machine makes use of him. There the movements of the instrument of labour proceed from him, here it is the movements of the machine he must follow. In manufacture the workmen are parts of a living mechanism. In the factory we have a lifeless mechanism independent of the workmen, who become its mere living appendage.[45]

Direct producers becoming appendages signifies the realization of real subordination or subsumption of the labour process by capital.

The reconstitution of the labour process specified by the transition from manufacture to modern industry conditions the cultural dimension of the process of proletarian class formation. The effects of the first stage, manufacture, on this process is rather less than clear — especially if its two phases of cooperation and detail labour are confounded. But for simple cooperation, the cleavage between capital and labour appears muted by the retention of a petty commodity producer labour process, the essence of which lies in a small number of artisans cooperatively exercising their craft skills with a maximum of autonomy from capital. For the phase of detail labour, the picture is somewhat clouded with the initiation of the transition from formal to substantive subsumption. Marx argued that since

> . . . handicraft skill is the foundation of manufacture, and since the mechanism of manufacture as a whole possesses no framework apart from the labourers themselves, capital is constantly compelled to wrestle with the insubordination of the workmen.[46]

Commonly, then '. . . there runs the complaint of want of discipline among the workmen'.[47] On the other hand, because of the variety of skill levels associated with detail labour, workers were divided into the classification of skilled and unskilled with mobility mediated by apprenticeship.[48] This pattern of integration into the production process could well structure class formation in non-radical directions.[49]

The second period, modern industry, is far clearer on the question of class formation. Marx identifies the effects of modern industry below:

> . . . the character of independence and estrangement which the capitalist mode of production as a whole gives to the instrument of labour and to the product, as against the workman, is developed by means of machinery into a thorough antagonism. Therefore, it is with the advent of machinery, that the workman for the first time brutally revolts against the instruments of labour.[50]

The real subordination inherent in capitalism finds its fullest expression in modern industry engendering a radical component in proletarian class formation. Most significantly, radicalism manifests itself most strongly precisely at the point of transition when machinery first undermines the labour process characteristic of manufacture;[51] comparatively, then, modern industry in its consequences appears much more radical than does either phase of manufacture.

Marx's conclusion here is founded upon the particular ways in which the labour process is restructured by modern industry. Because machinery dispenses with both physical power and skill, women and children become direct producers thereby depreciating the value of labour power from the man to his family.[52] Because the pace of production is controlled by machinery (i.e. its owners), the labour process itself is intensified both by increasing the speed of machinery and by giving the direct producer more machinery to tend.[53] Because machinery symbolizes a shift in the organic composition of capital, of the ratio of dead to living labour, a relative surplus populaton of the unemployed is created subject to the vagaries of the accumulation process. Thus, potential labour power as well is structured by capital; the effects of capital spread beyond the specific site of production. It is in the context of this sort of analysis that Marx argues

> ... only since the introduction of machinery has the workman fought against the instrument of labour itself, the material embodiment of capital. He revolts against this particular form of the means of production, as being the material basis of the capitalist mode of production.[54]

In conclusion, though the detail labour phase of the manufactory stage may result in problems of insubordination on the part of labour from the perspective of capital, the transition to modern industry (which is also the definition of industrialization) provokes the more radical consequences in proletarian class formation.[55] This transition, from formal to substantive subsumption of labour power by capital, corresponds with a transition in the foundation of exploitation, from absolute surplus value to relative surplus value. These correspondences — simultaneously at the level of the organization of production, at the level of the labour process, and at the level of exploitation — shape in a radical direction proletarian class formation.[56]

Because in Marx's view, urbanization was so intimately connected with industrialization, it may be dealt with rather briefly. Marx defined urbanization as the separation and opposition of town and country which, simply because it provided for the separation of capital from landed property, equally provided for the development of independent capital.[57] This separation permitted property and labour to be governed by exchange relations within a context structured by capital and the division of labour.[58]

Once this process had become manifest, a division of labour amongst the cities themselves developed in which there was specialization in terms of production and trade. As well as serving as the foundation for long-distance exchange, towns also specialized in production, giving rise to the manufactory.[59] In this sense, urbanization and industrialization were concomitants.

The other feature of urbanization relevant to this argument is identified by Marx when he noted that '... modern history is the urbanization of the countryside, not, as among the ancients, the ruralization of the city'.[60] The urbanization of the countryside was constituted by such processes as the destruction of rural trades complementing agricultural production thereby bringing about one type of rural depopulation, and the domination of the countryside by the cities through the exchange relations found on long-distance trade.

Urbanization, then, is intimately related to industrialization. It too had a role to play, especially in the creation of agrarian protest for the reasons outlined above. So both urbanization and industrialization reinforce some of the essential properties of the other.

In light of the above, it is necessary to specify concepts such as capitalism, and industrialization and urbanization in terms of their association with the periods of production, themselves defined according to the organization of the labour process. This provides the basis for a conceptually rigorous periodization of history. It also provides the context for the assessment of revisionist history on which Bowles and Gintis rest their empirical case.

Capitalism and Educational Transformation

Relating the foregoing argument developed by Marx to that of the revisionists tends, at first glance, to lend them credence. Industrialization produced a radical dimension to proletarian class formation, with urbanization contributing in the form of agrarian protest. Together they provided the context for the intervention of mass education to meet this threat to the social order. But the plausibility of this explanation depends of course upon the interpretation of industrialization and urbanization.

Beginning with New England, much of Katz's argument is based on Essex County, Massachusetts in the 1850s. Using material provided by Thernstrom, the following picture emerges for Essex County in 1875. Of all the manual workers, 41.5 per cent were semi-skilled and 41.2 per cent were classified as artisans. (The remaining 17 per cent were labourers described by Thernstrom in terms of the very short and casual nature of their jobs.) While presumably artisans correspond with self-employment or with one of the phases of manufacture, it is difficult to know how to treat the semi-skilled classification. However, within this particular category, the factory operative subdivision presumably corresponds with the factory system; they comprise only 7.6 per cent of the total.[61] It is difficult to draw unambiguous conclusions from this for one cannot derive from census categories the concrete organization of the labour process. But the division of workers into manufacture and modern industry appears to be at best relatively equal. And this a quarter century later than the period with which Katz was concerned.

What is clear is the uneven nature of the transition to the industrialization. Precisely because of this unevenness, one would anticipate uneven class formation. It is in this sort of situation that the possibility of attributing the behaviour of only one segment to the entire class becomes a danger.

It will be recalled that Katz made much of the situation of shoemakers, his description indicating that they were caught in the throes of industralization. He buttresses his argument by showing that they voted to reject the high school in Beverly by 73 per cent to 27 per cent. But he does overlook the fact that, when artisans are taken as a whole, the vote was almost evenly divided — 47 per cent to 53 per cent.[62] So the working class was not nearly as united as examination of the shoemakers alone would suggest.

Points made in a recent article by Hogan have some relevance here. He argues that the shoemaking industry in Lynn, Massachusetts was transformed into a system of wage labour *before* industrialization, before mechanization and modern industry.[63] Corresponding to this stage of manufacture was what Hogan called the 'politics of defense' by newly subsumed petty commodity producers, '. . . the politics of a working class subject to formal subordination but not yet to real subordination'. Despite (or because of) the reconstitution of the shoemaking labour process within the contours of manufacture, shoemakers '. . . failed to developed organizational strength prior to 1860'. Only after the Civil War, when the labour process was reconstituted by industrialization, did the politics of real subordination appear, assuming the form of militant trade unions.[64] Temporally, this is a period quite distinct from the conjuncture of the common school.

It is difficult to draw unequivocal conclusions from the above. The status of industrialization is unclear, but the period seems to be characterized more by manufacture than by modern industry. Even shoemakers — the advanced segment of the working class — likely laboured more within the context of detail labour. The contradictory behaviour of artisans generally tends to be lost in Katz's emphasis on the shoemakers where he appears to equate their behaviour with the artisan class as a whole. But even the shoemakers exhibited defensive as opposed to radical politics. Whether this was an adequate or even the most significant factor in the historical conjuncture of educational transformation is unclear. Perhaps it can be stated that the role of industrialization *vis-à-vis* educational transformation in Massachusetts is somewhat doubtful.

But what of the role of capitalism? Most interesting in this context is a revision by Katz of his earlier position. When explaining educational reform, he argues that the focus '. . . should be on the spread of wage-labour and the values associated with capitalism rather than urbanization and industrialization'.[65] Since capitalism is based on wage labour, and as wage labour preceded industrialization, Katz argues that the connection between industrialization and educational transformation fails on temporal grounds, precisely the position put forth above.[66] Capitalism in general, not industrialization (nor urbanization) in particular, was responsible for educational reform.

This is superior to his earlier formulation. But capitalism/wage labour is not, as has been shown above, an undifferentiated entity. Rather, it is characterized by developmental states within which the labour process is differently structured by capital. Thus it appears that Katz is proposing, in his denial of industrialization (i.e. the transition to modern industry), manufacture and educational reform as concomitants. Although it is not made explicit, it also appears that Katz is referring to the detail labour phase of manufacture rather than the phase of simple cooperation when utilizing the concept of capitalism. To the extent that this is the case, serious implications for the Bowles and Gintis' position arise in that they appear to treat as coterminous the modern factory system and educational reform with their emphasis on structural replication in the conceptualization of the correspondence principle.

If this is so, Katz's argument ultimately rests on the class actions of detail labourers, the most extreme of whom — shoemakers — were characterized above as practicing defensive politics. If educational reform — no longer associated with industrialization — is to be associated with capitalism, it must, in the last instance, be associated with the defensive politics of shoemakers whose class formation was structured more by their formal than their real subordination by capital. Whether this was adequate to provoke educational reform is unclear. As argued above, the role of industrialization is doubtful; as argued here, the role of capitalism, though less doubtful, is uncertain.

Comparatively, the case is far clearer in mid-nineteenth century Ontario. Beginning with the size of the production unit, the census of 1851 for all of Ontario reveals that the average number of employees per establishment ranges from a high of 9.5 for foundries to a low of 1.7 for grist mills.[67] The case for Markham Township, bordering Toronto, is much the same. Here the figure ranges from a high of 12 for foundries to a low of 1.8 for saw mills.[68]

These relatively small production units appear indicative of an economy in the manufacture state; indeed, perhaps indicative of the phase of simple cooperation. Lending credence to this assertion is the corresponding nature of the class formation identified by Pentland. He describes what he calls the feudal pattern of labour relations and argues that it is associated with these small production units. Primiarily because of the poorly developed labour market (especially with the shortage of skilled workers) in the Ontario of the time, employers — in order to retain their workers— created a cultural unity which overlay production units. This was based on repeated personal contact with workers in which the owner was paternalistic and benevolent, assuming many social costs (for example keeping workers on in periods of slack production). Because this tended to transcend the capital-labour cleavage, there was little foundation for the development of a radical consciousness.[69] And this is precisely what one would expect from a labour process constituted by the phase of simple cooperation.

In a more recent study, Palmer comments on the absence of significant industrial employment prior to 1850; industrial capital began to structure the social landscape of Toronto and Hamilton only by the 1880s.[70] Prior to 1850 were the years of staple exports within a situation of colonial subordination (the Corn Laws and the Navigation Acts). Prior to 1850 were the years of

> . . . primitive accumulation in which the social relations of labouring life, the nature of political rule, cultural developments, and investment and exchange patterns were all setting the stage for the new industrial capitalism to break the fetters that a staples economy had erected everywhere.[71]

It was left to the last half of the nineteenth century to see the rise of the factory system under the aegis of entrepreneurial capitalism.[72]

Prior to 1850, the proletariat in Upper Canada was scarcely constituted. Turning now to its cultural formation, Palmer identifies the period of the 1880s as a unique moment in that here consciousness and solidarity reached their peak.[73] It was in this period that the working class was transformed into an oppositional, alternative movement, thus presenting to capital the greatest threat of the century.

In conclusion, both industrialization *and* capitalism have a doubtful empirical status. Though the situation was ambiguous for New England, it is far clearer in the case of Ontario. And, as one would expect in light of the theoretical argument advanced earlier, the radical restructuration of proletarian class formation with the concomitant potential of radical (rather than defensive) class politics failed to realize. Again, this was especially true of Ontario with the predominance of a feudal pattern of labour relations in the industrial sector.

Given the argument advanced in the previous section, one would anticipate that if the formative role of industrialization is in doubt, then so must the role of urbanization. This will now be examined, devoting particular attention to Ontario, for the Canadian revisionists in particular, place heavy reliance on urbanization.

Both American and Canadian revisionists tend to conceive of urbanization as the concentration of population in geographical areas. Taking them at their word, the population of the largest city in Upper Canada, Toronto, remained at 3.2 per cent of the total population from 1838 to 1851. The total urban population of the province stood at 7.3 per cent of the total in 1848 and 7.5 per cent of the total in 1851.[74] It is quite clear that defined only in terms of the concentration of population, urbanization was not a process of singular relevance to the social structure of Upper Canada at this time.

Given this, it was only in the latter half of the nineteenth century that the period of industrialized capitalism appeared engendering proletarian consciousness and solidarity. This is clearer in the instance of Upper Canada than Massachusetts, but is plausible for both.

Though the contradiction between capital accumulation and reproduction asserted itself during this era, educational transformation was fundamentally complete by the middle of the century. The parameters of the Upper Canadian system are briefly reviewed below.[75]

The Act of 1846 created a new, executive-appointed General Board of education whose responsibilities were the entire province. Its responsibilities were to generally advise the Chief Superintendent and to carefully examine all books in use in the common schools, making appropriate recommendations. The Board also had the authority to refuse the government grant to schools using disapproved books. In this way, central control over the curriculum became manifest, a control which was to be extended by the 1850 Act to the employment of teachers, in that they were to regulate the classification of teachers and to oversee the operation of the normal school.

This latter act also established the Boards of Public Instruction for each county, the purpose of which was to certify teachers and to select textbooks in accordance with the regulations laid down by the Council of Public Instruction.

The Chief Superintendent was required by the 1846 Act to sit on the General Board of Education, to ensure that the legislative grant was applied only to the purposes for which it was intended, and to promote the establishment of school libraries. In the area of curriculum, he was to discourage the use of unsuitable books and to provide for the use of approved, uniform ones. The Act of 1850 maintained these provisions, and provided some additional powers. The Chief Superintendent was now to prepare general rules and regulations for all common schools. He was empowered to certify all teachers who satisfactorily completed normal school, thereby transcending more local certification procedures. Finally, there were county and local superintendents who were to act at the behest of the Chief Superintendent. Thus, both curriculum and teachers were subjected to the centralized construction of bureaucratic procedures.

The outstanding feature of this system was the extent to which, by 1850, it was centralized and controlled by the state. In the context of the period, it was a modern public system. This does not seem to have been a peculiarity of the historical experience of Upper Canada. To a lesser extent, the situation in Massachusetts was also peculiar. And this 'peculiarity' seems to be a constant when one considers comparative developmental patterns as well.

Given the correspondence principle, one would anticipate that a more highly developed capitalist society would possess a system of education more advanced (especially in terms of its public and bureaucratic properties) than that of a less industrialized society. In this respect, it is instructive to compare England, Massachusetts, and Ontario of the mid-nineteenth century.

Johnson describes the English system of education in 1846 as being weakly related to the state, as having a dominant Anglican presence at the local level, and as possessing a decentralized pattern of provision — hardly characteristic of an advanced common school system[76]. Following a visit to Ontario, the editor of the *Massachusetts Teacher* described the Upper Canadian system of education in the November, 1855 issue as follows:

> So much has been written and said about the Prussian System of Schools, that well-informed teachers have become familiar with most of its prominent features; but a system of education in some respects more complete and more imposing than that of Prussia has sprung upon our borders, which appears to have attracted less general attention among us.[77]

The quintessence of the Prussian system of education lay in its extreme centralization and control by the state. And it seems significant that this evaluation came from Massachusetts, itself undergoing radical educational reform.

Accordingly, a reasonable rating of the three systems of education in terms of developmental level would be Ontario, Massachusetts, and England in descending order. But when the extent to which each society is urban-industrial capitalist is assessed, the opposite order appears to be the case. In other words, the least advanced society possessed the most advanced form of education. The fact that the most industrialized, urbanized, capitalistic society was characterized by the most 'archiac' system of education points to the difficulties faced by the interpretations produced by the correspondence principle.

In this light, it is interesting to examine a study which manifests precisely these problems. It is an analysis of educational reform in nineteenth century Ontario done by Schecter.[78] It is especially interesting in that Schecter explicitly utilizes Bowles and Gintis' theory, arguing that reform was the product of the contradiction between accumulation and reproduction. However, he remarks on one unique feature characterizing educational reform in Ontario; here transitions in the educational system may presage changes in the economy because '... school reform preceded industrialization in Canada ...'[79]. While this may be the opposite of what one might expect, Schecter attributes temporal misphasing to the international system of capitalism arguing that '... the practice and ideology of that reform movement was as much a response to the social transformations of capitalism elsewhere as it was to the social reality of British North America'.[80] So it was to the containment of social contradictions raised by a transition to industrial capitalism that had yet to occur that early Upper Canadian reformers were addressing themselves. It appears that while Schecter uses the model of capital accumulation in theory, his actual explanation depends on the model of diffusionism.

In reviewing Schecter's study, Curtis is led to the conclusion below:

> The Canadian case ... presents a notable peculiarity ... which ... resides in the fact that the Upper Canadian educational system, as organized in the 1840s, was a specifically capitalist or industrial school system, while capitalist industrialization in Upper Canada was only slightly developed.

This is a telling point against the historical validity of the correspondence principle. When combined with the historical evidence presented above, evidence informed by the use of the model of capital accumulation, the point is more persuasive. Finally, the observations made directly above on apparently anomalous developmental pattern makes this point even more persuasive.

Conclusion

In light of the evidence presented above, it is not surprising that Curtis feels compelled to speak of the relative autonomy of education from economic development in Upper Canada.[82] Educational reform cannot be properly understood within either the revisionist or the reproduction (i.e. correspondence) versions of the social control paradigm.[83]

Though using different terminology, Hogan makes much the same case. Making particular reference to the correspondence principle, he argues that '. . . the expansion of schooling in the early nineteenth century was more an issue of political reproduction than economic reproduction'.[84]

Both Curtis for Upper Canada and Hogan for New England agree that the correspondence principle does not adequately explain the genesis of the common school. It seems clear from the above analysis that, when a rigorous periodization of the history in question is done through the Marxist categories constituting the model of capital accumulation, there was little with which the social relations of education as institutionalized by 1850 to correspond. The contradiction between accumulation and reproduction had yet to make its presence felt, the forces of production had yet to be fettered by the social relations of production, the labour process was characterized by the stages of simple cooperation or, perhaps, detail labour. To have schools reproducing factory social relations within the production context enumerated above seems a doubtful proposition. Precisely because the correspondence principle is so carefully specified theoretically, the difficulties in periodization faced by the revisionist branch of the social control paradigm are greatly exacerbated when one superimposes the capital accumulation model on their empirical foundation. In a sense, the excellence of Bowles and Gintis' theoretical elaboration is responsible for this conclusion. For it is only through that excellence that doubt becomes possible.

If not correspondence, then what? Here it is useful to return to Curtis and Hogan. What is striking is that two investigators, working independently and in the context of two quite different societies, have arrived at such similar observations. Below is Curtis:

> . . . educational reform in mid-nineteenth century Upper Canada sought to reconstruct political rule in society by reconstructing the political subjectivity of the population. . . . educational reform sought to build political subjects, and in so doing also constructed the state.[85]

And now Hogan:

> Even to the 1880s, almost the exclusive purpose of the public school system was to insert children into the ideological — particularly

> political — practices of the society, what was called 'citizenship' or 'character training'.[86]

This double emphasis on the political/ideological as opposed to the economic foundations of schooling suggests an intervention by education into the cultural practices and thus the formation of classes. This in turn permits a way of thinking about educational transformation rather different than that provided by the correspondence principle. By way of conclusion, a few very general comments about educational reform in Upper Canada will be made from this perspective.

That educational reform denoted an intervention into the cultural practices of subordinate classes there can be little doubt. To take only one example — an example demonstrating that even the seemingly trivial was not beyond the concern of reformers — Ryerson advocated the inclusion of music in the curriculum because by '... furnishing the young with interesting moral songs,' education would '... displace in their social amusements many of at least a questionable nature'.[87] Music was to negate various constituents of cultural practices. But to realize such ideological functions, education itself had to be transformed.

The nature of this transformation can be comprehended through the structural concepts of centralization and bureaucratization. Centralization designates the type of articulation of the state with education.[88] Educational transformation in Ontario meant that the central government both structured the form of education available and secured the legal/repressive conditions necessary for the existence of the new common school system by the state's intervention into private or civil society.[89]

Bureaucratization is characterized by its two-fold nature. First, it represents the means whereby local control over education was relocated from local areas to the state. And secondly, it created a social boundary whereby local groups were excluded from participation in and control over local schools. In Ontario this meant the elimination of the prior forms of education which, while minimally funded by the government, were controlled by local users. From a situation in which schools were integrated into the reproduction of local cultures, schooling, given the contours of its transformation just described, intervened into local cultural practices. The state appropriated the community life of the earlier society and absorbed within itself the powers communities had created and exercised through cooperation; it then used these transformed powers to govern in its own interests.

This is the essential meaning of educational transformation. The concept best geared to comprehend it is not correspondence — the reflection of the economic structure in the superstructure — but rather hegemony. Now the problematic of hegemony revolves about the attempted securing of the consent of the subordinate by means of the intervention of the state to articulate and structure the nexus between the processes of cultural production and cultural reproduction, thereby attempting to ensure the more general process of the reproduction of the social formation as a totality.[90] It is secured through the intervention of the state into civil society, provoked by an appropriated crisis of authority.[91] Resistant cultural practices are, as Hall points out, castigated by labelling them social problems in order to create moral panics, thereby underwriting the crisis of authority.[92] The result is intervention into the cultural reproduction of subordinate class forms by the state through centralization and bureaucratization.

Moreover, as Hall points out, hegemony does not conceptualize a relation of correspondence between base and superstructure in which the internal structure of the latter is determined by the requisite of structurally replicating the former. In place of this determinist articulation is the notion of the relative autonomy of the state from civil society, emphasized above by Curtis. For Hall, one way of thinking about relative autonomy is through the notion of 'coupling'. By this he appears to mean the coexistence of two quite distinct but nevertheless interrelated spheres or regions, a relation founded on the political/ideological role performed by the state in attempting to secure the reproductive conditions necessary for the maintenance of the social formation.[93] Though the state responds to the agenda set by the base, there is no theoretical requirement that it structurally correspond with the base. Because of the relative autonomy permitted by the concept of coupling, there is no prior necessity to appeal to the effects on the labour process of the process of capital accumulation to interpret educational transformation. The paradigm of hegemony is, then, more appropriate for the empirical circumstances of the two societies discussed above.

There were numerous factors in mid-nineteenth century Ontario upon which to sustain a moral panic. Due to an urbanization greatly exacerbated by the Irish famine migrations, poverty, crime, and vagrancy were widespread. But of far greater salience was the political threat of populism based in the countryside. The populists were radical democrats who were not only presenting an alternative vision of the organization of society but also, through their political practices (assuming the concrete form of a populist rebellion and a populist political party, the Clear Grits), attempting to realize it.[94] Though the likelihood of their success was doubtful, it did not seem so to the authorities of the time, who saw them as a stark threat to stability. Educational reform was directed to their political/cultural practices.

As a general rule of thumb, it may be said that populism develops when petty bourgeois structures of production are confronted with capitalism. That this confrontation occurred in mid-nineteenth century Ontario was due to its articulation with Britain on the basis of long-distance trade with the staple wheat in one direction, manufactured goods in the other. In short, Ontario was incorporated on a peripheral basis into the international capitalist order.[95]

It is here that the Marxist conception of urbanization becomes especially relevant. Ontario was urbanized — in terms of the bifurcation and opposition of town and country. The division of labour among towns into production and mercantile exchange did in fact occur, but on a pattern consistent with the peripheral status of Ontario. Production tended to be concentrated in English cities while Upper Canadian cities specialized in mercantile exchange, as the points of articulation with England in long-distance trade. Corresponding with this was the relation of these towns with the countryside; as the foundation of dependency was wheat, rural producers were dominated by an impersonal, fatalistic system of exchange, located in the cities, over which they had little control. This had much to do with the manifestations of agrarian protest noted above.

What educational reform actually did was to construct a public in the sphere of civil society. This required a centralized educational administrative bureaucracy, arising on the base of conflicts deep within civil society. As Curtis points, 'schools, scattered throughout civil society, were to be . . ., "pure state spaces", places purged of the conflicts, struggles, and stresses of civil society'.[96] Reform created a domain of administrative/managerial/bureaucratic logic 'above' politics which appropriated civil society in this classless form.[97] Within the boundaries of this form people were to become individuals independent of class-based configurations of cultural practices.

As Cole notes in his assessment of the correspondence principle, the theory of hegemony has, as its advantage, the removal of the element of determinism among the levels constituting a social formation — levels whose articulation is often characterized by unevenness, contradiction, even the absence of correspondence.[98] Educational formation was relatively autonomous of production relations both in Upper Canada and Massachusetts. Marxist theory must take this into account.

Notes

1 Bowles, S. and Gintis, H. (1976) *Schooling in Capitalist America: Educational Reform and the Contradictions of Economic Life*, New York, Basic Books.
2 *Ibid*, p. 151
3 Gintis, H. and Bowles, S. 'Contradiction and reproduction in educational theory' in Barton, L. *et al* (Eds) (1980) *Schooling, Ideology and the Curriculum*, Lewes, Falmer Press; Dale, R. *et al* (Eds) (1981) *Education and the State: Volume 1: Schooling and the National Interest*, Lewes, Falmer Press; and reproduced as chapter 2 of this volume (p. 19).
4 *Ibid*, p. 18 and p. 28.
5 Bowles, S. and Gintis, H. (1976) *op. cit*., p. 147
6 *Ibid*, p. 131
7 *Ibid*, p. 132.
8 Dreeben, R. (1968) *On What is Learned in Schools*, Reading, MA, Addison-Wesley.
9 Bowles, S. and Gintis, H. (1976) *op. cit*., p. 144.

10 *Ibid*, p. 157.
11 *Ibid*, pp. 157–60.
12 *Ibid*, pp. 174–5.
13 *Ibid*, p. 159.
14 *Ibid*, pp. 232–3.
15 *Ibid*, p. 224.
16 *Ibid*, p. 174.
17 HOGAN, D. (1981) 'Capitalism, liberalism, and schooling' in DALE, R. *et al* (Eds) *Education and the State: Volume 1: Schooling and the National Interest*, Lewes, Falmer Press p. 35.
18 CURTIS, B. (1983) 'Preconditions of the Canadian state: Educational reform and the construction of a public in Upper Canada, 1837–1846', *Studies in Political Economy*, 10.
19 *Ibid*, p. 99.
20 *Ibid*.
21 *Ibid*, pp. 101–2.
22 BOWLES, S. and GINTIS, H. (1976) *op. cit. pp. 230–1.*
23 KATZ, M. (1968) *The Irony of Early School Reform: Educational Innovation in Mid-Nineteenth Century Massachusetts*, Boston, MA, Beacon Press, p. 11.
24 LAZERSON, M. (1975) *Origins of the Urban School: Public Education in Massachusetts*, Cambridge, MA, Harvard University Press, p. ix.
25 KATZ, M. (1975) *Class, Bureaucracy and Schools: The Illusion of Educational Change in America*, New York, Praeger Publishers, p. 161.
26 *Ibid*.
27 KATZ, M. (1968) *op. cit.*, pp. 38–9 and pp. 221–2.
28 HOUSTON, S. (1972) 'Victorian origins of juvenile delinquency: A Canadian experience', *History of Education Quarterly*, 12; HOUSTON, S. (1974) 'The impetus to reform: Urban crime, proverty and ignorance in Ontario, 1850–1857', PhD thesis, University of Toronto; and PRENTICE, A. (1977) *The School Promoters: Education and Social Class in Mid-Nineteenth Century Upper Canada*, Toronto, Oxford.
29 KATZ, M. (1968) *op. cit.*, pp. 222–3.
30 *Ibid*, pp. 81–3.
31 MARX, K. (1965) *Capital*, V.1, Moscow, Progress Publishers, pp. 14–6.
32 JONES, G. (1975) 'Class struggles and the industrial revolution', *New Left Review*, 90, p. 49.
33 ALTHUSSER, L. and BALIBAR, E. (1972) *Reading Capital*, London, New Left Books, pp. 225–53.
34 HOGAN, D. (1982) 'Education and class formation: The peculiarities of the Americans', in APPLE, M. (Ed) *Cultural and Economic Reproduction in Education: Essays on class, Ideology and the State*, Boston, MA, Routledge and Kegan Paul, p. 38. Hogan's article is apropos as it is developed with reference to Massachusetts.
35 *Ibid*, note 20, p. 28.
36 MARX, K. (1965) *op. cit.*, chapters 14 and 15; SWEEZY, P. (1972) *Modern Capitalism and Other Essays*, New York, Monthly Review Press, pp. 127–46.
37 MARX, K. (1965) *op. cit.*, p. 318.
38 *Ibid*, p. 305.
39 *Ibid*, p. 308–10.
40 Simple co-operation '. . . does not, in itself, represent a fixed form characteristic of the capitalist mode of production. At the most it appears to do so, and that only approximately, in the handicraft-like beginnings of manufacture . . .', *ibid*, p. 317.
41 *Ibid*, p. 313. See also pp. 318–19.
42 *Ibid*, p. 320.

43 *Ibid*, p. 340.
44 *Ibid*, p. 372.
45 *Ibid*, p. 398.
46 *Ibid*, p. 346.
47 *Ibid*, p. 347.
48 *Ibid*, p. 330–31. Marx notes that apprenticeship was in force to the end of the period of manufacture, p. 346.
49 SWEEZY, P. (1972) *op. cit.*, p. 130. He sees manufacture as essentially conservative for it '. . . creates a highly differentiated labour force, dominated, numerically and otherwise, by skilled workers who tend to be contentious and undisciplined, but incapable of sustained revolutionary activity'.
50 MARX, K. (1965) *op. cit.*, p. 407.
51 For an example, see SCOTT, J. (1974) *The Glassworkers of Carmaux: French Craftsmen and Political Action in a Nineteenth-Century City*, Cambridge, MA, Harvard University Press. In this regard, Marx as well argued that antagonism between the worker and marchinery as the material embodiment of capital '. . . comes out most strongly whenever newly introduced machinery competes with manufactures handed down from former times'. See MARX, K. (1965) *op. cit.*, p. 407.
52 MARX, K. (1965) *op. cit.*, pp. 372–73.
53 *Ibid*, p. 388.
54 *Ibid*, p. 304.
55 SWEEZY, P. (1972)*op. cit.*, p. 47. Here he summarizes his conclusions in tabular form.
56 Reality is not quite so neat as this. For instance, the real subsumption of the labour process may dimly manifest itself in the detail phase of manufacture. And because of the efficiencies achieved through the division of labour in manufacture, a component of the total surplus value is based on relative surplus value. Although there may be a coexistence of real and substantive subordination, and of absolute and relative surplus value, one of these two forms will be dominant, depending on the particular period in the organization of production.
57 MARX, K. (1973) *The German Ideology*, New York, International Publishers, p. 69.
58 *Ibid*, p. 68.
59 *Ibid*, pp. 71–2.
60 MARX, K. (1965) *Pre-Capitalist Economic Formations*, New York, International Publishers, p. 78.
61 THERNSTROM, S. (1964) *Poverty and Progress: Social Mobility in a Nineteenth Century City*, Cambridge, MA, Harvard University Press, table 9, pp. 197–8.
62 KATZ, M. (1968) *op. cit.*, p. 273
63 HOGAN, D. (1978) *op. cit.*, note 20, pp. 68–9.
64 *Ibid*, pp. 41–4.
65 KATZ, M. (1978) 'Origins of the institutional state', *Marxist Perspectives*, 1, 4, p. 15.
66 *Ibid*, pp. 15–6.
67 Adapted from *Census of Canada: 1870–1871*, Vol. 4, table 9, pp. 198–9.
68 Adapted from Public Archives of Canada, Manscript Census of Markham Township, 1851.
69 PENTLAND, H. (1959) ' The development of a capitalist labour market in Canada', *Canadian Journal of Economics and Political Science*, 25, 26, pp. 452–5.
70 PALMER, B. (1986) 'Listening to history rather than historians: Reflections on working class history', *Studies in Political Economy*, 20, p. 67. See also PALMER, B. (1979) *A Culture in Conflict: Skilled Workers and Industrial Capitalism in Hamilton, Ontario, 1860–1941*, Montreal, McGill-Queen's University Press; and PALMER, B. (1983) *Working Class Experience: the Rise and Reconstitution of Canadian Labour, 1800–1980*, Toronto, Butterworths.

71 Palmer, B. (1986)*op. cit.*, p. 68.
72 *Ibid*, p. 69.
73 *Ibid*, p. 65; and Palmer, B. (1983) *op. cit.*, p. 106.
74 Adapted from *Census of Canada: 1870–1871*, Vol. 4. Urban population is defined as the total population living in what the census classifies as cities and towns. Figures necessary to determine the total urban population are unavailable prior to 1848.
75 The account of centralization and bureaucratization which follows is drawn substantially from MacDonald, P. (1980) 'The transformation of a pre-capitalist education formation: The development of education in nineteenth century Ontario', Ph D Thesis, University of Toronto, pp. 221–6.
76 Johnson, R. (1970) 'Educational policy and social control in early Victorian England', *Past and Present*, 49, p. 98.
77 Public Archives of Ontario, R. G. 2, Series E-1; Hodgins, J. (page proofs), 'Historical Sketch of Education in Upper and Lower Canada'.
78 Schecter, S. (1977) 'Capitalism, class and educational reform in Canada', in Panitch, L. (Ed), *The Canadian State: Political Economy and Political Power*. Toronto, University of Toronto Press.
79 *Ibid*, p. 379.
80 *Ibid*.
81 Curtis, B. (1983) *op. cit.*, p. 102.
82 *Ibid*, p. 103.
83 *Ibid*, p. 113.
84 Hogan, D. (1979), 'Capitalism, liberalism, and schooling', *Theory and Society*, 8, p. 394.
85 Curtis, B. (1983) *op. cit.*, p. 100.
86 Hogan, D. (1979) *op. cit.* p. 393.
87 Ryerson, E. 'Report on a system of public elementary instruction for Upper Canada, 1846', in Hodgins, J. (Ed) (1894–1910), *Documentary History of Education in Upper Canada*, Vol. 6, Toronto, Warwick Bros. and Ritter, p. 186.
88 Althusser, L. (1971) 'Ideology and ideological state apparatuses', in Althusser, L. (1971) *Lenin and Philosophy and Other Essays*, New York, Monthly Review Press.
89 This intervention into civil society by the state is the manifestation of the construction of hegemony by the state. See Gramsci, A. (1971) *Selections from the Prison Notebooks*, New York, International Publishers, pp. 242–7.
90 Hogan, D. (1979) *op. cit.*, pp. 37–8.
91 Gramsci, A. (1971) *op. cit.*, p. 210.
92 Hall, S. *et. al. Policing the Crisis: Mugging, the State, and Law and Order*. London, Macmillan Press, pp. 208–217.
93 Hall, S. 'Review of the Course', Open University Course E202, Unit 32. See also the quotation in Apple, M. (1978) *Education and Power*. Boston, MA Routledge and Kegan Paul, pp. 16–17.
94 MacDonald, P. (1980) *op. cit.*, pp. 367–93.
95 *Ibid*, pp. 307–27.
96 Curtis, B. (1983) *op. cit.*, p. 114.
97 *Ibid*, p. 115.
98 Cole, M. (1983) 'Contradictions in the educational theory of Gintis and Bowles', *The Sociological Review*, 31, 3, p. 474; and chapter 3 of this volume. (pp. 35–6)

6 *Facing the Complexity of Power: For a Parallelist Position in Critical Educational Studies**

Michael W. Apple

Introduction

The important work of Samuel Bowles and Herbert Gintis did not start leftist criticism of schooling in the United States. Indeed, both popular and scholarly criticism had become relatively widespread by the late sixties and early seventies. In the curriculum field, for example, stimulated in large part by the arguments of Dwayne Huebner and James Macdonald,[1] serious questioning of the relationship between schooling and forms of domination and exploitation had already established itself as part of a growing tradition. What Bowles and Gintis did, however, was to focus attention directly, in a structural fashion, on the capitalist economy per se. In so doing, they provided a more coherent lens with which to view the schooling process.

There were gains and losses in this, of course. Thus, in providing a more coherent economic focus, they also underplayed the complex workings of culture and politics. Yet, in my mind, given the political and educational context at that time the gains significantly outweighed the losses. Any assessment of *Schooling in Capitalist America* must be grounded in an appreciation of what it accomplished. A large portion of the current analyses of the ways in which the economic, cultural, and political spheres are articulated in education could not have been done if Bowles and Gintis had not labored before.

For these reasons, I do not wish to spend too much time criticizing *Schooling in Capitalist America*. I have engaged in sustained examination of some of its tendencies (its tilt toward economism, determinism, and reductionism) and have provided parts of an alternative theory in a number

*The arguments presented here are based on a larger treatment in my *Teachers and Texts: A Political Economy of Class and Gender Relations in Education*, New York/ London, Routledge and Kegan Paul, 1986.

of volumes.[2] Instead, after briefly pointing to a number of areas where the theory behind it was weak, I shall describe some of the most significant gains made in the decade or so since it was published, gains that I think push us considerably beyond such initial formulations. Finally, since Gintis and Bowles have engaged in serious self reflection on the conceptual and political lacunae within their earlier research — especially in its neglect of an analysis of the contradictions of liberal policies and discourse[3] — I want to suggest a few of the issues that they and we still need to contend with if we are to successfully build more democratic educational programs and defend the progressive tendencies that now exist in some schools.

Once again, however, my own ability to do this is dependent on insights that Gintis and Bowles were more than a little helpful in providing. Their continuing work was and is an advance over a good deal of previous positions. I approach this, then, not as an anonymous critic, but as a colleague who has learned and benefited from their own labors, even when I am in sometimes serious disagreement with them.

Bringing the Economy Back In

It is not to fall back into the trap of reductionism to recognize that in this society, as in all others, there exist general priorities and interests that provide what might be called its historical center of gravity.[4] We do live in a capitalist society and that means something to the 'knowledge that, how and to' that tends to be enacted. As I shall argue later, I do not think that class dynamics and the economic relations of capitalism explain everything of social importance to critically minded educators; but to ignore their utter import is to cut oneself off from some of the most insightful analytic tools we possess.

Robert Heilbroner has described capitalism as a 'stratified society in which the accumulation of wealth fulfills two functions: the realization of prestige, with its freight of unconscious sexual and emotional needs, and the expression of power, with its own constellation of unconscious requirements and origins'.[5] Prestige, power, and wealth are part of a system, then, that requires some to have them while others do not.

This is not actually or even primarily a Marxist point. Adam Smith, surely no marxist for temporal as well as ideological reasons, put it this way. 'Wherever there is great wealth, there is great inequality. For one very rich man, there must be at least five hundred poor, and the affluence of the rich supposes the indigence of the many.'[6] The difference here, though, is that the more Marxist oriented approach extends these insights into a complex and critical theory of how the economy, government, and culture of people interact to create such exploitation. Thus, it is not the mere fact of focussing on, say, economic structures which produce severe inequalities that is at issue. It is *how* one does it that counts. This is, in part, what got Bowles and Gintis into difficulty.

Some of the criticisms that Bowles and Gintis' correspondence theory was subjected to are briefly summarized by Geoff Whitty. Even though *Schooling in Capitalist America* helped to establish neo-marxist theory in a number of areas in education, 'it was a relatively crude piece of marxist theory, based upon some highly questionable statistical data, and, perhaps strangest of all, one that minimized the significance of the overt (as opposed to the hidden curriculum of schooling) in securing social reproduction and the legitimation of inequality'.[7] It soon became clear that there were theoretical flaws in their arguments — ones concerning their account of the rise of mass compulsory schooling, their picture of the dynamics of the capitalist system of production, and their characterization of the supposed correspondence between education and paid work.[8]

As Whitty goes on to say, all too many accounts that were influenced by the conceptual apparatus stressed by or lying behind Bowles and Gintis (and Bowles and Gintis were often more subtle than some of their followers) were characterized by the following.

> Schools were seen merely as part of the ideological apparatus of the state whose role was to secure the hegemonic control of the bourgeoisie and the perpetuation of the capitalist mode of production. Class domination was stressed at the expense of class conflict and, whether via a correspondence between schooling and the economy or via their relative autonomy, control and its legitimation appeared to be secured with little difficulty.[9]

Before we chastize Bowles and Gintis too readily, however, we need to remember one rather important fact. In the justified debates during the past decade about the reductionist tendencies of 'orthodox' marxist theories, we have tended to forget how very mechanistic and reductionist were and *continue to be* many of the major alternatives that they were reacting to. Thus, while at one end of the spectrum may lie the reductionism of 'vulgar marxism' — where all aspects of the evolution of a society are seen as stemming in some mechanistic fashion from the self-expansion of capital— at the other end of that spectrum 'is the vulgar reductionism of theoretical economics, which perceives capitalism merely as a neutral field of property rights in which monadic individuals pursue their private utility-maximizing ends'.[10] The explanations generated out of this latter model of understanding embody a determinism as ironclad as the most simplistic Marxism[11]. And while Bowles and Gintis may have leaned too much toward a mechanistic perspective, they really were considerably less socially simplistic than what passes for 'neutral' economic theory today. They did establish a framework for the political economy of schooling that, with some reconstruction — especially with the addition of a more detailed analysis of the State — continues to be very influential today.

For example, a recent book by Carnoy and Levin, *Schooling and Work in the Democratic State*, marks a continuation of the basic problematic of Bowles and Gintis. While it partly rejects correspondence principles, it is clearly still attempting to solve the relationship between schooling and paid work. Their stress on contradictions and struggles within the State is an advance over the early work in *Schooling in Capitalist America*, yet it is very much within the tradition it established. The central problems that *Schooling and Work in the Democratic State* wishes to explore are best summed up in the words of the authors.

> In our view, the challenge today is to explain how the public school can at one and the same time be an institution that reproduces the unequal class relations of capitalist society and an institution that is more democratic and equal than the workplace for which it prepares students. We reject both a mechanistic correspondence between work and school and a clear separation of the two. Rather we believe that though schools do reproduce unequal class relations, the fact that they do so imperfectly merely reflects the social conflict that characterizes the capitalist society they serve. What is the relation of schooling and educational reform to social conflict? How is that social conflict related to the dynamics of the workplace? How do schools reproduce social relations? In their institutional role do schools primarily reproduce ideology (the dominant culture), or do they primarily reproduce the social relations and division of labor in production?[12]

The position that Carnoy and Levin take in answering these questions is that the fact that schools are structurally connected to the political as well as economic sphere creates tensions that are fundamentally contradictory. These tensions — what Gintis and Bowles later call the contradictions between 'property rights' and 'person rights' elsewhere[13] — are built into the very structural dynamics of schooling and make the school a site of conflicting demands, conflicts, and compromises.

As Carnoy and Levin put it:

> . . . [The] relationship between education and work is dialectical — composed of a perpetual tension between two dynamics, the imperatives of capitalism and those of democracy in all its forms. As both a product and a shaper of social discord, the school is necessarily caught up in the larger conflicts inherent in the capitalist economy and the liberal capitalist state. These conflicts reside in the contradiction between the unequal relation underlying capitalist production and the democratic basis of the liberal capitalist state. The school is essential to the accumulation of capital and the reproduction of the dominant relations of production,

> and it is valued by parents and youth as a means to greater participation in economic and political life.[14]

While *Schooling and Work in the Democratic State* is not simply Bowles and Gintis redux, it is very clear that *Schooling in Capitalist America* casts a long shadow. Nearly all current major analyses of the political economy of schooling still have to contend with its claims. Contending with its claims, however, does not mean that progress has not been made that goes beyond their early research, especially in our understanding of the complexity of the cultural/ideological, political, and economic determinants of education.

For A Parallelist Position

In order to understand how far we have come, it might be wise to situate *Schooling in Capitalist America* into the kind of scholarship that I believe has made the most progress in critical educational work in the past decade. Here I am referring to those who have been dissatisfied with the reductive tendencies that have been all too common in some marxist investigations.

A significant portion of the program of analysis that stands behind this other work has been influenced (not determined) by a *culturalist* marxism, one that is self-critical and that has been considerably tempered and made much more flexible. This influence is usually based on three main premises.

> The first is that cultural processes are intimately connected with social relations, especially with class and class formations, with sexual divisions, with the racial structuring of social relations and with age oppressions as a form of dependency. The second is that culture involves power and helps to produce asymetries in the abilities of individuals and social groups to define and realize their needs. And the third, which follows the other two, is that culture is neither an autonomous nor an externally determined field, but a site of social differences and struggles.[15]

Certain important elements should be noticed here: the anti-determinist position of the last sentence in the quotation; and the emphasis not only on struggles over economy but culture, not only class but sex and race. These premises bear in important ways on how we think about education since, as a primary agency in the production and reproduction of 'legitimate' culture and as a set of institutions with very real connections to the social relations of production and the social division of labor, education has not only been one of the things that is struggled over, but is a major institutional site in which these struggles take place.

Usually, however, the way we have talked about these things historically has not been particularly 'culturalist'. Culture has taken a back seat and most of the examinations have stressed the connections between our institutions of education and the 'occupational ladder' in the economy. Formal schooling, it has been argued, corresponds to and helps reproduce the social division of labor in the economy.

Even though as a number of people have demonstrated and as I noted earlier, this research has been conceptually and empirically problematic and rather too deterministic,[16] this has been a progressive step. For instance, so much as been written about the connections between the school and the labor market that it is hard not to think about schooling in class terms. From the early functionalist work of Bowles and Gintis to the later analyses of Bernstein, Willis, Arnot, Giroux, Carnoy and Levin, and myself, there has been a clearer recognition that our educational system can only be understood 'relationally'.[17] Its meaning, what it does culturally, politically, and economically, is missed if our analysis does not situate the school back into the nexus of dominant class relations that help shape our society. (I shall not go into detail on the historical growth of relational analyses of class in education since this has been done elsewhere).[18]

The recognition that schools need to be understood in this way has had its benefits to be sure. But it has also led to a number of problems as well. Less attention has been paid to the other constitutive dynamics around which our society has been organized. Here I am talking about gender and race. It would be impossible, for example, to understand the history of the United States labor market, its urban economies and governmental policies, its popular cultural forms, and so much more, without integrating an analysis of racial formation into one's assessment. As Michael Omi and Howard Winant put it, racial formation is a complex process that is, at once, political, cultural, and economic.[19] Economic and class analysis, while providing important elements of understanding to be sure, cannot do justice to the realities of racial oppression. Furthermore, by directing our attention to the primacy of class relations, it undervalues political processes and actions that have their roots in racial identity and the cultural forms of people of color, thereby repelling 'many politically active persons whose awareness of racism it cannot address, but only distort and deny'.[20]

These same points about class and race need to be made about gender relations as well. We do gain insights into women's realities by talking in class terms. For instance, in our kind of society, women have a double relation to wage labor. They are both paid and unpaid workers. (This notion of *unpaid* labor is important and is something I shall return to.) Unpaid domestic labor, relations of consumption, and their connections to paid work are all critically important in illuminating both how our economy functions and the 'shaping of women's consciousness'.[21] This consciousness and these relations have a long history, of course, for women's ties to wage labor and the unpaid labor in the home or on the farm have changed markedly over time. We need to remember, for example, that at the end of the eighteenth and the beginning of the nineteenth centuries, the lack of an 'adequate supply of workers' and the continuing need for cheap labor in the early mills in New England created conditions that made *women* the first industrial proletariat in the United States.[22]

It is essential that we know this, but stopping there would cause us to underemphasize the role that cultural forms played in the formation of a specifically women's response to certain of these economically and class based conditions. (Further, it would lead us to assume that these conditions were only produced by the economy.) Thus, for instance, for many working class and middle class women in later periods of American history, the definition of themselves as, say, the primary purchasers of commodities for the home was used by these women to expand their sphere of control outside as well as inside the home. Consumption practices, the 'labor of purchasing' (and it *is* a labor process), were not only a way in which the economy locked them into their class location. These practices were employed by women to increase their social space and freedom, and to remove themselves from patriarchal relations in the home.[23] A specifically women's cultural politics evolved, one that is missed in discussions of class and economy. Furthermore, as Barrett and others have demonstrated, it is simply not possible to reduce patriarchal relations which have their own specificities and histories to a reflection of class relations. An analysis of a dominant 'mode of production' cannot fully account for the historical relations between men and women,[24] relations that bear on education, the home, and the paid workplace fully as much as class based ones.

Two things are worthy of note from this discussion. First, cultural forms and practices often have their own politics. They may be related to and limited by class relations and the economy, but they also are 'relatively autonomous'. They have something of a life of their own and provide important grounding for action that may not simply reproduce existing relations of domination and exploitation. Second, there are at least *three* elements operating in this situation, class *and* race *and* gender. Thus, an analysis of dominant power relations in our society needs not only a theory of class but just as much of a sensitivity to patriarchy and race as well. For my purposes here I shall focus primarily on class and gender, but in no way do I want to minimize the significance of racial domination.

Patriarchal structures and class structures are both subtle, complex, and wide ranging. They have their own dynamics and are not reducible to each other, though unfortunately those scholars on the left who stress class as the fundamental category of analysis tend to merge feminist issues back into the 'real' problems of class relations. As Heidi Hartmann has put it in arguing against such reductive tendencies, 'The marriage of Marxism and feminism has been like the marriage of husband and wife depicted in English common law: Marxism and feminism are one, and that one is Marxism.'[25] Such a position has, of course, been challenged conceptually and politically. These criticisms have caused a particular set of questions to come to the forefront in our investigations in a number of fields. What is the relationship between gender and class? How are these relationships produced and reproduced in particular sites such as the home, the paid workplace, and the school? Are these dominant relationships contested by real women and men as they go about their daily lives or are they largely accepted as the way the world really is?[26] One cannot study the role of education in society without taking these issues very seriously.

These are complicated issues as you would imagine. But the attempt to deal with class and gender together, without slighting either, is one of the most serious agendas we face. However, these attempts face other difficulties if they are to do justice to the actual people who are in these sets of relations. This bears on the point I made a few pages ago about cultural forms and practices.

For example, the problem is not only how we might fruitfully examine both class and gender together, but also how we combine structuralist insights about the relationship between the school and the social and sexual division of labor with a culturalist perspective that places human agency and the concrete experiences of people at the center. How do we show the role of the educational system as one site in the production of these divisions without at the same time falling into the many traps that bedevilled earlier attempts at doing this, attempts that often turned people into the puppets of structural forces?[27] Can we get inside institutions and illuminate what actually happens, how people act (often in contradictory ways) within the conditions set by the institution and the larger society, and point out possibilities that exist for altering dominant relations?

In the past, only a relative handful of books have been able to successfully combine a structuralist focus on the objective conditions within a social formation and the culturalist insistence on seeing these conditions as ongoingly built, and contested, in our daily lives. All too often, authors choose betwen seeing culture as a mere reflex of economic relations as Bowles and Gintis tended to do or else tend to fall into a naive romanticism about the power of 'resistance' by women or men on the shop floor, the home, the office, or the school. Unfortunately (or, perhaps, fortunately) reality is much more dense and contradictory than that.

Oddly, progress on discerning the relationship between class and gender and between, say, culture and economy has been stimulated both by advances in and debates about the class analytic program itself in education. While the literature in class analysis in education has progressed rapidly over the past decade, it is in two areas that the most headway seems to have been made. The first is the growth of understanding of the labor process. Originally stimulated in large part by Harry Braverman's work and the debates this engendered,[28] not only has the labor process outside the school been insightfully investigated, but the actual work settings of educators have been explored more and more rigorously. Forms of control of the curriculum, of the teaching act itself, and specific administrative strategies have been situated within the larger dynamics of the transformation of paid labor over time and the contradictory needs of the State to support capital accumulation and to legitimate both itself and the accumulation process. Discussions of how teachers are being deskilled as more and more of the curriculum, pedagogy, and evaluation are standardized or prepackaged, of the 'proletarianization' of teaching as teachers' working conditions, control, and autonomy worsen, and of the accompanying ideological tensions that result from these processes have all become increasingly visible.[29]

I believe that these were significant gains in our understanding. Paradoxically, however, though focussing largely on teachers as classed actors these gains have led to some very important challenges to the limitations of class analysis, per se, since it has come to be increasingly clear that the labor that is being 'degraded' and controlled in schools is largely *women's labor* in a whole array of cases.[30] Thus, once again, the need to integrate class and gender together has been seen as a very real issue. Bowles and Gintis might have been able to deal with gender issues more thoroughly if they had chosen to focus their attention on the labor process *inside the school* as much as they did on the labor process in the larger society.

The second area in which considerable progress has been made concerns a rejection of imposition theory. In early formulations of the problem in education, it was often assumed that dominant classes had self-identified and coherent interests. These powerful groups identified an institution that wasn't meeting these interests and then imposed equally coherent strategies on these institutions to guarantee that dominant interests were in fact met. Now, of course, some of this strategizing does go on. Witness the growing influence of capital on the bulk of the national reports on education and in many of the state legislatures throughout the United States and eleswhere.[31]

Yet, this kind of theory also assumes too easily that institutions like the school or in the larger State are populated by mere homunculi, puppets whose strings are pulled by classes in dominance. What it forgets is that most institutions not only came about because of conflict, but are continuously riven by conflicts today. Furthermore, people employed in these institutions at all levels often have their own interests they try to pursue based on their own material circumstances and histories. Many times, these interests will cohere with those of dominant groups, perhaps especially now when capital and the right are resurgent. At times, though, these same people will mediate, transform, and attempt to generally set limits on what is being imposed from the outside. They will also try to employ such 'impositions' for their own ends, ends that will have a good deal to do with their own class, race, and gender location.[32]

To take one example, right now conflicting definitions of 'legitimate' culture and over the teaching of workplace skills, norms, and values are being fought over in education. The school and the State in general are part of a 'contested terrain'. Many groups within that terrain are struggling to maintain their positions or increase their power as documents such as *The Paideia Proposal* and *A Nation At Risk* demonstrate.[33] Not only capital, but the new middle class and the 'old humanist' fraction of the middle class that resides largely in the universities, right wing populist groups (who are normally made up of indviduals from the working class or lower middle class whose moral and economic world seems threatened as capitalism transforms their public and private lives), as well as teachers and other groups of women, people of color, workers, and so on, all are contesting the balance of power and culture in education. Capital and the right may be ascendent, but that doesn't mean that their ability to pressure textbook publishers, educational policy makers, the government, students, and teachers will be unmediated by groups with their own ideological and economic interests.[34]

Thus, while impositions may be tried, they do not occur without a struggle. The key to winning, to establishing hegemony, is usually that group which can establish the parameters of the terms of the debate, that group which can incorporate the competing claims of other groups under its own discourse about education and social goals. As we are seeing all around us, the current discourse is increasingly framed in economic terms. It is the language of production, rationalization, and standardization. It is muting the voice of democracy, participation, and equality. This more democratic voice is still alive, to be sure, but it is harder to hear it above the machinery of the mechanization of education.

The dominant discourse is not only increasingly economic, however. It is also framed in gender terms. For the current conservative restoration rests not only on an ethic of the accountant's profit and loss sheet and on 'productivity' and accumulation. It rests on a return to past moments of gender and race relations, a return to a romanticized past when people 'knew their place'.[35] This cannot be fully explained as a simple working out of the logic and conflicts of capitalism without missing something in the process.

In the preceeding discussion, I have taken what is commonly known as the *parallelist* position. That is, I have argued that we should not automatically assume the primacy of class relations over those of gender and race. These latter two dynamics, and the complex and immensely *contradictory* interconnections among all three, must be given equal weight in the analysis of any concrete situation. Of course, we may find that class has primacy in a situation, but it would have to be proven, not assumed at the outset. Second, I have argued for both a greater emphasis on cultural processes that are related to but not reducible to the workings out of economic relations and for greater attention to be paid to conflicts not only about what the State should do but within it as well. Finally, I have noted that a focus on the labor process both inside the school and on the productive and reproductive labor of women would help illuminate many of the points I have stressed.

How do most economically oriented studies, from the earlier work of

Bowles and Gintis to the more recent analyses stand on these positions? First, their very evident insights about class and the economy need to be recognized. In many ways, even with their reductive view of how capitalism actually works in all its complexity, the return of the economy to a prominent place in educational theory was and is warranted. It is less insightful about these other dynamics (i.e. gender and race), sometimes seemingly adding them in as afterthoughts.

For example, there are significant problems in any theory that privileges paid work. It cannot, except as some sort of conceptual 'add on', deal adequately with the unpaid productive and reproductive labor of women in the home, for instance. It can lead to a form of class reductionism, as well, that is more than a little susceptible to the feminist criticisms that have been so very devastating to traditional marxist assertions.[36] If I were to point to one of the areas in which Bowles and Gintis and the scholars who have followed the path they established could have strengthened their discussion immeasurably, it would be right here. They do not integrate fully enough into their analysis a theory (one might call it socialist feminist) that could account in a comprehensive way for the structures that produce some of the most significant experiences and sets of social relations of 51 per cent of the world's actors.

Thus, we must recognize that social movements that are not only class-based ones are increasingly important. The State is influenced by and itself influences the formation of these social movements. We need to elaborate these insights into a theory that could account for political and cultural, as well as economic action, and into one that would allow for the ultimate irreducibility of gender and race dynamics.[37] This would have important implications for politics inside and outside education and would also lead to an even more subtle analysis of the State, one that would parallel the advances currently being made on the study of gender and race in the economy and politics. This would certainly complement the current discussions of the central place of democratic conflicts in the State itself.[38]

What does this mean? As I argue in *Education and Power* an adequate theory that links schooling to our social formation must not oversimplify.[39] It must see capitalism not simply as an economy but as a 'way of life'. This requires an approach not only to the economy, but one that is a theory of the *social totality*, of the complex and contradictory interconnections within and among the economic, political, and cultural/ideological spheres, with the economic being even more powerful in times of crisis. Such an account would embody, hence, not a monocausal set of explanations (for example, economy explains all), but a theory of *over-determination* in which what schools do is 'caused' by the complicated and contradictory relations both among these spheres and within them, and by the class, race, and gender dyamics and conflicts that help constitute them. As I argued, schooling is involved in the production as well as reproduction of agents, knowledge, social relations, and ideologies. The educational system as a whole is also involved in their distribution and in the legitimation both of these processes and of itself as part of the State. This occurs through conflict and struggle. It is not something that is automatic, brought about by correspondence. And this means that there will be genuinely contradictory elements in schools, elements that embody good sense as well as bad sense, that will be progressive and will need to be *defended* not just criticized.

Thus, it is of vital importance that we remember that even with the role schools have been shown to play in the production and reproduction of race, gender, and class relations of this society, historically the educational system and its internal policies and practices *have* been built out of conflicts. Many of the results of these conflicts have been compromises that signify victories, not losses, for the majority of people. Carnoy and Levin make exactly this point when they say that the fact that struggles over education have been at least partly successful in the past is documented by the fact that schooling itself tends to be more equally distributed than, say, economic capital, income, or employment status. 'Schooling produces relatively more equal outcomes than the workplace and other institutions of the larger society.' Even though our formal institutions of elementary and secondary education bear some very real organizational resemblance to paid workplaces such as offices and factories, and even though they do engage in 'screening and preparing youth for inequality', when compared to these other workplaces, schools are clearly more equal and participatory.[40] Since schools *are* part of the State, of the political sphere, and, as Gintis and Bowles claim in their self critical work, the State has been a site of conflict between property rights and person rights, we should *expect* that schools will be more democratic than these other institutions.[41]

This is perhaps best summed up by Carnoy and Levin.

> Educational institutions are not just producers of dominant class conceptions of what and how much schooling should be provided; public schools also reflect social demands. Attempts by the capitalist state to reproduce the relations of production and the class division of labor confront social movements that demand more public resources for their needs and more say in how these resources are to be used. The capitalist state and its educational system are therefore more than just a means for coopting social demands, or for simply manipulating them to satisfy dominant class needs. Social demands shape the state and education.[42]

Extending a number of themes I argued in *Education and Power*, though still somewhat too economistically, they conclude that:

> The educational system is not an instrument of the capitalist class. It is the product of conflict between the dominant and the dominated. The struggle in the production sector, for example, affects schools, just as it conditions all state apparatuses. Fur-

> thermore, because the state, including the educational system, is itself the political arena, schools are part of social conflict. Education is at once the result of contradictions and the source of new contradictions. It is an arena of conflict over the production of knowledge, ideology, and employment, a place where social movements try to meet their needs and business attempts to reproduce its hegemony.[43]

These arguments do not provide support for any logically consistent notion of correspondence, nor do they lend support for a class reductive position. Obviously, giving more parellel status to gender and race dynamics complicates matters considerably. The recognition that culture and the State are linked to and relatively autonomous from the economy does little to lessen that complexity. These involved relations — conflicts between (*and* within) race, class, and gender formations, over political, cultural, and economic power, over social and educational goals within the State — are real. Why pretend, because of some odd commitment to orthodoxy, they do not exist?

Here, I find the arguments advanced by Stuart Hall, one of the most insightful marxist theorists, to be essential. As he states:

> The task of critical theory is to produce as accurate a knowledge of complex social processes as the complexity of their functioning requires. It is not its task to console the left by producing simple but satisfying myths, distinguished only by their super-left wing credentials. (If the laws and tendencies of the capitalist mode of production can be stated in a simplified form because they are essentially simple and reducible, why on earth did Marx go on about them for so long — three incompleted volumes, no less?) Most important of all, these differences and complexities have real *effects*, which ought to enter into any serious calculations about how their tendencies might be resisted or turned.[44]

These points are grounded in an emerging set of arguments now being confronted within the leftist community. It is a set of arguments that are not only important for education, but for our political thought in general. And, actually, they come close in some important respects to the position Gintis and Bowles have taken in some of their more recent work. Not only must we reject the class reductionism still so pervasive in democratic socialist thought, but we also need to question the notion that only economic struggles 'really' count in the long run. To only stress the latter is to ignore the fact that — if I may speak technically for a moment — people are constructed by a variety of discourses, in a multitude of institutions from the paid and unpaid workplace to the family, the school, the media, and so forth. In *political* terms, none of these has a necessarily privileged place. It is the effect of all of these together that matters. Thus, interventions and struggles in each are important.

Laclau and Mouffe summarize these points theoretically in the following way: 'Judicial institutions, the educational system, labour relations, the discourses of resistances of marginal populations, [of women and people of color], construct original and irreducible forms of social protest, and thereby contribute all of the discursive complexity and richness on which the programme of a radical democracy should be founded.'[45] Our task is to make concrete linkages between our own actions in the educational arena and those of these other arenas. From this, a shared, yet pluralist, 'discourse of democracy' in schools and these other arenas can grow. In this way, we can assist the movement to have person rights win out over property rights.

The Double Edged Sword of 'Transportability'

A number of the points I have argued in the preceeding sections of this chapter are compatible with the positions taken by Bowles and Gintis in the articles and books[46] that have appeared since the publication of *Schooling in Capitalist America*. They continue to be among the most provocative and insightful writers we have on the left. In this final section, I wish to briefly examine what their latest position can offer in helping us understand the possibilities of extending the 'discourse of democracy', of person rights, in education.

Gintis and Bowles have argued that discourses over person rights developed in one sphere are *transportable* to others. Demands for and discourses about political rights by women, for example, spill over into the economic sphere. They are appropriated and used in the struggle for economic equality.[47] In asserting this, Gintis and Bowles have become considerably more flexible in their position since they allow for the possibility that conflicts in one sphere may have a serious impact on another. This is a very real advance beyond correspondence theories and beyond a simple base/superstructure model. Further, it gives more weight to politicized educational and cultural action than before. This is very important since it implicitly recognizes that there may be cultural preconditions to all political and economic action.

However, Gintis and Bowles largely limit their discussion to the positive moment of such transportability. For them, progressive action in the State, even under the conditions of liberalism, can establish some of the discursive conditions for progressive action in the economy. This is a real contribution. It allows for the efficacy of cultural and political effects as well as for those generated by economic struggles. But, what they have ignored is the transportability of such a discourse of person rights not only from one sphere or site to another, but *to an opposing and often reactionary group* which is able to use such meanings for its own purposes. That is, what they do not fully recognize is that there is *no guarantee* that the trajectory of such 'transportable discourses' is necessarily in a progressive direction. The opposite of this is exactly the case right now. The growth of the new right, symbolized by Reaganism in the United States and Thatcherism in Britain, provides an excellent case in point.

The new right has to be explained by what went before it. The social democratic accord was disintegrating in the midst of an economic, political and ideological crisis. But such an accord established the terrain upon which the new right emerged. Thus, the new right had to displace social democratic elements and then had to harmonize these disaggregated elements within its own discourse. A period of accord or settlement in which an historic compromise is reached is then followed by a period of rupture or break.[48] The new right both participated in this rupture and sought to rearticulate elements of that compromise with its own emerging tendencies.

In sum, what the right has done in many ways is to take many of the elements 'which are already constructed into place, dismantles them, reconstitutes them into a new logic, and articulates the space in a new way, polarizing them to the right'.[49] One of its major successes was in translating the possessive individualist and free market ideologies of monetarism into 'the language of experience, moral imperative, and common sense'.[50] This was done through its appropriation of populism and the language of democracy.

Hall notes that the discourses of populism and democracy are *not* the intrinsic property of any one class. They can be articulated differently in different historic conditions as the result of specific ideological conflicts.[51] Rightist populism (and it is a populism in many ways) takes the themes of nation, family, authority, standards, and traditionalism and brings them together with themes that have had a particularly important history in the United States, those of self interest, competitive individualism, and anti-statism.[52] These are condensed, as it were, in one particular historical conjuncture. Progressive elements such as a concern for fairness and justice for the 'people' are taken out of their original context and connected to the imperatives of profitability and accumulation.[53] 'We' are hard working and deserving; 'they' are immoral, or simply uncaring state bureaucrats, or elitist.

What the new right had to do was reinterpret the very meaning of inequality and recast the means of achieving it. Thus, whereas previously affirmative action programs in education and elsewhere took racial and sexual equality into account by using race and sex categories to repair previous imbalances, the new right was successful in altering the very meaning of equality and person rights away from what they saw as 'preferential treatment'. This was a form of undeserved privilege in their minds and should be replaced by a strict criterion of color blindness. State intervention on the side of such 'preferential treatment' went too far. It 'debilitated, rather than uplifted its target populations'. The real victims of such discrimination had become not people of color or women, but white males.[54]

The right's ability to rearticulate and organize around earlier themes is very visible here. Forces of reaction have appropriated the idea of racial and sexual equality developed under the social democratic accord and rearticulated its meaning for their own purposes. The right has 'repackaged the earlier themes — infusing them with new political meaning and linking them to other key elements of conservative ideology'.[55]

A hegemonic bloc can be reformed in this way. By integrating under one discourse the rearticulated themes of equality (which earlier periods of struggle for person rights by disenfranchised groups had made legitimate) with conservative anti-statist, religious, and economic themes, an umbrella is created under which a large portion of the population can stand. Thus, a new collective identity can be formed around an innovative political project.[56] Person rights concerning popular democratic or egalitarian ideals such as justice, equality of opportunity, and individual rights can be fused with traditional and often contradictory American ideological themes such as respect for authority, a lack of trust in central governments, the defense of traditional morality and 'free enterprise' (and the ever present resistance to demands for further rights by new class, racial, or sexual groups).[57]

The implications of these points are striking. In essence, I am arguing that — depending on the balance of forces — seemingly progressive discourses can have complicated *trajectories*. They can be transported from one social sphere to another — as when the struggle for equal political representation is taken up and used as a set of principles to support the redistributive economics of comparable worth, changes in the paid labor market sought by feminist groups, anti-sexist and anti-racist school practices, and so on, or when the tactics and goals of the Black movement are taken up by other oppressed groups in their own particular struggles. However, there is no guarantee that these discourses will be employed for their original ends. Because they *are* popular discourses built out of the struggles of real people over education, health and welfare, political and economic rights, and so forth, they can be continually reappropriated by right-wing forces and used against these same people as we are seeing right now. These dual trajectories are inherent within the themes themselves.

Because of this, the struggle for a genuine democracy in education as in so many other areas of our public and private lives needs to be guided not by any notions of correspondence, but by a clear sense of the contradictory tendencies in our social formation, of the real cultural, political, and economic groupings and conflicts that create the conditions in which we live. It also needs to be guided by a better understanding of the ways successes can be reappropriated by dominant groups unless we continue to organize and build on past gains. But this must not be an isolated act. Only by building coalitions with other progressive groups from the ground up in the economic, political, and cultural spheres can there be hope that when gains in one site *are* transported to another, they will indeed have lasting democratic effects. These democratic effects are not automatic, but require hard, practical action to keep the discourse and practice of person rights from being reappropriated by the right's hegemonic project.

With this in mind, it is correct I think to give Bowles and Gintis the last words. Whether a society based on the common good,[58] not the needs of the few, comes about 'will depend in large measure on the ability of democrats first to understand, and then effectively pursue, the historic project of the expansion and deepening of democratic personal rights in the face of the tenacious and no less expansionary claims of property'.[59] Struggles in education have always had an important place in this historic project to expand and deepen person rights. It is up to us to help ensure that this continues.

Notes

1 See HUEBNER, D. (1966) 'Curricular language and classroom meanings' in MACDONALD, J.. and LEEPER, R. (Eds) *Language and Meaning*, Washington, Association for Supervision and Curriculum Development; and APPLE, M. W. (1985) 'There is a river: James B. Macdonald and curricular tradition', *Journal of Curriculum Theorizing*, 6, 3, pp. 9–18.

2 APPLE, M. W. (1979) *Ideology and Curriculum*, Boston/London, Routledge and Kegan Paul; APPLE, M. W. (1982a) *Education and Power*, Boston/London, Routledge and Kegan Paul; APPLE, M. W. (Ed) (1982b) *Cultural and Economic Reproduction in Education*, Boston/London, Routledge and Kegan Paul; and APPLE, M. W. and WEIS, L. (Eds) (1983) *Ideology and Practice in Schooling*, Philadelphia, PA, Temple University Press.

3 GINTIS, H., and BOWLES, S. (1980) 'Contradiction and reproduction in educational theory' in BARTON, L., MEIGHAN, R., and WALKER, S. (Eds) *Schooling, Ideology and the Curriculum*, Lewes, Falmer Press; DALE, R. *et al* (Eds) (1981) *Education and the State: Volume 1: Schooling and the National Interest*, Lewes, Falmer Press; and reproduced as chapter 2 in this volume; and GINTIS, H. (1980) 'Communication and politics', *Socialist Review*, 10, 2/3, pp. 189–232.

4 HEILBRONER, R. L. (1985) *The Nature and Logic of Capitalism*, New York, Norton, p. 85.

5 *Ibid*, p. 53.

6 SMITH, A. (1976) *The Wealth of Nations*, Oxford, Clarendon Press, pp. 709–10.

7 WHITTY, G. (1985) *Sociology and School Knowledge*, London, Methuen, pp. 25.

8 *Ibid*, p. 26.

9 *Ibid*, p. 29. See also the volumes by APPLE, M. W., (1979) (1982a) and (1982b) *op cit.*, APPLE, M. W. and WEIS, L., (Eds) (1983) *op cit.*; and GIROUX, H. (1983) *Theory and Resistance in Education* South Hadley, Bergin and Garvey.

10 HEILBRONER, R. L., (1985) *op cit.*, pp. 192–3.

11 *Ibid*, p. 193

12 CARNOY, M. and LEVIN, H., (1985) *Schooling and Working in the Democratic State*, Stanford, Stanford University Press, pp. 3–4.

13 GINTIS, H. and BOWLES, S., (1980/81/88) *op cit.*; and GINTIS, H., (1980) *op cit.*

14 Carnoy, M. and Levin, H., (1985) *op cit.*, p. 4.
15 Johnson, R. (1983) 'What is cultural studies anyway?' Occasional Paper SP No. 74, University of Birmingham Centre for Contemporary Cultural Studies, p. 3.
16 See Apple, M. W. (1982a) *op cit.*; and Giroux, H., (1983) *op cit.*
17 For further discussion of the concept of relational analysis, see Apple, M. W. (1979) *op cit.*
18 Apple, M. W., and Weis, L., (Eds) (1983) *op cit.* For a brief overview of this history, see also Carnoy, M. (1984) 'Marxism and education' in Ollman, B. and Vernoff, E. (Eds) *The Left Academy: Marxist Scholarship on American Campuses Volume Two*, New York, Praeger, pp. 79–97; and Whitty, G., (1985) *op cit.*
19 Omi, M. and Winant, H. (1983) 'By the rivers of Babylon: Race in the United States', *Socialist Review*, 13, 5, p. 40.
20 *Ibid*, p. 39.
21 Vogel, L. (1983) *Marxism and the Oppression of Women*, New Brunswick, NJ, Rutgers University Press.
22 Kessler-Harris, A. (1982) *Out to Work: A History of Wage-Earning Women in the United States*, New York, Oxford University Press, p. 148.
23 This is treated in more detail in Leach, W. (1984) 'Transformations in the culture of consumption: Women in department stores, 1865–1900', *Journal of American History*, 71, 2, pp. 319–42.
24 See the exceptional discussion in Rothaus, L. (1986) 'Labor, intimacy and class: Ideologies of feminine subjectivity in the punk subculture', unpublished manuscript, University of Wisconsin-Madison, Department of Educational Policy Studies. These points are of major importance. Too often, most marxist investigations focus all too heavily on production as paid work. They privilege the labor process outside the home to the extent that the relationship between schooling and patriarchal relations is made epiphenomenal. Recent feminist arguments, then, about the 'productivist' bias in some Marxist work need to be taken very seriously.
25 Hartmann, H. (1981) 'The unhappy marriage between Marxism and feminism: Towards a more progressive union' in Dale, R. *et al*, (Eds.) *Education and the State Volume 2: Politics, Patriarchy and Practice*, Lewes, Falmer Press, p. 191.
26 For some of the debate over these issues, see Barrett, M. (1980) *Women's Oppression Today*, London, New Left Books; Vogel, L., (1983) *op cit.*, Apple, M. W. (1982a), *op cit.*, and Apple, M. W. (1986b), *Teachers and Texts: A Political Economy of Class and Gender Relations in Education*, New York/London, Routledge and Kegan Paul.
27 See Apple, M. W. (1982a), *op cit.*; and Giroux, H., (1983) *op cit.*
28 See Braverman, H. (1974) *Labor and Monopoly Capital*, New York, Monthly Review Press; Edwards, R. (1979) *Contested Terrain*, New York, Basic Books; Wood, S. (Ed.) (1982) *The Degradation of Work?*, London, Hutchinson; and Apple, M. W. (1982a), *op cit.*
29 An overview of this material can be found in Apple, M. W. (1982a), *op cit.*; Harris, K. (1982) *Teachers and Classes*, Boston/London, Routledge and Kegan Paul. See also a number of the chapters in Apple, M. W. and Weis, L., (Eds) (1983) *op cit.*
30 Apple, M. W. (1986b), *op cit.*
31 *Ibid.* See also, Apple, M. W. (1986a) 'National reports and the construction of inequality', *British Journal of Sociology of Education*, 7, 2, pp. 171–90.
32 Apple, M. W. (1986a) *op cit.*
33 Adler, M. (1982) *The Paideia Proposal*, New York, Macmillan; and National Commission on Excellence in Education (1983) 'A nation at risk', *Education Week*, 27 April, pp. 12–16.
34 Apple, M. W. (1986b), *op cit.* Basil Bernstein's analysis of the place of the 'new middle class' is also very hopeful here. See Bernstein, B. (1977) *Class, Codes and Control*, Volume 3, Boston/London, Routledge and Kegan Paul, especially chapter 8.

35 Hall, S. (1980) 'Popular-democratic vs. authoritarian populism: Two ways of taking democracy seriously' in Hunt, A. (Ed.) *Marxism and Democracy*, London, Lawrence and Wishart, pp. 157–85.

36 See, for example, Barrett, M. (1980) *op cit.*; Apple, M. W. (1986b), *op cit.*

37 Omi, M. and Winant, H. (1986) *Racial Formation in the United States*, New York/London, Routledge and Kegan Paul. See also Laclau, E. and Mouffe, C. (1985) *Hegemony and Socialist Strategy*, London, Verso.

38 Omi, M. and Winant, H. (1986) *op cit.* Much of the recent work on the state is nicely analyzed in Carnoy, M. (1984) *The State and Political Theory*, Princeton, NJ, Princeton University Press.

39 Apple, M. W. (1982a), *op cit.*

40 Carnoy, M. and Levin, H., (1985) *op cit.*, p. 2. See also pp. 12–31.

41 *Ibid*, p. 24. See also Gintis, H. and Bowles, S. (1980/1981/1988) *op cit.*; Gintis, H., (1980) *op cit.*; and Apple, M. W. (1982a), *op cit.* The historical range of many of these conflicts can be seen in Reese, W. (1986) *Politics and the Promise of School Reform*, New York/London, Routledge and Kegan Paul; Wrigley, J. (1982) *Class Politics and Public Schools*, New Brunswick, NJ, Rutgers University Press, and Hogan, D. (1985) *Class and Reform*, Philadelphia, PA, University of Pennsylvania Press.

42 Carnoy, M. and Levin, H., (1985) *op cit.*, p. 47.

43 *Ibid*, p. 50.

44 Hall, S. (1981) 'The whites of their eyes: Racist ideologies and the media' in Bridges, S. and Brunt, R. (Eds.) *Silver Linings: Some Strategies for the Eighties*, London, Lawrence and Wishart, p. 36.

45 Laclau, E. and Mouffe, C., (1985) *op cit.*, p. 192.

46 See especially Gintis, H. and Bowles, S. (1980/1981/1988) *op cit.*; Gintis, H. (1980) *op cit.*, and their exceptionally interesting new volume, Bowles, S. and Gintis, H. (1986) *Democracy and Capitalism*, New York, Basic Books.

47 *Ibid.*

48 Hall, S., personal conversation.

49 Hall, S., (1983) 'The great moving right show' in Hall, S. and Jacques, M. (Eds.) *The Politics of Thatcherism*, London, Lawrence and Wishart, p. 25.

50 *Ibid*, p. 28.

51 Hall, S., (1980) *op cit.*, pp. 174–5.

52 Hall, S., (1983) *op cit.*, p. 29.

53 *Ibid*, p. 31.

54 Omi, M. and Winant, H., (1987) *op cit.*, p. 208.

55 *Ibid.*

56 *Ibid*, p. 217.

57 *Ibid*, p. 217–8.

58 For an outstanding analysis of both the concept of the common good and a set of concrete proposals to reach it, see Raskin, M. (1987) *The Common Good*, New York/London, Routledge and Kegan Paul.

59 Bowles, S. and Gintis, H., (1986) *op cit.*, p. 213.

7 *'Experience' as Analytical Framework: Does it Account for Girls' Education?*

AnnMarie Wolpe

Inequalities in education are experienced by different classes and fractions within them and nowhere is this more obvious than amongst women. Since the nineteenth century women have campaigned for better education, yet what form changes in education should take and how these are to be effected remains problematic. One crucial reason for this is that there is no consensus about the causes of the specificities of women's position in education.

This chapter begins with a brief presentation and assessment of the original explanation by Bowles and Gintis (1976) of educational differentials as these affect women. In their later review (1981) of *Schooling in Capitalist America* (reproduced as chapter 2 in this Volume) they accord importance to the role of experience in understanding 'the school as an arena of structured social interaction'. This view of Bowles and Gintis and the work, in a similar vein, of feminist writers is then examined. The chapter concludes with a schematic presentation of an alternative analytical framework which takes account of the experiential while, at the same time, not losing sight of the structural conditions in education.

Bowles and Gintis on Women

In order to address the questions relating to women, the discussion will begin with an overview of their conception of the economy, its relation to the family, what part education plays in relation to the economy, and then, finally, how women fit into this analysis.

Despite the risk of oversimplifying a complex and important work, suffice it to say that for them the inequalities 'stem from the property market institutions of capitalism, from the social relationships of work and from the dynamics of uneven development'.

We seek only to support our earlier assertion that the roots of

> unequal incomes and inequality of opportunity alike lie not in human nature, not in technology, not in the educational system itself, but in the dynamics of economic life (Bowles and Gintis, p. 89)

Inequalities cannot be ascribed to innate qualities of individual actors. Rather some of these inequalities are manifest in differential earning capacity which arise

> . . . largely from the class structure and the structure of racial and sexual privilege. In a more proximate sense, differences in wages or salaries are associated with differing personal characteristics of workers and differing institutional, geographical, and sectional situations facing them. . . (*ibid.* p. 91).

At the macro level, differences in earning capacity may be attributed to class, with gender and ethnic structures also relevant. There is what they term the 'structure of racial and sexual privilege' which results in the wages and earnings of women and black workers being determined largely by employment conditions.

As is well known, more and more women have, since the 1950s, entered the labour force. Bowles and Gintis point out that the demand made by the changing capitalist system for increased numbers with technical skills results in an 'expansion [that] has required the integration of blacks, women and middle class youth into this corporate wage-labour system.

They also point out that there has been an increase of 'highly qualified female workers', but their status in the labour market has not improved. As they correctly say, occupational growth was limited for them 'to the low level, white collar jobs associated with bureaucratized production'.

Moving from the macro level to the next order which is the individual subject, they claim that specific personal elements come into operation. These personal characteristics are derived from the 'cognitive capacities', 'personality traits', 'modes of self-presentation' which in turn are acquired during the processes of education. Here is one of the links with education which will be commented upon below.

Work affects and determines the personal lives of people. Thus they say:

> . . . the nature of work is a fundamental determinant of personal development (*ibid*, p. 68)

and

> The nature of work provides a pattern of prerequisites which affect the nature of personal development in families and school. In short the quality of work has an impact on the individual extending far beyond immediate satisfaction on the job (*ibid*, p. 71).

Work, therefore, must be seen as contributing to the formation of personal development.

There are two aspects to family life which Bowles and Gintis highlight. The first is that the family is the site of production which is 'geared primarily not to profits but rather towards the satisfaction of needs of the nuclear family'. And it is here that sexual differences arise because 'The family as a social as well as biological reproduction unit cannot but reflect its division of labor as a production unit'.

The second aspect, to which they apportion great significance, is the role of the family in the transmission of sets of ideologies appropriate not only to the maintenance of a capitalist system but also to the 'shackling' of women to the home and a perpetuation of their conditions of inequality. And this occurs in a family formation that they say is 'stagnant'. Patterns of 'consciousness and motivation' and the 'hierarchical division of labour' are generated by and transmitted through the family.

> ... like the educational system, the family plays a major role in preparing the young for economic and social roles. Thus the family's impact on the reproduction of the sexual division of labour, for example, is *distinctly greater than that of the educational system*. (*ibid*, p. 143) (my emphasis)

Thus,

> [The family] facilitated the submission of the next generation of women to their inferior status in the wage-labor system and lends this alternative to child-rearing and domesticity an aura of inevitability, if not desirability (*ibid*).

Women adopt the ideology and 'normally embrace their self concepts as household workers'. This is transmitted to children through 'sex-role stereotyping of boys and girls'. From their account family life plays a far more important and determining role in the future life styles of women than does schooling. According to them both boys and girls are affected by the ideological inputs they receive but differentially: ideological formations are derived from the family situation for girls but boys from their schooling. They do not offer an account of why this should be so, why girls are relatively unaffected by their schooling. Why should girls escape the ideological pressures which, according to Bowles and Gintis, constitute the main effect of schooling on pupils? Such a claim is obviously difficult to sustain.

This early conditioning spills over into the work situation. In addition to the restriction placed on women's earnings because of employment conditions and male 'sexual privilege', women are further handicapped by their 'submission to their inferior status' as a direct outcome of socialization processes within the family. Whilst all children learn about the labour system, girls accept the 'inevitability' that their future domestic roles is preferable to their inferior status in the labour market. The family influence sets the scene for their future lives.

What constitutes the link between the economy and the education system? This is predominantly through the internalization of appropriate ideologies relating to work, the legitimation of the system of inequality, and the channeling of the future generation of workers into their appropriate situations in the workplace.

To begin with it is through the education system that the youth acquire the appropriate attitudes towards their future work in 'alienated and stratified work relationships'. These ideologies are successfully transmitted by the schools.

In their main work Bowles and Gintis are particularly concerned with the way in which the education system legitimates the economic inequalities which exist in society. Education

> ... legitimates economic inequality by providing an open, objective and ostensibly meritocratic mechanism for assigning individuals to unequal economic positions. The educational system fosters and reinforces the belief that economic success depends essentially on the possession of technical and cognitive skills (*ibid*, p. 103)

Pupils leave school with the appropriate consciousness about the work they will do in the future and will believe that they have had equal chances with everyone else. Bowles and Gintis support their 'legitimization hypothesis' through the use of fascinating empirical data. They conclude:

> In summary, the ostensibly objective and meritocratic selection and reward system of US education correspond not to some abstract notion of efficiency, rationality and equity, but to the legitimatization of economic inequality and the smooth staffing of unequal work roles (*ibid*, p. 108)

This is effected through the reward system operating in schools and colleges.

> ... the basis for assessing merit — competitive academic performance — is only weakly associated with the personal attributes indicative of individual success in economic life. Thus the legitimation process in education assumes a largely symbolic form (*ibid*, p. 123)

The role of education, therefore, is specific. It is but 'one of several institutions which serve to perpetuate this structure of privilege'.

This overview provides the basis for a presentation of Bowles and Gintis' analysis as it affects women. Take earnings as the starting point. Apart from class relations which relate to all workers, by virtue of being female women are destined to fill particular jobs which are low paid because of employment conditions and the 'structure of sexual power relations'. The latter are rooted in domesticity which is intricately connected to their work.

> . . . the occupational emphasis on full-time work, the dependence of promotion upon seniority, the career-oriented commitment of the worker, and the active discrimination against working women conspire to shackle the women to the home while minimizing the likelihood of a joint sharing of domestic duties between husband and wife. (*ibid*, p. 143)

Whereas the economy and its link to education play a crucial role in determining men's life chances this is not the case with women. As pointed out above the family's influence is greater than that of the education system in terms of reproducing the sexual division of labour and the construction of women's consciousness and motivation unlike the education system which, by definition, is responsible for these developments amongst the males. More specifically the ideologies which have specific reference to work and the development of specific characteristics of future workers which are all attributed to schools must, therefore, affect males. Girls' ideas have, according to their analyses, been formed in the family. Schooling cannot be as important for women because of the greater power of the family structure and its teaching on sex-roles. In one fell swoop they eradicate any importance of education in girls' lives.

In the course of their review Gintis and Bowles reaffirm their main thesis in their earlier work and that is that schooling is the 'preparation of students as future workers'. In the course of their discussion on the continuing contradictions which include the inability of education to conform to the demands of capitalism, they give an example involving women which also confirms the analysis on women given above in regard to the influential role of the family. However they claim that women have achieved equal ' formal status' with men and this will have an impact on their education, although they do not specifiy how this will occur. They say that the 'formally equal status of women as citizens . . . virtually ensures that the state political system will come to supply relatively equal education to men and women' (p. 23 of this volume).

It is possible to take issue with the two authors about their notion that 'formal equal status has been attained'. For example, moves to have the American constitution definitively altered to achieve this were defeated a few years ago. But this is not the place to enter into debate about the interpretation that may be put on what constitutes formal equal status and how effective this is. What is of interest is that they see this as leading, automatically, to a position in which women will receive 'relatively equal education to that of men' which presupposes, correctly, that that is not the case at the present. But given that previously they did not regard schooling as having a major impact on women's lives because of the prescriptive force of family indoctrination, changes in relation to education presumably cannot be regarded as highly significant; changes for women need to be effected in the family. They argue, as before, that the differentiation between men and women lies in 'the reproduction of hierarchical relations in the capitalist enterprise [which] has depended on the subordination of women to men'. The site of this domination is located in the family. So it is still the family which is *the* important locus for female subordination. Even if women were to attain equal education they would still remain unequal to men because of the economy and, in the final analysis, the family. They have a solution to the problem. They say that equality could be attained through applying the 'principle of democracy'.

> The subordinate economic postion of women can be overturned by applying the principle of the equal rights of citizens to the area of hiring and promotion, in place of the property norms of free contract and hierarchical authority. Similarly the principle of democracy and reciprocity in personal relations is quite adequate to express the basis for a non-patriarchal reorganization of family life (*ibid*, p. 51).

So both spheres in which women are discriminated against could be altered through rational forces. Earlier in the article they introduce the notion of rationality when they refer to democratic discourses effecting change. Thus the three goals of education — egalitarianism, developments of indviduals' capacities, and 'the smooth integration of individuals as fully functioning members of society' — could be achieved. This, presumably, could also apply to 'sexual power relationships' and could be a means of resolution of inequalities there.

Their analysis relating to women in their review has not significantly altered. The family still remains the site of women's subordination. Education is still a legitimating force for economic inequalities and a conduit pipe for channeling people into the work force. Women's role in the labour force is prescribed through their gender, family formation and class position. Women are destined to remain in their lower earning jobs because they are women. It is not the education system which can be held responsible, particularly given their acceptance in the 'relatively equal education' women are likely to receive.

Experience in Education

In their review Gintis and Bowles argue as follows:

> Our formulation rectifies an earlier preoccupation of both liberal and Marxian analysis with the overt content of schooling (p. 18 of this volume).

They are correct to suggest that the study of the content has not provided all the answers to the many problems in accounting for the forms education takes. But in dismissing this as a 'preoccupation' they seem to be ruling it out of existence altogether because they wish to replace this with analyses of experience. 'Experience', they say, provides a 'consistent analytical framework for understanding the school as an arena of structured social interaction'. Their focus on experience is consistent with their concern throughout their major work with the *individual* actor. Throughout their book reference is made to the individual and the personality development of the individual, an aspect of their work which has been generally overlooked in the past because of the tendency to concentrate on the link between schooling and the macro economic level.

Now the part experience plays in the educational process has been the focus of attention of analysts concerned with the individual subject and has spawned a large and interesting literature. It has been the subject of much debate for a number of years and reflects a range of different theoretical approaches. As Hammersley (1986) has noted:

> the study of classroom interaction has a quite surprisingly long history, and one of its distinctive features is a baffling array of approaches with different purposes, foci and terminologies. Despite this diversity, however, much of the most recent work in the field shares a fundamental idea which contrasts with the older 'classroom observation' tradition . . . the central aim [of the new work] has been to discover the assumptions, rules, strategies, etc. which underlie and produce classroom interaction. Nevertheless, within the boundaries of that common theme, there are still some major differences of approach. (p. 93)

Indeed much of the book is taken up with the representation of these different approaches by a number of writers. Whilst the contributors in this book wrestle over definitions and approaches there is one remarkable absence. There is absolutely no reference to any of the work conducted by feminists over the past decade. It is as though feminist concern with classroom interaction and the experience of girls in school is quite irrelevant. This is so even in the chapter by Furlong and Edwards (1986) dealing with sociolinguisitics, an area in which a great deal of feminist work has been undertaken.

Furlong and Edwards are concerned primarily with language in classroom situations. It is in regard to this latter work that their omission of feminist work is remarkable. They do not refer, for example, to Spender's work (1980) at all in spite of the enormous influence it has had especially amongst teachers. Even should they have reservations about the work their failure to acknowledge its existence is surprising, to say the least. On the surface this confirms some of our worst fears about the lack of concern, particularly by male academics, for gender inequalities.

Feminist Contribution to Analyses Based on Experience

The other side of the coin is to be found amongst some feminist writers who cast aside 'male-defined and male-oriented theories' and claim that feminist methodology is directly opposite to 'traditional male emphasis [which] has been on objectifying experiences'. Such writers Stanley and Wise (1983), Mahony (1985) and others add to this list Marxist feminists as well, rejecting the latters' work on the grounds of its abstract nature and its lack of concern with everyday experiences. In criticizing such work, some writers tend to a reject theoretical debates and rationality as well, according to Currie and Kazi (1987). I do not wish to engage with this isolationist debate[1] nor to defend what appears to be a flight from theory, a trend that is unfortunately all too prevalent in feminist work (and indeed in the social sciences as well). However, part of the conceptual basis for the development of this viewpoint may be located in the use of the concept of patriarchy and this, as will be discussed below, is what marks off much of the recent feminist work on the role of the experiential in girls' education from the mainstream work mentioned above.

And yet feminist concern with the experiencing subject share two common elements with that of the social sciences including deviancy studies and 'new histories'. These social sciences have not only wished to extend their range of understanding of social situations but have also wished to break away from what they have seen as limiting and restricting mainstream analyses. As Johnson (1979) said in regard to the historians these developments can be

> best understood as an opposition, often rooted in political experiences, to all externalizing, mechanical or functionalist accounts of the social world and an insistence on getting inside the minds, perceptions and the feelings of the historical agents themselves (p. 64).

Although the feminist work also represents an opposition 'rooted in political experiences', some feminists have claimed a uniqueness for their methodology because of the focus on the individual woman's experience. The reason for this is the close alignment this perspective has to the political slogan that the personal is political.

Much work on girls and education has been informed by this approach which focusses on the experiential. This has been largely confined to girls' reactions to certain aspects of boys' and teachers' behaviour, particularly in the classroom. This is registered in terms of girls' oppression and the detrimental effect of boys' and teachers' behaviour on girls' progress. It has presented girls as victims of boys' oppression.

This approach has received popular acceptance because, it would seem, in vividly describing certain aspects of classroom interaction it is able successfully to raise practitioners' consciousness about the effects that their behaviour may have in the classroom. Further it highlights certain aspects of behaviour which appear to be amenable to alteration. This has led to what Davies (1984) referred to as the 'do-able' tactics directed towards reducing sexist practices that can be immediately adopted in the schools and has resulted in sets of guidelines put out by several local education authorities and teachers[2].

Whilst the strategies have proved extremely useful, particularly in terms of heightening educators' awareness of sexism, it would be wrong to think that they have, or can, alter drastically the education system to the benefit of girls. It is highly questionable that the disadvantaged position of girls in education can be attributed to the behaviour of boys and teachers. Thus, although the behaviour of boys and teachers may be altered and girls' *experiences* in education improved considerably, it does not automatically follow that the level of their attainment and the subjects they study will be extensively changed, nor that conditions of their future employment will alter.

Gaby Weiner (1986) called this type of approach 'radical'[3] in which 'inequality is a direct outcome of women's subordination to men'. This subordination is of primary importance and supercedes economic factors. Its theoretical paradigm is patriarchy.

The concept of patriarchy has been utilized to meet the failure of traditional Marxist analyses to take direct cognizance of gender inequalities and to account adequately for women's oppression[4]. There is a vast literature dealing with this topic from pschyoanalytical theory to an undifferentiated notion of male domination of women. It is this latter formulation which dominates the literature in education.

The employment of the concept is seductive because it appears to provide an instant explanation of men's domination of women since recorded history. There is a fundamental essentialism implied in the concept. Men dominate by virtue of their maleness: men *qua* men oppress women. Patriarchal relations prevail irrespective of other social conditions. Patriarchy in this sense is ahistorical and unchanging. It assumes a homogeneity within both genders; other factors such as class and ethnicity are rendered more or less unimportant. In the final analysis power relations between the two genders are determined by biological factors — maleness or femaleness. Power relations are unspecified and unvaried.

Once adopted patriarchy becomes a 'universal' explanatory tool. In the sphere of education, patriarchy and patriarchal relations become catch all terms in relation to knowledge, classroom practice, curriculum, school organization and so on. For example, Spender (1982) says that through patriarchy men control knowledge, which is derived from their own experience. They may use women's ideas if they find them useful, but if not they discard them. Whyld (1983) says that 'Our culture, knowledge and traditions have been selected and designed by males for the interest and encouragement of males'. De Wolfe (1980) talks about 'patriarchal learning and suggests that this should be replaced at least in women's studies by learning which is informed by 'feminist philosophy' which 'has always stressed the importance of shared experience and cooperative learning in a situation in which there are no leaders and no experts' unlike patriarchal learning. In all these different arenas, which are held to be important for girls' educational development, their apparent failure to 'achieve' is attributed to the operation of patriarchal relations. The effect of men's power is seen in all aspects of schooling so knowledge is patriarchal, the form of assessment is patriarchal, hierarchical school organization is patriarchal, sexual oppression is the outcome of patriarchy and so on.

Using this theoretical base has an unintended consequence of deproblematizing these areas. Labelling knowledge and all these other aspects of the schooling process as patriarchal suggests that as such they have a basic common element derived from male culture and therefore are counter to women's development. The remedy for this malady is to replace all such elements with equivalent female inspired aspects, such as de Wolfe envisaged. It is assumed that this substitution will create the conditions which will ensure the progress of all women and an overall improvement in their life chances. This preempts the continued investigation of all such areas. Problems with schooling are reduced to accounts of male culture.

Initially the studies on classroom interaction were concerned to fill the lacuna of mainstream social science which treated the school population as composed solely of boys. Studies on gender differences, and here my own work illustrates this point clearly, were concerned to make girls 'visible'. We were successful up to a point, although, to begin with, our work circulated largely amongst women academics and dedicated teachers; it remained outside the mainstream (and still does to a certain extent) of sociology of education. But we were able to demonstrate that many different classroom practices and elements of the curriculum contribute to the reinforcement of already existing patterns of gender differentiation. Our research, then, was, and is, a form of protest against conventional analyses.

Classroom dynamics have become one of the major foci for feminists. The findings have been derived from classroom observations, reports by girls, interviews, reports by and on teachers. The starting point for the analysis of girls in the education system is that they are disadvantaged in relation to boys as a whole. This disadvantage is apparent in many facets but the root cause in 'radical' analysis is attributed to boys' overall behaviour. What they do and how teachers react to them is seen to effect all girls directly and indirectly. In this context boys have become cast as the villains of the piece, the ones who are largely responsible for the failure of girls to 'achieve' and to leave schools trained and able to compete on an equal footing with boys in the labour market.

This view is encapsulated in a statement made by Arnot (1984) in which she claims that the outcome of feminist analyses has made the 'discussion of boys' education urgent' because 'often it is the *boys* who are the problem for girls in schools'. Drawing on three pieces of research, she says:

> In research such as that conducted by Walkerdine [1981], Stanworth [1983], and Fuller [1980], we get glimpses of the extent of boys disruption of the classroom; their noisiness, their sexual harassment of girls and female teachers, their demands for attention and their need of disciplining and their attitudes to the girls in their class as the silent or the 'faceless' bunch. (p. 38)

In this statement the conclusions of three research projects are combined to create a generalization about all boys and their behaviour. These three pieces of research to which Arnot refers are highly diverse studies which use different techniques and samples. The basis for their comparability lies in the commonality of the subjects — that is male — and the conclusions derived from stated reactions or interpretations all relate to male behaviour.

Walkerdine's paper was based on 'an examination of some observations collected in two nursery schools', Fuller's on eight fifth-form girls of 'West-Indian parentage' in a comprehensive school and Stanworth on ' "A" level classes in the Humanities department of a college of further education with a large fifth form intake'.

The size of each study's sample is not at issue, rather other factors. There is the nature of the samples, each of which differed in regard to age and ethnicity; the class backgrounds of each group are unknown. Secondly there is an assumption that the research methodologies provide a basis for comparison of data. But how was the research conducted; what were the theoretical underpinnings in each piece of research which determined the nature of the questions posed and the subsequent interpretation of the data? These aspects are not taken into account.

More specifically there are the following points. Stanworth (1983) recognized that here depiction of 'the quality of classroom life' had still to be established amongst younger pupils, and yet this point is overlooked when her findings are appropriated and contribute to a stereotypical view of all ages of boys. How typical were the exchanges reported on in the nursery school of all the boys in the class? Walkerdine did not present the material as though it was the case but rather in terms of different discourses surrounding sexuality amongst some very young children. Fuller's study (1980) focussed on adolescent girls of West Indian origin. Were her interpretations of these girls' reactions to boys to be taken as representative of all boys in secondary schools? Stanworth's research

> draws upon detailed individual interviews with teachers. and with a sample of their male and female pupils, in seven 'A' level classes. The objective was not to produce a description of events in the classroom as they might appear to an impartial observer, but rather

> to capture the quality of classroom life as currently experienced by pupils themselves (p. 23).

Notwithstanding such questions, these totally diverse studies have become the reference point and the basis for informed statements about all boys, irrespective of age, or stage of education, or class position. The common denominator is boys and so in spite of different research strategies and techniques, size of sample, and other factors these studies are deemed comparable. From these and other sources a stereotypical view of boys has been created. Boys are the problem. Boys are noisy, disruptive, harass girls sexually, demand teachers' attention, need to be disciplined, and hold pejorative views about all girls. These characteristics are said to exist amongst all boys from the age of nursery school upwards.

This representation has become part of conventional wisdom. There are a number of studies which seem to confirm and reinforce these generalizations. Take the question of boys' monopoly of teachers' attention. Arnot (1984) referring to Delamont (1980), Spender (1982) and Clarricoates (1980) says

> their work has shown how teachers tend to concentrate their time and energy upon boys in their classrooms, extending more approval *and* more disapproval to boys than to girls (p. 38).

Stanworth (1983), in what has proved a classic of its genre, found that 'trivial tokens of personal attention from teachers are the very signs that pupils looked for in deciding whether or not they are regarded with favour by their teachers'. As boys receive a disproportionate amount of attention from teachers, she concludes that girls' self-esteem is lowered. Although she does not specifically say so the unintended consequence of this is a lowering of girls' level of achievement, a conclusion which Mahony (1985) reaches.

In building up her case against co-education schooling, Mahony draws attention to different aspects of boys' behaviour. It includes boys' monopoly of physical and linguistic space, their style and gesture in the classroom, behaviour outside the classroom, their language, physical molestation of girls and so on. This together comprises what Mahony calls the environment in which the *message* to girls perpetuate their inferior status. When discussing the monopoly of linguistic space she refers to teachers' behaviour, girls' behaviour and boys' behaviour, all of which constitute a norm and form the basis for the 'environment' in which girls find themselves. 'It is

1 normal for teachers to ignore girls for long periods of time, but not for boys;
2 normal for boys to call out, move from their seats, push each other;

3 normal for girls to be addressed collectively, boys by their individual names;
4 normal for boys to dominate classroom talk.
5 normal for boys to talk rough and girls to talk soft. (p. 28)

Drawing on a fairly wide range of empirical detail the outcome of the radical position is to canvas for a return to single sex schools. So Lees (1986) in her recently published study on teenage girls has this to say about boys in the classroom:

> The co-ed/single sex distinction is important for girls because what steers the formal learning process in a sexist direction often stems from the presence of boys in the classroom, and their effects on teachers' attention and time devoted to girls, sexual harassment of girls and the ability of girls to hold their own in competition with boys. (p. 120)

So in the end the standard of girls' educational achievement is the direct outcome of their experience of school which is conditioned by the behaviour and the effect of behaviour of boys.

Criticisms of Radical Feminist Classroom Interaction Studies

There is a wide range of criticism which can be levelled against ethnographic studies in general. My concern here is not with this problem but with the specific 'radical' feminist analyses of girls' education which have focussed on the experiential culminating in a stereotypical protrayal of boys.

The starting point of radical analyses is the notion of patriarchy. The construction of reality is premissed on this basis. In accordance with partriarchal relations all boys are seen to be privileged in schools, as contrasted with all girls. Boys, it is argued, are accorded a higher status by virtue of their being male. This dominance permeates all relations in the school and is particularly manifest in the classroom.

The result of this emphasis is a plethora of data referred to above, which is said to express patriarchal power. This is assumed to be detrimental to girls, an assumption strengthened through verbal reports by girls on the way in which they experience classroom interaction. For example, as illustrated above, teachers' behaviour is said to have the effect of lowering girls' self-esteem thereby affecting their performance in school.

But how correct is this interpretation? Such data could be given quite different meanings. This was recognized by Eggleston (1976) who said in his introduction to Delamont's book:

> Increasingly we realize that the interactions of the classroom can

> have many more intepretations; that the behaviour of students and teachers carries important meaning about such fundamental matters as the nature of power knowledge and the social system. (p. 8)

So while classroom interactions may highlight the specific 'nature of power, knowledge and the social system' it depends on the construction of what constitutes the social system that is of importance. In the case of 'radical' analyses the social system is defined as a patriarchal one. Given a different analytical framework an alternate interpretation may be made as the following illustrates.

MacDonald (1981) provided interesting data when she was reviewing earlier American studies on teachers' behaviour. She pointed out that American social psychology literature on teacher behaviour from the 1950s and 1960s commented on what was then defined as discriminatory practices against boys. One researcher argued that the 'instructional and managerial interactions with boys were obvious strategies for social control'. By the 1970s the definition of this type of reaction had been recast in terms of boys gaining independence, autonomy and activity through teachers' constant attention and admonition. Whereas in the 1950s such behaviour on the part of teachers was defined in terms of being harmful towards boys, thirty years on this is seen in quite opposite terms — as advantageous to boys. Teachers' constant attention to boys is now good for boys, irrespective of the nature of that attention.

The interpretation conforms with notions of patriarchal power and control in which it is simply taken for granted that boys are privileged; everything that occurs confirms this, even the constant remonstrations of boys.

Closely associated with this is what Glaser and Strauss (1967) defined some years ago as 'exampling', a process which may not necessarily be consciously pursued. Furlong and Hamilton (1986) refer to 'exampling' defining it as 'this practice of fitting out an already formulated theory with supporting evidence'. They then quote Glaser and Strauss (1967):

> A researcher can easily find examples for dreamed up, speculative or logically deduced theory after the idea has occurred. But since the idea has not been derived from the example, seldom can the example correct or change it (even if the author is willing) since the example was selectively chosen for its confirming power. Therefore one received the image of a proof when there is none, and the theory obtains a richness of detail which it did not earn. (p. 5)

The research referred to above seeks to establish examples where such dominance may be seen to operate and concentrates its attention on such manifestations. All the instances have the 'confirming power' of the theory' which attributes to boys' behaviour power to determine the outcome of girls' education. And the conclusions drawn by the radical analyses illustrate this process of 'exampling'.

There are consequences which follow: sets of assumptions are made which are not questioned. For example, are all boys singled out for attention? It may be that some boys are consistently the focus of the teachers' attention, but this may not apply to all boys. Whatever the form of attention boys receive does this enhance their self-esteem? Even if it could be demonstrated that boys' self-esteem were advanced by their constant attention, why should it be advantageous to them in academic terms? If teachers do, in fact, spend a fair amount of time in reprimanding boys why should this be taken to improve their chances of acquiring knowledge, skills and qualifications?

Similarly in relation to girls' reports that their self-esteem is lowered: what are the consequences of this experience? Does this have direct effect on their academic attainment? Does it mean that girls' so-called silence (although even that is debatable as my own research data in a forthcoming book indicates) diminishes their capacity to learn? Is learning solely a function of praise and approval by teachers? Fuller's (1980) evidence suggests that the young women in her study were pro-education, but this did not result in their apparent conformity to school ethics. They effectively masked their intentions to do well.

> The black girls conformed to the stereotypes of the good pupil only in so far as they worked conscientiously at the schoolwork or homework set. But they gave all the appearance in class of not doing so, and in many other ways displayed an insouciance for the other aspects of the good pupil role (p. 59)

Obtaining 'academic qualifications was an integral part of this sense of control over their future' and a way out of a particular life style they disliked. This provides a totally different picture of girls' silence and supposed oppression.

Or take Walkerdine's (1985) concern with the 'regulation of speaking and silence'. She says:

> ... the issue of silence and speaking is not a simple matter of presence or absence, a suppression versus enabling. Rather, what is important is not simply whether one is or is not allowed to speak, since speaking is always about saying something. In this sense, what can be spoken, how and in what circumstances is important (p. 205).

In other words, Walkerdine places the verbal and non-verbal within a broader context. It is what is said, the manner in which it is said and the circumstances surrounding the verbal exchange that needs to be analyzed. It is not sufficient to assume that the exchange between teacher and pupil is straight forward·and a simple expression of overall male dominance

Further on Walkerdine refers to the multiplicity of individuals' subjectivities, a notion that she used in the earlier article on nursery school children's behaviour. In doing so she disputes the notion of 'voluntarism' which assumes that change can follow from subjects 'recognizing and choosing to stand outside the conditions of their own regulation'. Their silences have to do with other factors which she ties in with child-rearing practices and, in particular, how the family through the actions of the mother, positions the child. This type of analysis suggests a far more complex process than the rather simplistic accounts given by the 'radical' analyses above. The conclusion to be drawn from Walkerdine's analysis is that the placing of girls in single sex schools will not necessarily overcome their silences, nor necessarily result in a change in their self-esteem. It is too easy to assume that identifiable forms of classroom behaviour and interaction have a direct causal effect on the final outcome of a total educational experience.

To conclude the discussion on such work it may be as well to recall what Sharp (1986) had to say about ethnography. She defined it as revealing 'the effects of the social totality which itself produces the characteristics of the fieldwork situation and structures possible outcomes'. Much of the work of the 'radical' analyses discussed above confirms Sharp's statement and, incidentally, 'exampling' as defined by Glaser and Strauss.

But this is not to deny the value of observations of classroom interaction. They illustrate the process of classroom dynamics which go beyond the systematic observations that for so long dominated investigations. They emphasize the active part that pupils play in the classroom replacing the previous portrayal of pupils as passive subjects. The studies which have concentrated on girls have ably illustrated the ways in which girls are disadvantaged. However to treat social interaction as the sole cause of the limitations imposed on girls is to deny the existence of other factors which operate within and without the education system. It relegates all girls to a purely passive and reactive role, denying their active engagement in their own lives.

There is a number of structural factors which interact and affect the schooling system. These include the specificity of the labour market (as Bowles and Gintis emphasized), family life, peer-group culture, all of which are located within a class structure. Then there are factors specific to the schooling system: the hierarchically organized system, the content and organization of knowledge, forms of control and so on, which operate within a semi-autonomous structure within society (Poulantzas, 1975). The school processes cannot be reduced to experience of the subjects, or the effect of peer culture or specific aspects of knowledge. What goes on in school involves a complex set of relationships all of which need examination and analysis.

Where a Marxist-feminist analysis can make a specific contribution to an understanding of the education system is the identification and consideration of how gender differences exist in relation to all these factors. It enlarges the scope of the analysis and makes it far more complex than the tendency to account for the specificity of all girls' education on the basis of their experience within the classroom.

Schematic Outline of an Alternate Framework of the Schooling Process

I have discussed analyses which have concentrated on the experience of the individual subject. Bowles and Gintis (1976), notwithstanding their overall concern with the macro level, did raise questions about individuals' life chances, interpersonal relations and development of personality characteristics.

> To capture the economic impact of education we must relate its social structure to the forms of consciousness, interpersonal behaviour and personality it fosters in students (p. 9).

This concern led them to emphasize the role of experience of education when they reviewed their original book.

They did talk of specific groups such as women and ethnic minorities. They recognized the differentials between men and women, but in the final analysis women were seen as victims of their own domesticity and familial responsibilities. It was the family which was ultimately the cause of their inequalities. Although the education system might well affect consciousness in general, it was in the family that girls' and women's consciousness was forged.

'Radical' feminist writers on education, on the other hand, attribute a great deal of importance to the experience girls have of the education system. This experience is mediated by boys' behaviour, which is also taken as affecting teachers' behaviour. The combination of both culminates in girls' loss of self esteem and perception of oppression. It is this latter aspect which reflects the nature of boys' dominance, itself an aspect of male dominance in society in general.

There are several unintended consequences of the 'radical' analysis. It creates a stereotypical boy which is the reverse side of the stereotypical girl. This suffers from the defects that emerge from the use of stereotypes. Stereotypes are typifications or simplifications of common elements which refer to apparent, straight forward identifiable characteristics and predictions of how people will behave (Perkins, 1979). They embrace evaluative statements which often are judgmental, masking the complexities of social relations.

The set of sterotypical views about boys' behaviour has led to expectations about their behaviour as a whole, ignoring the widespread differentiation that does operate in schools. Further there is the tendency to take the effect of boys' behaviour as constituting the fundamental cause of girls' failures in school. In doing this there is the recourse to an essentialist view which refers not only to boys' nature but also to that of girls. Certain assumptions about standards and levels of attainment follow on from this. The first is that girls will attain high academic standards through a separation from boys. The second is that all boys do well in school and leave school with qualifications, particularly in sciences and mathematics those subjects which are always quoted when academic attainment is mentioned.

The consequence of such analyses is the failure to examine the specificity of girls' education. Factors relating to age differences, class factors, ethnic differences are largely overlooked when all girls are treated as comprising a homogeneous category on the basis of their biology. The consequence of the 'radical' position is to canvas for a return to single sex schools. To understand the specificity of girls' education a different approach is required.

Schools, like other aspects of the social system, reflect male dominance. It is mistaken, however, to think that this male dominance has a unilinear effect on the processes of schooling in general and girls' educational attainment in particular. Just as there is a complex set of interrelated factors which account for male domination at workplaces and in the home, so this is the case in schools. What happens in school is not a simple reflection of male dominance expressed in the form that boys' behaviour takes. Schools are concerned with control of the individual actor and the transmission of sets of ideologies and knowledge. Insofar as individual actors in the schools imbibe and act upon stereotypical notions of gender specific behaviour this is only part of their overall behaviour. School life is far more varied than this.

It is necessary to begin the analysis by placing schooling within a broader socio-economic context, as Bowles and Gintis did. It would mean taking account of the link between schooling and both the labour market and family formation, going beyond the ideological influences.

The relationship between schooling and employment is complex, not least because of the contradictions within the labour market itself and which escape resolution through the application of rational solutions. In the first instance there are varied, contradictory and opposing demands for quantities of labour power possessing differing skills and qualities. Apart from struggles between capital and labour there are the contradictions within the capitalist system itself. The attempt to translate these demands into the labour producing institutions such as schools and further and higher education institutions is difficult because of these contradictions. There are added problems because the education institutions are themselves the site of political and ideological struggles. Furthermore they 'have a strong relative autonomy with respect to the economy' (Bourdieu and Boltanski, 1977). The reproduction of the work force is, therefore, not a straightforward phenomenon, as Bowles and Gintis would have us believe.

When any one group is examined these external factors together with the specific conditions of that group must be taken into account. So when it comes to examining the relationship between schooling and employment of women, the specific conditions would have to include the nature of the employment available to women. This is determined by the work place itself, the agreements with organized labour and the availability of labour. Thus the nature of work that women perform in the labour market is not a simple straightforward outcome of their schooling. They may have high, low or minimal level of qualifications which may provide access to certain types of employment. They may have high or low levels of aspiration in regard to their work. But neither the availability of work, nor the nature of the work itself is directly determined by, or the outcome of, their level of qualifications, and/or their aspirations (Wolpe, 1978). Increased particip-ation in the labour force may 'structure' the work aspirations of succeeding generations, particularly the daughters as Furlong argues (1986), but aspirations alone will not change the nature of the available work[5]. But none of this is to suggest that schooling is irrelevant to future work; but its role is circumscribed.

There is, of course, a close link between work and ideologies held about work. When this is applied to family life, the work ethic is directly contradictory to the ideology about women's role in the family. Schools portray motherhood as the main goal for women. This is present in all parts of the curriculum, including the hidden curriculum, and is further reinfor-ced through different channels such as the pastoral system and welfare services. What constitutes family life is represented by the nuclear family. This view conveniently ignores changes that have occurred particularly in regard to single parent families and homosexual couples. Furthermore, it legitimates the specific exploitation of women who are employed in home work, part-time jobs and low level jobs generally because women are not regarded as main supporters or essential contributors to the family income. The form of division of labour in the family makes it possible for women to do outwork or part-time work. All of this is perpetuated through the ideology of woman as wife/mother and paves the way for both women and men to accept women's low level of pay and occupational chances.

All these factors are important and have an impact on schools themselves. However given all this and given the relative autonomy enjoyed by schools, the organizational and structural forms which charac-terize schools also need to be identified. These forms operate in a situation which is itself the site of struggle and conflict. Within schools sets of contradictions are apparent and these surface everywhere.

Before the specificity of girls' education may be examined the conditions within schools have to be established. To begin with there is the organizational context of the school which revolves around general forms of control. These forms of control are meant to ensure the conditions for the transmission of specific knowledge and ideas to the pupils.

Two distinct forms of social control may be identified. The first operates through disciplinary procedures and the second through the curriculum. Each of these will be schematically presented.

Disciplinary Control

Discipline is a necessary condition for the maintenance of the continued operation of the school[6]. This is often not fully recognized as the discourses which concentrate on moral order would indicate. Like prisons, hospitals and other large institutions, schools employ a range of instruments of discipline and require that all members of the institutions be subjected to control. Nor is this new. Schools have always had to use disciplinary measures although these have altered with changing social conditions.

In the present day the examination system operates as one of the major instruments of disciplinary control. Where public examinations are not normally pursued and more ritualistic forms of control over the physical movements of pupils have declined, control over the pupils becomes more problematic and difficult. Alternate methods of control have to be sought and become increasingly important if resistance to schooling, as witnessed in the high rate of absenteeism and low level of attainment, is to be successfully combatted.

Where the discipline resulting from a formal examination system of pupils is absent, the heavy responsibility on the individual teacher takes on a more central role in giving effect to alternative forms of disciplinary control of pupils. This is one of the reasons why classroom interaction assumes such importance in those schools where academic performance is comparatively low. Given the distinctive class membership of pupils who take examinations — middle class pupils predominate here — class factors become important in this sphere of control. Conventional wisdom correctly holds that middle class pupils are more likely to take their schooling seriously in that they will do homework and aim to enter public examinations. Working class pupils on the other hand are said to adopt a counter school culture. At the most general level class factors do operate as is reflected in the predominantly middle class composition of university and polytechnic students.

How do issues relating to gender appear and how may they be identified, particularly given that all pupils irrespective of any specific differences including gender are subjected to disciplinary measures? It is at the level of interaction between teacher and pupils that gender differences occur. Teachers, for example, do have expectations about the behaviour of boys and girls, reflecting cultural stereotypes. Such expectations may cut across expectations they hold about class differences and does affect their behaviour. In addition pupils themselves reflect their culture, and this has to be considered. Stereotypical views about gender also apply to teachers and have an effect that needs analysis. In regard to this latter point, for example, male teachers are thought to be better able to control classes than female teachers. This belief is reinforced by the hierarchical structure of the school, and by various aspects of sexuality which may be projected in the classroom consciously or unconsciously. The masculinity of male teachers is seen to be an advantage when it comes to controlling a class, while the femininity of women teachers is seen to be a negative element. In regard to classroom interaction in general, there are several factors which affect the interpretation of the data. Pupils like their teachers are active subjects and this applies to girls as well as to boys. Conventional wisdom projects the image of a quiet, well disciplined girl who passively does her work in the classroom. This image is enlarged upon by the 'radical' view which protrays girls as victims of boys' oppression. However, not only do girls fail their schoolwork and opt out at rates not dissimilar to that of boys but they too engage in resistance to school. So while examining the forms of disciplinary control, the way in which girls resist school and what form their counter school culture takes needs full investigation. Resistance to control is not the monopoly of one gender, although the form it takes may differ according to gender. Girls' resistance may occur in the way in which they dress for school; truancy and school avoidance while occurring amongst both boys and girls, may differ in accordance with how each group spends its time. In the classroom girls' resistance takes a different form to the boys: they may be quieter and less physically active than boys, but they nevertheless resist school lessons. What is interesting is the absence of discussions of girls' resistance from the literature (Davies' book is a noticeable exception) — this may reflect their more effective masking of their resistance, as well as the reluctance to recognize that deviancy and acts of violence do occur amongst girls and women.

The examination of disciplinary forms of control will end the portrayal of girls as the 'faceless' bunch in the literature. They are part of a complex interrelated process and many may be engaged in acts of resistance to school culture. This is not to deny the large numbers who are pro school and do attain a high level at the end of their school days. Some girls may well experience the behaviour of some boys as oppressive in co-education schools, but to suggest that this is the dominant part of their school life is to project a restricted view of what goes on in schools. All the active participants reflect cultural and class differences which include expressions about sterotypical views on gender.

Another dimension of the mental control is that which relates to moral order. Moral order is equated with sexual morality and sexual behaviour. Schools are charged with providing moral guidance to the pupils and this is effected through sex education or other parts of the curriculum which concentrated on teaching fidelity in marriage. Such provisions ignore emerging sexuality amongst the adolescents and the importance this plays in their lives, and the way in which masculinity and femininity mediate all aspects of school life.

Detailed analyses of how disciplinary control operates, its effect on girls and boys, and the forms of resistance by all pupils provide the starting point for understanding the processes of social interaction in schools.

Curriculum

The other form of control is achieved through the working of the curriculum, a complex and, obviously, a crucial component of schooling. It is an area which has been subjected to rigorous analysis. It will be taken as given that that which constitutes the curriculum comprises a knowledge base which itself is intricately tied in with class and power relations of the society. Bourdieu (1971), Young (1971) and numerous others have so ably established the link between schools through the working of the curriculum and the capitalist system.

Such analyses are at the macro level. But the way in which the curriculum operates in terms of controlling gender differences is less clear. To begin an analysis of this the following framework is proposed. First the elementary division which demarcates academic from non-academic knowledge needs to be established. The former has a higher status than the latter. These two sections are directly linked to mental and manual work respectively.

In addition not all parts of an academic curriculum enjoy equal status. Although there is no objective criterion which establishes the worth of one discipline over another, some academic subjects have higher status: the physical sciences and mathematics top the list. This is an area where further analyses need to be undertaken, but the importance of the hierarchy of such subjects should be related to the future pathways into occupations. Whatever the case, discussions on the nature of curriculum pursued by girls should take such factors into account.

To labour the obvious, pupils who pursue an academic curriculum are more likely to find a pathway into higher paid occupations than those in the non-academic streams. Girls who pursue academic curricula may gain access to higher paid occupations, although their scope is limited because of the structure of the labour market, as referred to above, the absence of women's power in it and the overall domination of women particularly in terms of the division of labour both at the work place and in the home. The comparison that can be drawn should be between girls and boys in the academic streams rather than the tendency to contrast all girls with a select group of boys. Too often it is assumed that all boys are advantaged as a group irrespective of the fact that only a relatively small percentage of boys may pursue academic subjects.

A similar distinction applies to non-academic subjects and presumably there is a difference in status between some of the subjects and the rationale for their inclusion in the curriculum. However these differences are seldom commented upon. What is of more importance for girls is the link that may be established between some of these non-academic courses and domestic or work roles.

This leads onto that aspect of the curriculum which is particularly relevant to gender differences. That is the hidden curriculum. Through its operation messages relating to gender differences specifically of an ideological nature are directly or indirectly transmitted. This is an aspect of work which has been well documented in the feminist literature (MacDonald, 1981; Whyld, 1983).

Throughout there is a need to compile concrete data: the distribution of girls and boys in accordance with the type of curriculum they are pursuing, the age at which they make decisions, the full picture of how these decisions are reached (including the structural constraints operating within the schools) and the class membership of the pupils. Such data would provide an adequate basis for comparison between girls and boys with like backgrounds.

This would move the discussion away from the commonplace comparisons that are drawn between all girls and the relatively small number of boys following a scientific curriculum at 'A' level. Such comparisons are meaningless. Rather the comparisons should mirror the wide differences which are reflected amongst school leavers. Too often the alarmingly large proportion of pupils who fail to attain passes in either academic or non-academic subjects is overlooked. In the course of emphasizing girls' failure to pursue certain academic subjects, the failure amongst boys is ignored. Approximately 40 per cent of all school leavers do not have any meaningful qualifications. This applies to boys even more so than the girls as recent figures indicate. (DES, 1984)

Discussions on girls' performance in school should avoid generalizations. They should be specific and take account of the conditions of the school, the nature of the curriculum girls follow, and locate the different elements of the curriculum within a broad context.

Conclusion

This brief schematic outline gives some indication of an alternate form of analysis that could be pursued in the course of establishing the specificity of girls' educational profiles. It is important to recognize that over the years progress has been achieved and the upward trend in the numbers of girls obtaining qualifications should not be forgotten. At the same time it is important to recognize that schooling in this country is in a state of crisis. There is an alarming number of girls and boys who leave school illiterate;

then there are those who have minimal qualifications and are unlikely to ever pursue further education. A country which fails to educate its future population cannot progress.

Our concern is not to compare all girls with an abstract notion of an achieving, well qualified and well educated male population. We should be examining the education system as a whole and tackling the problem of increasing and improving the education chances for all pupils, girls and boys alike. It is unrealistic to think that a return to single sex schools will aid all girls. It might well help those who are 'high fliers' and who wish to study the male dominated subjects such as physics and chemistry undisturbed by boys in their senior years but what of that large band who cluster round the lower percentile? Will their removal to single sex schools result in a sudden flurry of girls opting for academic subjects, and working hard at school? The available evidence suggests the contrary. For this large band of girls schooling in a co-education situation may prove problematic with some boys creating a hostile and aggressive environment. But this is not the single major problem. Their life chances are determined by their class and gender positions, both of which are mediated by a number of different institutional and developmental processes including their education, family life and peer culture. To effect a major improvement there obviously need to be changes all round which tackle the various areas in which discrimination occurs including their schooling, and division of labour in the family and work-place. This is unlikely to occur overnight and will prove a site of ongoing struggle which must go beyond the 'structural boundaries of liberal discourse' as Gintis and Bowles (1981) advocate (see Chapter 2).

It is possible to make a start within the schooling system in order to improve the life chances of girls and boys alike. There is an urgent need for the creation of an environment in which the essential aims of a true education may be effected for girls and boys alike. This, however, requires rethinking of all aspects of the curriculum, modes of teaching, the control of pupils, and a revitalization of all resources, in which particular attention is paid to the teachers who for too long have been undervalued and who are often unable to work creatively because of the difficult and often fraught situation in which they find themselves. Such a programme suggests a complete overhaul of an the education system in concrete terms and goes well beyond the call made by Gintis and Bowles for a reformulation of the philosophy of education. As they point out the education system is just one part of a social formation all of which requires change if socialist principles are to be realized for all irrespective of gender or ethnic differences.

Notes

1 In their article on academic feminism, Currie and Kazi (1987) examine some of the criticisms that have been levelled against academic feminist writers. Contrary to

those writers like Stanley and Wise (1983) who present experience of the individual as the basis for understanding social reality, they say that subjectivity has a material base. They also challenge social scientists who present social reality as 'something separated from and unrelated to human subjectivity'.

2 For details on some of the measures and strategies adopted either by individual teachers or LEAs see, for example, Cornbleet and Libovitch, (1983), Whyte *et al*, (1985).

3 I am following the use of the term 'radical' in relation to the debates in education in accordance with Weiner's (1986) definition. In this way Arnot and others who have employed Marxist analyses in relation to the labour process may also be included under this heading. Weiner identifies another perspective in the gender and the 'equal opportunities' debate in education which is the 'egalitarian' one. This strives for equality within the existing social structure and is concerned with 'equalizing current school resources and education benefits rather than in any deliberate attempt at positive discrimination in favour of girls'.

4 Patriarchy is by no means a new concept as Coward (1983) pointed out. It had become popular during the nineteenth century and had been developed by Henry Maine in the course of formulating a basis for understanding comparative law. This early usage was subsequently developed by anthropologists. But it was with the rise of feminism that the concept has been revitalized.

5 Furlong (1986) says:

> . . . increasing labour parket participation by women this generation will structure the work expectations of the next generation through family experiences. Similarly increasing numbers of women in positions of authority in this generation will result in more girls aspiring to such positions in the next generation. (p. 375)

He says that it is 'the images women hold about themselves' that prevents them from getting better jobs, but fails to provide the evidence that there are better jobs waiting for women to fill them. He ignores, in other words, the process of deskilling and the decline in numbers of women than in previous decades in management jobs. We may have appropriate images about the type of work we wish to do but this will not generate the work.

6 For a fuller discussion on the role of discipline and an analysis of it in the educational system see Wolpe (1985). I am not suggesting here that traditional disciplinary methods are the necessary condition for children to learn. This is the case given the present social conditions. But given a marked change in social conditions and the education system it is possible to envisage an alternative mode of regulation which would result in self discipline and a desire to learn.
discipline and a desire to learn.

References

Arnot, M. (1984) 'How shall we educate our sons?' in Deem, R. (Ed) *Co-education Reconsidered*, Milton Keynes, Open University Press.

Bourdieu, P. (1971) 'Systems of education and systems of Thought' in Young, M. (Ed) *Knowledge and Control*, London Collier-Macmillan.

Bourdieu, P. and Boltanski, L. (1977) 'Qualifications and jobs' in *Two Bourdieu Texts*, Stencilled Occasional Papers, Birmingham, Birmingham Centre for Contemporary Cultural Studies.

Bowles, S. and Gintis, H. (1976) *Schooling in Capitalist America*, London, Routledge and Kegan Paul.

Clarricoates, K. (1980) 'The importance of being Earnest ... Emma ... Tom ... Jane. The perception and categorization of gender conformity and gender deviation in primary schools' in Deem, R. (Ed) *Co-education Reconsidered*, Milton Keynes, Open University Press.

Cornbleet, A. and Libovitch, S. (1983) 'Anti-sexist initiatives in a mixed comprehensive school: A case study' in Wolpe, A M *et al* (Eds) *Is There Anyone Here From Education?*, London, Pluto Press.

Coward, R. (1983) *Patriarchal Relations*, London, Routledge and Kegan Paul.

Currie, D. and Kazi, H. (1987), 'Academic feminism and the process of de-radicalization: Re-examining the issues' *Feminist Review*, 25.

Davies, L. (1984) *Pupil Power*, Lewes, Falmer Press.

De Wolfe, P. (1980) 'Women's studies: The contradictions for students' in Spender, D. *et al* (Eds) *Learning to Lose*, London, Women's Press.

Deem, R. (1980) (Ed) *Schooling for Women's Work*, London, Routledge and Kegan Paul.

Deem, R. (1984) (Ed) *Co-Education Reconsidered*, Milton Keynes, Open University Press.

Delamont, S. (1980) *Sex Roles and the School*, London, Methuen.

Des (1984) *Statistics of Education: School Leavers CSE and GCE*, London, HMSO.

Eggleston, J. (1976) 'Introduction' in Delamont, S. (Ed) *Interaction in the Classroom*, London, Methuen.

Fuller, M. (1980) 'Black girls in a London comprehensive school' in Deem, R. (Ed) *Co-education Reconsidered*, Milton Keynes, Open University Press.

Furlong, A. (1986) 'Schools and the structure of female occupational aspirations' *British Journal of Sociology of Education*, 7, 4.

Furlong, V. J. and Edwards, A. D. (1986) 'Language in classroom interaction: Theory and data' in Hammersley, M. (Eds) *Controversies in Classroom Research*, Milton Keynes, Open University Press.

Gintis, H. and Bowles, S. (1981) 'Contradiction and reproduction in Barton, L. *et al* (Eds) *Schooling, Ideology and the Curriculum*, Lewes, Falmer Press.

Glaser, B. and Strauss, A. (1967) *The Discovery of Grounded Theory*, Chicago, Aldine.

Hammersley, M. (Ed) (1986) *Controversies in Classroom Research*, Milton Keynes, Open University Press.

Johnson, R. (1979) 'Culture and its historians' in Clarke, J. *et al* (Eds) *Working Class Culture*, London, Hutchinson.

Lees, S. (1986) *Losing Out*, London, Hutchinson.

MacDonald, M. (1981) *Class, Gender and Education*, Educational Studies, E353, Block 4, Miltion Keynes, Open University Press.

Mahony, P. (1985) *Schools for the Boys?*' London, Hutchinson.

Perkins, T. E. (1979) 'Rethinking stereotypes' in Barrett, M. *et al* (Eds) *Ideology And Cultural Production*, London, Croom Helm.

Platt, A and Whyld, J. (1983) 'Introduction' in Whyld, J. (Ed) *Sexism in the Secondary Curriculum*, London, Harper and Row.

Poulantzas, N. (1975) *Classes in Contemporary Capitalism*, London, New Left Books.

Sharp, R. (1986) 'Self-contained ethnography or a science of phenomenal forms and inner relations' in Hammersley, M. (Ed) *Controversies in Classroom Research*, Milton Keynes, Open University Press.

Spender, D. (1980) *Man Made Language*, London, Routledge and Kegan Paul.

Spender, D. (1982) *Invisible Women*, London, Writers and Readers Publishing Cooperative.

Stanley, L. and Wise, S. (1983) *Feminist Consciousness and Feminist Research* London, Routledge and Kegan Paul.

Stanworth, M. (1983) *Gender And Schooling*, London, Hutchinson.

Walkerdine, V. (1981) 'Sex power and pedagogy', *Screen Education*, 38.

Walkerdine, V. (1985) 'On the regulation of speaking and silence: subjectivity, class

and gender in contemporary schooling' in Steedman, C. *et al* (Eds) *Language Gender and Childhood* London, Routledge and Kegan Paul.
Weiner, G. (1986) 'Feminist education and equal opportunities: Unity or discord?', *British Journal of Sociology*, 7, 3.
Whyld, J. (Ed) (1983) *Sexism in the Secondary Curriculum*, London, Harper & Row.
Whyte, J. *et al* (Eds) (1985) *Girl Friendly Schooling*, London, Methuen.
Wolpe, A M. (1978) 'Education and the sexual division of labour' in Kuhn, A. *et al* (Eds) *Feminism and Materialism*, London, Routledge and Kegan Paul.
Wolpe, A M. (1985) 'Schools discipline and social control' in Barton, L. *et al* (Eds) *Education and Social Change* London, Croom Helm.
Young, M. (Ed) (1971) *Knowledge and Control* London, Collier-Macmillan.

8 *Beyond the Reproductive Theory of Teaching*

Dennis L. Carlson

In the following I want to examine and call into question some of the dominant images of teachers that have emerged from various critical theories of schooling over the past several decades. I also want to indicate some of the ways our view of schooling and of teachers' role in it needs to be modified so that it avoids the determinism and cynicism inherent in much critical discourse on the schools. From a political standpoint, the importance of a multi-faceted and less deterministic treatment of teachers and their occupational culture is considerable. It seems doubtful, for example, that any movement to transform the schools, as part of a democratic Left political agenda, can succeed without the active support of rank-and-file teachers. It consequently is important that the Left not 'write off' teachers as mere functionaries in an oppressive schooling process.

In keeping with these objectives, I divide my comments into two major sections. In the first of these I examine the structural-functional theory of schooling, most associated with the work of Samuel Bowles and Herbert Gintis in America, which apprehends teachers according to their 'objective' class location within the processes of social and economic reproduction. Teachers are viewed as members of the 'new middle class' serving the interests of capital; but they are also understood as subject to proletarianization, wich brings them into closer alignment with labor. In a second section I examine a less-deterministic and functional critical theory of schooling grounded in class cultural analysis. Here the emphasis is upon viewing teachers as active participants in reproductive processes, who in some ways accommodate themselves to the status quo and in other ways resist the role they are expected to perform within the schooling process. In particular I analyze accommodating as well as countervailing tendencies within teacher unionism and teachers' professional culture. I also analyze some of the ways gender issues in the culture impinge upon teachers' political role in the schools. Together with a structural-functional description of teachers' 'objective' class position and location, a class cultural description of teachers and teaching is needed to round-out the picture and counter somewhat the over-mechanistic and pessimistic appraisal of teachers that dominates structural-functional critiques.

Structural-Functionalism and Teaching

The dominant theory of schooling that has influenced the way critically-minded educators view teachers and teaching is grounded in a neo-Marxist structural-functional model. It is associated in Europe with the work of the French structuralists, most notably Louis Althusser and Nicos Poulantzas, and in America with the work of Bowles and Gintis as well as that of Harry Braverman (although Braverman's work does not directly address schooling.)[1] These various theorists of advanced capitalism differ in a number of ways; however, for our purposes I want to focus on their similarities. What the structural-functionalists all share is an understanding of the special role of the state in social and economic reproduction, a functional view of the schools as an apparatus of the state, and a reductionistic treatment of teachers as the agents or functionaries of schooling. According to Althusser, the school is the single most important institution of the 'ideological state apparatuses'. As a direct consequence of their differentiated as well as common experiences in state schools, students are socialized into appropriate personality traits, work norms, and world-views 'needed' in the economy. Bowles and Gintis refer to the 'correspondence' or the 'congruence' between '. . . the personality traits conducive to proper work performance on the job and those which are rewarded with high grades in the classroom'.[2]

To appreciate more specifically how teachers are treated within this structural-functional theory of schooling, we must understand a bit more about teachers' 'objective' location within the process of the appropriation of surplus value, which determines their class position. Structural-functionalism is associated with the notion that a 'new' class (or sub-class) is organized in late or monopoly capitalism, concurrent with the last great consolidation of industry and the growth of the state as a central legitimating agency, which began near the turn of the twentieth century. This class is variously called the 'new petit bourgeoisie', the 'professional-managerial class', and the 'new middle class'.[3] It is defined as an intermediary class between the two great camps in capitalist society: labor and capital. Its collective political function is to supervise the appropriation of surplus value in the production process, help extract more surplus value from labor, and indoctrinate workers (or future workers) with the values of discipline, respect for authority,etc., that are essential to the appropriation process. Included in this class, among others, are shop-floor supervisors and managers, efficiency experts and accountants, clerical workers, engineers, bureaucratic planners and technicians, *and* teachers. Teachers supervise, discipline, and indoctrinate future workers in the service of capital.

Structural-functionalists generally argue that because members of this class serve as agents of capitalist interests, and do not directly add anything of value to what is produced by human labor, their work cannot be considered 'productive'. Instead, along with management and capital, they live off the surplus value created by labor. Supposedly, there would be no need for this 'unproductive' labor under socialism, for the domination and indoctrination of labor and of future labor would no longer be necessary. Some 'unproductive' jobs would disappear; others, including teaching, would serve new, productive roles. Their work would become productive to the extent that teachers provided the young with important skills and knowledge that contributed to their capacity for socially-beneficial and personally-enhancing work in the community.

If teachers are potentially productive workers, in the structural-functionalist calculus, their position under advanced capitalism is clearly viewed as unproductive. Kevin Harris remarks in this regard:

> Teachers are the effective agents in schools ... Their political function qua teachers, then, parallels the political function of schooling ... Just as schooling is a direct form of political control over children, teaching is a direct political struggle with children, especially working-class children.[4]

Similarly, Walker notes that:

> The fact that a person is fulfilling the teaching function puts them in a relationship which perpetuates the elitism, the paternalism, the control of knowledge and the corresponding passivity and resentment which constitute significant class barriers between the two groups (teachers and working class children).[5]

Bowles and Gintis devote little attention to teachers or teaching per se, since their concern is with the overall process of schooling; but they do quote from Paulo Freire's account of the 'banking' concept of education, in which the teacher is viewed as the 'depositor'. According to Freire:

> Instead of communication, the teacher issues communiques and makes deposits which the students patiently receive, memorize, and repeat. This is the 'banking' concept of education ... The teachers and the students are taught ... The teacher chooses and enforces his choice and the students comply ... The teacher acts and the students have the illusion of acting through the action of the teacher.[6]

If teachers are understood as agents of capital and the state within structural-functional theory, they are also recognized more sympathetically as victims of exploitation and oppression themselves within the hierarchical, bureaucratically-organized school system. This other side of the structural-functional argument is based on notions of the proletarianization of the new middle class. Proletarianization as a system imperative is related to two aims of capital. The first is to gain even more complete control of the labor process at the 'point of production'. In the twentieth century, this has been achieved primarily through the rationalization and standardization of work tasks which allow management to dictate each step in the work process, along with new bureaucratic rules and procedures to which workers are held accountable. As Braverman argues, these new forms of scientific management and bureaucratic control have had the effect of de-skilling workers in complex craft knowledge and re-skilling them as followers of a routine work format. De-skilled workers consequently suffer from job routinization and close supervision, and they lack avenues for advancement within the job hierarchy. A second aim of capital in proletarianizing workers in these ways is to 'cheapen' the cost of their labor. By lowering the skill requirements necessary for work, management is able to buy labor more cheaply on the labor market by drawing from among the large pool of semi-skilled workers. Because members of the new middle class are paid employees, along with actual productive workers, they are susceptible to this same logic of proletarianization. This trend is evident even as the new middle class continues to serve the ideological and political functions of capital, a situation which places this class in an objectively contradictory position, torn between an identification with capital and with labor.

When we examine trends in teaching, we indeed find evidence to support Bowles and Gintis' contention that the concentration of decision-making power in education along with the quest for economic rationalization 'had the same disastrous consequences for teachers that bureaucracy and rationalization of production had on most other workers'.[7] Let me turn to three current aspects of the proletarianization of teaching. First, new instructional technologies and programmed instructional materials may be having the effect of de-skilling teachers in the traditional craft skills of teaching: that is, subject matter knowledge and pedagogic knowledge (knowledge of the learning process and human motivation). Teachers are re-skilled by these new instructional technologies and forms more as supervisors of a predetermined classroom production process, or 'classroom managers'. Their job becomes keeping students 'on task', disciplining those who disrupt the production process, and keeping track of production records: primarily through administering and recording standardized test data. Harris is led to the conclusion that if present trends continue, 'the proletarianized teacher will control children more and instruct them less'.[8] A second aspect of teachers' proletarianization has to do with the intensification of their labor. The demands of the pre-specified curriculum, repeated testing, and classroom supervisory duties have all made the school day more hurried, less relaxed, and less satisfying for both teachers and students. Michael Apple notes of this continuing intensification of teachers' labor, along with that of other workers in the economy: 'It has many symptoms from the trivial to the more complex — from no time at all to even go to the bathroom, have a cup of coffee, or relax, to having a total absence of time to keep up with one's field.'[9] The results of this intensification, according to Apple, may be a reduction in the *quality* of services provided by the schools. 'While traditionally 'human service professionals' have equated doing good work with the interests of their clients or students, intensification tends to contradict the traditional interest in work well done...'[10] Finally, the proletarianization of teaching is associated with the continuing cheapening of teachers' labor. For all the talk of raising teachers' salaries, their real wages continue to decline relative to other similarly educated workers. These trends were particularly evident during the fiscal crisis of the mid-1970s in local government, a crisis which may well be part of a larger continuing fiscal crisis of the state in advanced capitalism.[11]

To this point I have described, in a rather straightforward manner, the structural-functionalist theory of teaching and teachers, with its emphasis upon both the reproductive role of teaching and the proletarianization of teachers. Now let me examine each of these notions in a more critical vein, indicating some of the benefits as well as limitations inherent in this perspective. With regard to the view of teachers as agents of an oppressive schooling process, structural-functionalism has served an important purpose in revealing the inadequacies of the old liberal-pluralist model of schools and teachers as agents of social progress and equality of opportunity by indicating how the schools function to uphold the existing, highly-inequitable social and economic order. Of course, the state and state schools are not mere 'puppets' of elite interests, and their relative autonomy is enhanced by the fact that they are outside of the direct production and profit sphere and thus one step removed from direct economic determination. Nevertheless, if the schools are not mere 'puppets' of elite interests, there is general agreement on the Left that the state *is* decisively constrained by forces external to it, and that these constraints originate in the economic sphere.[12] Any political movement that hopes to challenge the present organization and functioning of the schools must begin with a recognition that the state, and state schools, *are* heavily determined by the reproductive needs of capital and cannot be made to serve fundamentally differing purposes short of a socialist reorganization of society. This means that teachers are in a very tight position in schooling, and that their efforts to develop cooperative relations in the classroom with their students based on 'mutual respect and trust' are in the face of the objectively-structured conflict between teachers and students, particularly between teachers and working class and disadvantaged students, that has to do with the functional role schools play in the reproduction of inequality and the domination of future labor.

But the functional description of teaching, taken alone, is not only inaccurate in its overdeterministic conflation of teaching and schooling, it is also politically disempowering, for it promotes a pessimism about working in the school with teachers that the Left should do its utmost to fight rather than encourage. Wexler (1982) has gone so far as to argue that by enhancing political apathy, terms such as 'reproduction', 'socialization', and 'hegemony' may actually contribute in a paradoxical way to reproductive forces.[13] One response to the reproductive theory of teaching has been to abandon teachers as potentially progressive forces in the schools and to view them as 'the enemy'. This is the general view of teachers that emerges from the so-called 'self-fulfilling prophecy' studies of the late 1960s and early 1970s. Rist, for example, concluded that kindergarten and elementary school teachers in the inner-city school he observed favored middle class children in various ways and set higher expectations for them than for poorer children, particularly those on welfare, and that these teacher expectations tended to become self-fulfilling within the context of the school world.[14] In a similar way, Bowles and Gintis talk of 'the professional educator's profound mistrust of, and even fear of, the families of black and poor children . . .'[15] An equally one-sided and disempowering response is to encourage idealistic and committed teachers to 'drop out' of the system, since they supposedly can do little positive within it. This simplistic image of teachers is vividly portrayed in the numerous personal accounts of 'teaching in the system', particularly the inner-city school system, that came out of the late 1960s. In these accounts, a few idealistic and highly-committed young teachers are almost always seen as exceptions to the general rule, and their tenure in the system proves short.[16] For critically-minded teachers currently working, or planning to work, in public school systems, such perspectives can be devastating. In criticizing structural-functional accounts of teaching, Sarup comments: 'If all that teachers are doing is directly reproducing pupils as units to be slotted into the labor market their job hardly seems worth doing.'[17]

The effect is to reinforce a politically naive strategy of abandoning pulic schools in favor of teaching in 'free schools' in the supposedly less-colonized private sphere. Although this political response is less popular today than it was a decade or more ago, it has continued to influence serious Leftist scholarship on the schools in America and has even led some critics to endorse the voucher system for 'privatizing' state schooling. According to this proposal, parents would receive lump sum allotments to be spent on the education of their children in the private schools of their choice. Everhart has recently called on Leftists to support a voucher plan based on the presumption that since the public schools cannot be reformed sufficiently from within, they must be 'gotten around'.[18] He dismisses public school teachers as possible allies in fighting corporate state interests in the schools, since it seems 'unreasonable to expect most teachers in the public school system as it is presently constituted to defy vested interests and favor a liberatory education which, in the end, might seriously challenge their own role as members of the state bureaucracy'.[19] As for teachers' collective associations and unions, Everhart concludes that because 'such agencies as the National Education Association (NEA) and the American Federation of Teachers (AFT) serve as powerful lobbies at the state and federal levels, ... legislators cannot help but pay close attention'.[20] Finally, as bureaucratic professionals 'most educators in these associations possess a minimal sense of class consciousness and see themselves more as educational technicians than as sharing major class or cultural interests with their students'.[21]

I do not mean to imply that the building of counter institutions within capitalist society is totally without merit; but it may not be the most effective strategy to bring about the transformation of contemporary forms of schooling. Taken as a primary strategy it may actually play into the hands of conservative more than progressive political forces. After all, the voucher plan itself is a legislative proposal sponsored by the political right in America and endorsed by the Reagan administration. Business interests see in it a means of turning over control of the schooling process to the supposedly more 'efficient' or 'cost-effective' business community, which would also, one presumes, be more narrowly economistic in its approach to preparing the young with the skills and dispositions desired of workers in the labor force. It seems likely, therefore, that any 'free market' approach to schooling that might be adopted in America would only encourage the further proletarianization of teachers as well, since the push for privatized schooling has been associated with attacks on teacher unions as 'impediments to change'.

The structural-functional reproductive theory of teaching, then, encourages a cynicism about 'working in the system' and an effort to build counter institutions: both of which seem short-sighted as political strategies. But what of the political implications of the proletarianization of teachers? Here, I think, structural-functionalism is more helpful politically, although this image of teachers also has limitations. Proletarianization suggests an increasing identification of teachers with working class discontents and political interests. Not only does proletarianization link teachers' occupational interests with a broad working class movement for change, it also, and more directly, links their interests to certain fundamental changes in the schools. For example, opposition to proletarianization also implies opposition to the further bureaucratization and centralization of decision-making in the schools, to dominant management ideologies and production metaphors, to an objectified curriculum with more standardized testing, and to the general predetermination of learning 'inputs' and 'outputs' that all act in one way or another to de-skill and subordinate teachers.

If the notion of proletarianization provides some basis for looking to teachers as potentially radical advocates of change in the schools, unfortunately the structural-functional model will take us no further in exploring this possibility, since it is basically a theory of how the systems *function* to uphold the status quo. As Connell comments: 'It is difficult for discussions of the reproduction needs of an *a priori*-defined structure to come up with explanations that are anything other than functional. This is a chronic problem in structuralist Marxism's accounts of class, ideology, and the state.'[22] Functional explanations are of some heuristic value, first in describing how a particular institution reproduces class relations; and second, in depicting the objective relations that individuals enter into in institutional settings over which they experience no direct control.[23] But functionalist explanations are never sufficient in themselves. They need to be integrated with a less deterministic and reified theory of social processes and actors. Classes, occupational groups, and individuals are not merely analytic abstractions; they are historically-embedded agents of action, and their actions and beliefs have real consequences that cannot be totally determined. Marx recognized class as an objective category in some of his more economic writings. This is the working class 'in itself', created by capital as part of the appropriation of surplus value and defined by its relation to the production process. But elsewhere Marx clearly uses class in a cultural and historical sense, the working class 'for itself' as it makes itself, even if this 'making' of a class is not always an entirely self-aware or politicized process that directly challenges the hegemony of capital. Both an objective *and* a cultural conception of class are essential to our understanding of teachers. Unfortunately, the structural-functional theory of schooling helps us understand only the former.

Class Culture, Resistances and Accommodations, and Teaching

Since the mid-1970s,and particularly with the publication of Willis' *Learning to Labour* in England, some critical theorists of schooling have begun to emphasize the active production of class culture — including culturally-specific resistances — within the overall dynamic of social and economic reproduction.[24] Willis' ethnographic study is of a group of delinquent working class youths, 'the lads' as they call themselves, in a secondary modern school in Britain. In it he shows how 'the lads' construct their own counter-school culture and actively resist their subordination in the classroom and the alienating conditions of their school labor. But ironically, Willis also shows how 'the lads' thereby contribute to their own domination as members of the working class. For example, 'the lads' rejection of school credentials and intellectual knowledge, and their refusal to compete for grades, involves an active resistance to domination and an insightful appraisal of the ideology of individual competition and advancement. But it also locks 'the lads' into a pattern of school failure that solidifies their future status as members of the manual working class. In these ways, Willis concludes that working class domination involves a form of 'self-induction' by the young into working class orientations towards work and authority through the schooling process rather than the simple imposition of culture through indoctrination, as implied in most structural-functional accounts.

This class cultural theory, that Willis applies to an understanding of working class students, may be applied as well to teachers, although to this point we lack good ethnographic data on teachers. Its relevance is in understanding the everyday practices and beliefs of teachers as they 'make' their roles in schools and classrooms, both as they resist their treatment as proletarianized functionaries of the state, and also as they participate in, or acquiesce to, existing relations and ideologies in schooling. In sketching out the basis for a class cultural theory of teaching, I want to refer to two sets of concepts that have been widely used in cultural studies, and which get to the heart of the class cultural argument. These concepts are *penetrations* and *limitations*, and *resistances* and *accommodations*.[25] We may think of penetrations as ideological and resistances as behavioral,but both terms designate a similar rejection of domination. Willis uses the term penetration 'to designate impulses within a cultural form towards the penetration of the conditions of existence of its members and their position within the social whole'.[26] Resistances are corresponding behavioral responses that challenge, in some way, the pregiven 'definition of the situation'. For example, in the industrial sphere, 'goldbricking', 'soldiering', production line stoppages, and other forms of worker resistance represent attempts to sabotage and subvert the official production goals, or make the work situation more tolerable, or gain some informal control of work. The notions of penetrations and resistances imply a largely untapped strength and resiliency among oppressed groups as they daily engage in a form of guerrilla warfare against the institutional authority and work processes that most visibly oppress them. The other side of the picture is that ideological penetrations are typically limited in important ways that stop short of seriously challenging the status quo. Willis uses the term limitation to designate those 'blocks, diversions, and ideological effects which confuse and impede the full development and expression of working class discontents'.[27] They thus promote an accommodation with the system, in which resistance is kept largely circumscribed and defensive, aimed at gaining a measure of protection and freedom *within* dominant structures.

One interesting case study of teachers along these lines is provided by Wolcott in *Teachers Versus Technocrats*, an ethnographic account of teachers in one school district and their reactions to a new 'innovation': in this case, a planning-programming-budgeting system, designed at a nearby university-based research and development center and mandated by the central school administration.[28] The system called for more quantification of learning outputs, more testing, and more record-keeping among teachers. Wolcott identified a spectrum of responses to the new system, ranging from resistance to compliance, with active and passive forms of each. Some of these responses were: *routine acceptance* ('I don't like it, but I use it' [197]; or 'I'm going through the motions' [199]); *antagonistic acceptance* (complaining loudly but in the end swallowing the 'bitter medicine' [199]); *innovative acceptance* (modifying the form or intent of the innovation so that 'we're still doing what we've always done' [200]); a *wait-and-see attitude* (which can eventuate in a decision to either go along or resist at a later date); *dropping out* (leaving the system or quietly doing the minimum); *heel dragging* ('Just drag your heels a little bit and wait. It will all pass' [202]); *dialogue management* with the system coordinators (involving 'playing dumb' or 'playing silent'); and *consciously subverting the program* (by, for example, reporting false data. According to one teacher: 'I cheated. I put what I thought would look good. I think 75 per cent looks good. I put in 80 per cent' [206]). The overall image Wolcott projects is of a fragile compliance by teachers, with a good deal of on-going resistance on a number of levels. These resistances do not seriously challenge the prerogative of school management in imposing the new system on teachers; but they do impede the system's effectiveness once it is adopted, and they represent at least a partial penetration of the managerial ideology that lies behind changes.

The final picture that emerges from a class cultural analysis of teachers' everyday working lives is one of great specificity and detail. Through ethnographic studies of teachers' actual work experiences, such as Wolcott's, we can see that the processes of social and economic reproduction operate in an often paradoxical rather than deterministic manner, with room for reappropriations and resistances by teachers within the schools. However, the focus upon individual resistances — which are not typically politicized in an overt fashion and which remain largely individualized expressions of discontent — means that the class cultural theory of schooling has also, and somewhat ironically, tended to perpetuate a pessimistic view of teachers' potential to radically rethink their position and mount a serious challenge to the status quo. Teachers' everyday resistances are important, but so long as they remain depoliticized and 'kept in the closet' of the self-contained classroom, it is difficult to see how they represent a serious threat to system stability. As Jean Anyon remarks in this regard: 'While accommodation and resistance as modes of daily activity provide ... ways of negotiating individually felt social conflict or oppression, this individual activity of everyday life remains just that: individual, fragmented, and isolated from group effort. It is thus politically weakened.'[29]

Part of what is needed in the formulation of a sufficient class cultural theory of teachers and teaching, to counter this individualistic focus, is an analysis of teachers' collective occupational culture: specifically teacher trade unionism and teacher professionalism. Teachers' trade union movement emerges out of teachers' objective structural position as educational laborers who must fight on-going efforts at further proletarianization, and it thus builds linkages with the broad working class. Furthermore, teachers have risen to a position of considerable strength and influence within the labor movement in America over the past two decades, since the beginning of the collective bargaining era. While membership in industrial trade unions continues to decline under the pressure of industrial reorganization and repressive anti-union tactics by the business community and the state, public education remains an important and growing sector for union organization. Labor historians and theorists have been both divided and ambivalent over the question of the political potential of the labor movement, and this uncertainty applies equally well to teacher trade unionism. Marx laid the foundation for both pessimistic and optimistic appraisals in his observation that: 'Trade unions work well as centers of resistance against the encroachments of capital, but they fail generally from limiting themselves to a guerilla war against the effects of the existing system, instead of simultaneously trying to change it'.[30] American scholarship on the labor movement has been strongly influenced by Wright Mills and his argument that rather than form a power block independent of corporate and state interests labor leaders have been coopted into the 'power elite' and serve as 'managers of discontent'.[31] Rank-and-file union membership is often treated as narrowly economistic in its interests and as lacking in wider class allegiances.

Certainly, teachers have adopted a heavily 'bread and butter' orientation to their labor contract since the collective bargaining era began in the 1960s. But if teacher unions, like other trade unions, have been heavily economistic, much of this is due to the fact that they have been limited to such a sphere of bargaining by law, the courts, and the police power of the state; and there seems little reason to presume that they have voluntaristically narrowed their concerns to economic remuneration, even if they have often acquiesced to bargaining on this level. In fact, there is evidence that teachers have sought, with limited success, to expand the scope of bargaining beyond the wage package, into the sacrosanct realm of managerial prerogative. Recent teacher contracts and court decisions in some districts have recognized teachers' demands for: membership on school advisory committees, involvement in establishing student disciplinary procedures, a voice in textbook selection, participation in the formulation of in-service training programs, input into teacher evaluation, and involvement in the adoption of new or experimental school programs.[32] Of course, there are clear limits as to how far school management can safely go in granting teachers these concessions without significantly obstructing the schools' reproductive functions. Teachers cannot push beyond a certain point before they face intransigence. After all, the existing functioning of the schools does not allow for teachers to regain significant control over their working lives. If it did, teachers might choose goals and priorities in the classroom other than those of the state or capital. But to the extent that teachers begin to demand and expect what the institution cannot readily provide, they reveal its limits, and they present dominant interests with a serious problem of control and legitimation.

A second aspect of teachers' collective occupational culture that shows signs of both accommodating and countervailing tendencies is professionalism. As a legitimating ideology, professionalism has its roots in the development of the 'new middle class'. It has always been in the interests of dominant groups to promote among the public the belief that this intermediary stratum of workers, which actually serves the political control needs of capital and the state, is politically neutral or disinterested. The traditional professional values of service to client, highly specialized or esoteric knowledge, and technical expertise all become useful in legitimating the role of the new middle class. To the extent that the activities performed by these workers can be treated as professional services, requiring decision-making by public-spirited experts, conflicts and disputes involving these 'services' can be removed from the overtly political realm where the class nature of the conflict is more easily revealed.

In education, professionalism has been presented as a means of ensuring that school policy-making, administration and practice are kept out of politics. Specifically, the professionalization of teaching has been used to reassure the public that those who direct childrens' educational experiences apply the latest knowledge from the 'science of education' to tailor instruction to each child's special 'needs'. It has obviously been in the interests of elite groups in education to promote such a professional ideology among teachers as well as the public, so that teachers' idealism is tapped and they do not begin to seriously question the role of the schools in social and economic reproduction. But in a contradictory way, teachers' professional aspirations also create a problem for the system so that dominant groups are ambivalent about referring to teachers as professions. On the one hand, teachers need to be perceived both by themselves and the public as professionals for legitimation reasons; but on the other hand, professionalized workers may also come to expect respect at the workplace and real involvement in decisions affecting their work. Once teachers take seriously professional ideals of having skilled crafts which they can provide in service to client and community, professionalism is turned against the continuation of oppressive structures and practices in education and teachers' discontents are less easily contained. For these reasons, its seems shortsighted for the Left to treat professionalism as merely or exclusively a legitimating ideology. The reappropriation of professionalism by teachers provides a reservoir of sentiment that at least potentially aligns teachers' occupational interests with transformative change in the schools.

Finally, teachers, like other social actors, occupy more than an objective class location, and they must be understood in more than class cultural terms. They assume other identifications and participate in other forms of struggle that have political significance. Gender identities and struggles, in particular, have historical roots and dynamics in teaching that cannot be conflated to the influence of class. Teachers' domination as workers in the school bureaucracy has been coextensive with their domination as women. Because of this, Anyon has called for research on the 'intersection' of class and gender; Connell talks of the 'joint dynamics' and 'simultaneous effects' of class and gender in the schools; and Walker and Barton talk of the need to 'interrelate socialist and feminist struggle' among teachers and other workers.[33] There are a number of rather direct ways in which patriarchy and bureaucratic control work together against teachers. For example, women compose 66 per cent of all public school teachers and 80 per cent of elementary teachers in America. Yet they hold only 18 per cent of elementary school principalships, 2 per cent of secondary principalships, and 1 per cent of the nation's superintendencies.[34]

The divisions among gender lines in education have made it easier for school administrators to differentiate their interests from those of teachers and cooperate in the disempowerment of teachers. Teachers often complain that administrators 'treat us like children', and this at least partially reflects the way women get treated generally in the economy and culture. According to Acker, commonsense assumptions about the general level of teacher incompetence and the 'low regard for the intellectural capacities of teachers, perhaps especially women teachers', provide a rationale for locking teachers out of a significant role in school decision-making.[35] The feminization of teaching also provides a hidden rationale for devaluation or 'cheapening' of teachers' labor; and the fact that women's labor is devaluated in the economy means that teaching is often relegated to the status of the semi-professions. The status hierarchy among professional educators is thus gender as well as class-linked. To some extent these divisions are perpetuated through a vicious cycle of self-fulfilling expectations. If elementary teaching is defined as 'women's work', many men who might otherwise find teaching at the elementary level rewarding decide not to puruse it because it represents a threat to their masculinity. This, then, reinforces the feminization of elementary teaching. For teachers to wage a concerted effort to regain significant control over their working lives, it becomes apparent that they will need to address these gender divisions within their ranks and challenge dominant notions of 'masculine' and 'feminine' work. They will also need to raise to an explicit level of discussion and political action the patriarchal as well as class-linked character of the system that keeps them subordinated, and that prevents many of their students from realizing their full potentials in the schools as well.

Conclusion

In this chapter I have sought to establish a critical framework for the study of teachers as political actors, inextricably involved in conflict over the purposes and direction of public education. I have argued that teachers have too often been treated in a deterministic fashion in the dominant structural-functional theory of schooling, leading to an overly-pessimistic appraisal of their real or potential role in the ongoing conflict between the two great camps in capitalist society: capital and labor. Structural-functionalism has presumed, simplistically, that questions as to the political role of various strata of workers in the labor force can be answered primarily through an analysis of their 'objective' class location and function. In contrast, I have argued that while this is a needed line of analysis, it is less important strategically than an assessment of the cultural conditions and circumstances which encourage teachers to define their interests in an expansive rather than restrictive way: that is, as part of a majority movement for social change that seriously challenges existing structures, ideologies, and practices.

This implies, I think, that the Left needs to redirect its attention back *within* the institution of schooling and those actors engaged in one way or another in politically-meaningful work in the schools, rather than view the schools from the outside, as a solid 'black box' of reproductive processes. If schooling, as a state function serving primarily reproductive interests, is not likely to be disestablished under advanced capitalism, and if apathy or dropping out of teaching only reinforces reproductive forces in the schools, then we must begin to look once more to teachers in the formulation of progressive political strategies. We must neither dismiss teachers as part of the oppressive apparatus of social control nor presume that because schools are basically determined institutions that teachers can do nothing politically worthwhile within them. We need an understanding of schooling that is more empowering than disempowering and that includes teachers as part of the solution rather than the problem: that is, as part of a broad-based movement to transform the schools and society and 'liberate' teaching itself.

Because I have argued against a pessimistic appraisal of teachers' political interests in the schools does not mean that what I have to say should be interpreted as an optimistic appraisal. Both political pessimism and optimism are simplistic distortions of a complex reality. The historical development of teachers' occupational culture, as I have suggested, has in some ways accommodated teachers' interests with those of the status quo, and served to incorporate their interests with those of elite groups; just as other elements of that same culture have been associated with countervailing ideologies and practices that have not been fully contained and that represent a significant challenge to the existing control and operation of the schools. Before teachers can make more effective political use of their power in the schools and society, they will need to engage in a good deal of critical self-examination — both as individual practitioners and as an occupational group — aimed at assessing their situation in the schools, what is possible and not possible, and how they might fit into a broader movement for change. Teachers are not capable of independently making the schools alter their current course or change their oppressive nature under capitalism. But teachers can play a significant and perhaps pivotal role in a movement that does have such a potential. This means that it is important to establish linkages between teachers and other workers, and between teachers' interests and those of other oppressed groups in society. It also implies work with teachers to help them demystify their own practice and occupation in capitalist America.

Notes

1 Althusser, L. (1971) 'Ideology and ideological state apparatuses', in Brewster, B. (translator) (Ed) *Lenin and Philosophy and Other Essays*, London, New Left Books; Poulantzas, N. (1975) *Classes in Contemporary Capitalism*, London, New Left Books; Braverman, H. (1974) *Labor and Monopoly Capital*, London, Monthly Review Press.

2 Bowles, S. and Gintis, H. *Schooling in Capitalist America*, London, Routledge and Kegan Paul, p.9.

3 Poulantzas uses the term 'new petit bourgeoisie'. See also Carchedi, G. (1977) *On the Economic Identification of Social Classes*, London, Routledge and Kegan Paul; and Ehrenreich, B. and J. (1979) 'The professional-managerial class' in Walker, P. (Ed) *Between Labor and Capital*, Boston, MA, South End Press, pp. 5–48.

4 Harris, K. (1982) *Teachers and Classes; A Marxist Analysis*, London, Routledge and Kegan Paul, p. 90.

5 Walker, P. (1979) 'Introduction' in Walker, P. (Ed) *Between Labor and Capital*, Boston, MA, South End Press, p. xix.

6 Cited by Bowles, S. and Gintis, H. (1976) *op cit.*, p. 40.

7 Bowles, S. and Gintis, H. (1976) *op cit.*, p. 204.

8 Harris, K. (1982) *op cit.* p. 73.

9 Apple, M. (1983) 'Work, gender and teaching', *Teachers College Record*, 84, spring, p. 618.

10 *Ibid.*

11 See O'Connor, J. (1973) *The Fiscal Crisis of the State*, New York, St. Martin's Press; Weitzman, J. (1979) *City Workers and Fiscal Crisis; Cutbacks, Givebacks, and Survival* New Brunswick, NJ, Rutgers University Press.

12 The issue as to *how much* relative autonomy the state has in carrying out its functional role within advanced capitalism is one of considerable dispute among neo-Marxists. For a discussion see Miliband, R. (1983) 'State power and class interests', *New Left Review*, 138, March–April, pp. 57–68.

13 Wexler, P. (1982) 'Ideology and education: From critique to class action', *Interchange*, 13, 3, pp. 53–68.

14 Rist, R. (1970) 'Student social class and teacher expectations: the self-fulfilling prophecy in ghetto education', *Harvard Educational Review*, 40, August, pp. 411–51.

15 Bowles, S. and Gintis, H. (1976) *op cit.*, p. 38.

16 See for example Herndon, J. (1968) *The Way It Spozed to Be*, New York, Simon and Schuster; Holt, J. (1964) *How Children Fail*, New York, Pitman Publishing; Kozol, J. (1967) *Death at an Early Age*, New York, Houghton Mifflin; Levy, G. (1970) *Ghetto School; Class Warfare in an Elementary School*, New York, Bobbs-Merrill.

17 Sarup, M. (1982) *Education, State and Crisis; A Marxist Perspective*, London, Routledge and Kegan Paul, p. 49.

18 See Everhart, R. (Ed) (1982) *The Public School Monopoly: A Critical Analysis of Education and the State in American Society*, Cambridge, MA, Ballinger Books;

Everhart, R. (1983) 'Leftist agendas, educational vouchers: Toward a critical appraisal', *Interchange*, 14, 3, pp. 46–64.

19 Everhart, R. (1983) *op cit.*, p. 51.

20 *Ibid.*

21 *Ibid.*

22 Connell, R. W. (1983) 'Crisis tendencies in patriarchy and capitalism' Sonnell, R. W. (Ed) in *Which Way is Up? Essays on Sex, Class and Culture*, London, George Allen and Unwin, chapter 3, p. 36.

23 See Wright, E. O. (1983) 'Gidden's critique of Marxism', *New Left Review*, March–April, pp. 11–35.

24 Willis, P. (1977) *Learning to Labour: How Working Class Kids Get Working Class Jobs*, Farnborough, Saxon House. See also Apple, M. (Ed) (1982) *Cultural and Economic Reproduction in Education; Essays on Class, Ideology and the State*, Boston, MA, Routledge and Kegan Paul, for a description of the class cultural perspective.

25 The first set of terms is used by Willis. The second set of terms has been used by Genovese, E. (1972) in *Roll, Jordan, Roll: The World the Slaves Made*, New York, Vintage Press, to describe the response of black Americans to their enslavement; and by Anyon, J. (1983) in 'Intersections of gender and class: Accommodation and resistance by working-class and affluent females to contradictory sex-role ideologies' in Walker, S. and Barton, L. (Eds) *Gender, Class and Education*, Lewes, Falmer Press, pp. 19–38.

26 Willis, P. (1977) *op cit.*, p. 119.

27 *Ibid.*

28 Wolcott, H. (1977) *Teachers Versus Technocrats; an Educational Innovation in Anthropological Perspective*, Eugene, OR, University of Oregon Press.

29 Anyon, J. (1983) *op cit.*, p. 34.

30 Cited in Banks, J. A. (1970) *Marxist Sociology in Action; A Sociological Critique of the Marxist Approach to Industrial Relations*, London, Faber and Faber, p. 48.

31 Mills, C. W. (1948) *The New Men of Power; America's Labor Leaders*, New York, Harcourt Brace; Mills, C. W. (1954) 'The labor leaders and the power elite' in Kornhauser, A. *et al.*, (Eds) *Industrial Conflict*, New York, McGraw-Hill.

32 See Bailey, W. and Neale, D. (1980) 'Teachers and school improvement', *Educational Forum*, 45, November, pp. 69–76; Retsinas, J. (1982) 'Teachers: Bargaining for control', *American Educational Research Journal*, 19, Fall, pp. 353–72.

33 Anyon, J. (1983) *op cit.*, Connell, R. W. (1983) *op cit.*, Walker, S. and Barton, L. (1983) 'Introduction' in Walker, S. and Barton, L. (Eds) *Gender, Class and Education*, Lewes, Falmer Press, p. xi

34 Cited by Marshall, C. (1984) 'The crisis in excellence and equity' *Educational Horizons*, Fall, p. 24.

35 Acker, S. 'Women and teaching: A semi-detached sociology of a semi-profession' in Walker, S. and Barton, L. (Eds) *Gender, Class and Education*, Lewes, Falmer Press, p. 127.

9 *Black Feminist Pedagogy and Schooling in Capitalist White America*

Gloria I. Joseph

Acknowledgements

I wish to acknowledge the theoretical research of Dr. Linda James Myers and Dr. Charlyn Harper, and the anti-racist works of Dr. Robert Moore. The contributions of these three scholars have been influential and instrumental to this chapter. Drs. Myers and Harper's research on Afro-centric conceptual systems has been basic to the world view embodied in Black feminism. Dr. Moore's studies and research in the area of white racism represents an extremely insightful and indepth analysis and understanding of the racist mentalities and patriarchal powers that underpin North American society.

Schools and schooling in capitalist America are very little different from other institutions and their methodological processes in capitalist America. Institutions operate from a well-programmed blue print which is designed to serve the people in an unequal and hierarchical manner. To 'serve the people' can be readily translated into 'to serve the devil'. The heinous nature of capitalist America gives easy rise to a feeling of existing in a living hell for the majority of the exploited, who indeed exist for the benefit of those with and in power. The educational system orchestrates an internecine relationship between teachers and students. This relationship which results in miseducated, misguided, misinformed youth, and adults, (leaders), who use 'disinformation' tactics and chicanery, operates today with maximum success in keeping the inequalities and hierarchies that characterize capitalist America.

In *Schooling in Capitalist America*, Bowles and Gintis state: 'The major characteristics of the educational system in the United States today, flow directly from its role in producing a work force willing and able to staff occupational positions in the capitalist system. We conclude that the creation of an equal and liberating school system requires a revolutionary transformation of economic life.[1] That was written in 1976. In 1903, the great scholar and Afro-American leader, W E B Dubois, stated: 'The problem of the twentieth century is the problem of the color-line, the relation of the darker to the lighter races . . . in Africa and Asia, in America and in the islands of the sea'.[2]

The integration of DuBois' prophetic words, with the quote from Bowles and Gintis, gives a greater sense of realism and accuracy to the current educational system in capitalist America.

The exclusion of the race question as a distinct entity, in any theoretical discussion of capitalist America is a serious omission and any analysis which does not specifically address the racial dimension is incomplete and inadequate. Racial relations and the US educational system have an extremely inglorious past which presently demands acute attention. It could be argued that every relationship is unique and race relations have no patent on uniqueness; that no general theories are adequate, and from this point of view, most theories are too general. However, there is ample evidence to indicate that relations between races have a long and important history which is not reducible to relations between the sexes or classes.

The American dream has never worked for Blacks, and that is a truism that must be remembered whenever analysis and discussion concerning the future of the nation's population are in progress. To say that '. . . the creation of an equal and liberating school system requires a revolutionary transformation of economic life', is to disregard the dynamics of the racial dimension. The absence of a sharp focus on racism inhibits the social change desired. I am in agreement with the statement that the role of the educational system in America today is to produce a work force willing and able to staff occupational positions in the capitalist system. However, this statement is basically applicable to the white population in America. There exists a significantly large body of Blacks and Latinos who are not in the economic work force at all. A most radical approach to dealing with the problems of radical educational change would be to focus on the Blacks, Latinos, Native Americans, — the domestic Third World people — as the vanguard. Historically in the USA those fighting raism have been in the vanguard of social movements. The struggle for racial equality, which serves as a generational linkage, provides the nation with a focus that is the antithesis of the avaricious , necrophilic, aggressive, materialistic, selfish, attitudes that characterize the dominant Western perspective. The history of non-whites in the USA, a history which is grounded in a spirituality, which places interpersonal relations among people as opposed to the acquisition of objects, as being of highest value, should be a major focus of education. Education has always been central in anti-racist struggle, for education — or the denial of it — has been integral to the maintenance of a racist society. In Puerto Rico and among Native People in North America, education was used by the United States to force children to speak English, to learn US history, to adopt 'American' culture, all part of an effort to destroy the fabric of traditional culture and society, in order to better control subjugated peoples. For similar reasons, it was made illegal in the south to teach African people held in slavery to read or write. I am arguing for and advocating an educational system that uses the history of Blacks, Latinos and Native Americans. In America — their values, struggles, exploitation — as building blocks towards developing revolutionary education which equals 'truthful history!' 'An understanding of history is critical in shaping an awareness of the present and the vision for a viable future.'[3]

In the struggle to ensure that the young be allowed to learn accurate and inclusive history of African Americans, Asian Americans, Chicanos, Native Americans, Puerto Ricans, women of all groups, and the history of menial-jobs-working-class people, we will necessarily be informing ourselves and others of what that history is, how it shaped our present and how those who came before us have struggled to create necessary change. Learning that history will help to shatter the prevailing mythology that inhibits so many from acting more decisively for social change and the creation of a more just society and viable future for all.

Schooling in white capitalist America reproduces capitalist social relations of production and this system of education is, and has been, detrimental to the livelihood of Blacks. My participation in this educational system is done within the degrees of contradiction that I have allowed myself. That is to say that since morally I cannot contribute to the continuation of the exploitation of Blacks, in my role as educator I view the educational system as a system in its own right constituted by intrinsic imperatives, and capable of creating building blocks for radical changes in the structure of American capitalist society. It is in this spirit that I introduce the Black feminist pedagogy which I feel complements and goes beyond the Marxist sociology of education.

The economic and political status of Afro-American women, as an oppressed group in the USA provides its members with a distinctive experiential reality, and disparate explanations of that reality as well. As a subordinate group, (subordinate to the dominant Eurocentric masculine corporate powerhouse), Afro-American women have a well developed alternative way of producing and validating knowledge about their experienced reality. The validations of their experienced realities differ markedly from explanations offered by the dominant Eurocentric masculine viewpoint.

Afro-American women's lives have been greatly affected by the intersection of systems of racial, sexual and class oppressions. However, they have developed a unique Black female culture whose purpose is to foster authentic Black female self-definition and self-valuation that counters and transcends the multiple structures of oppressions that they face. [4]

Literature on Black women reveals that Afro-American women do not see themselves as objects; do not identify with those in power; and have produced an independent Black women's point of view about their specific experiences with oppression. By and large, the literature tells us that Afro-American women have a realistic, common-sense, rational view of their relationship to the dominant society and do not operate on false illusions about their chances for survival or success.

The existence of a functional Black women's point of view assumes that there is an extant body of specialized knowledge that can be identified as Black feminist thought, and this existing body of knowledge is an authentic representation of a Black women's viewpoint. In other words it can be assumed that a unique, self-defined Black women's consciousness exists concerning Black women's material reality and that this point of view on reality has been authentically articulated in a body of knowledge which can be labeled BLACK FEMINIST THOUGHT!.[5]

The feminist sociologist, Chandra Talapade Mohanty, in a brilliant paper on *The Social Construction of Black Feminist Thought*, concludes that there are four criteria that appear to characterize an alternative epistemology (how we know what we know) used by Afro-American women in evaluating and validating their point of view/perspectives. They are (i) the use of dialogue in assessing knowledge-claims; (ii) the centrality of personal expressiveness; (iii) the ethic of personal accountability; and (iv) concrete experience as a criterion of meaning.[6] These criteria will be demonstrated in the section of this chapter where classroom examples of Black feminist pedagogy are presented. The practice of Black feminist pedagogy embodies these four criteria.

Black feminist pedagogy is designed to raise the political consciousness of students by introducing a world view with an Afro-centric orientation to reality, and the inclusion of gender and patriarchy as central to an understanding of all historical phenomena. The presence of an independent Black women's point of view using an alternative epistemology is fundamentally significant because its existence challenges not only the content of what currently passes as 'truth' but simultaneously challenges the process of arriving at that truth. Specifically I am presenting a pedagogy with a structure of an underlying philosophy that will generate a new political consciousness. This is akin to the philosophical structure the ideology of the great Brazilian educator, Paulo Freire, who developed a unique method of teaching reading which was formulated on his discovery that adults, can begin to read in a matter of forty hours if the first words they decipher are charged with political meaning.

Similarly political, social, and economic concepts, from a curriculum planned and taught by teachers possessing a Black feminist perspective/consciousness, would introduce a radical educational methodological imperative.

The introduction of a Black feminist perspective as the radical construct in the pedagogy that I am discussing, regards gender and patriarchy as critical in the constructing of society. (And that patriarchy reflects white men's world views, perspectives and interests.)

Black feminist pedagogy embodies a philosophy that is a philosophy of liberation. Black feminism's major premise is the active engagement in the struggle to overcome the oppressions of racism, heterosexism, and classism as well as sexism. It encompasses a world view with the inclusion of gender and patriarchy as central to an understanding of all historical phenomena, and addresses Third World women at home and abroad. The Black feminist perspective of which I speak intrinsically encompasses the application of an Afro-centric orientation to reality that is rooted in history, a reality that is informed by an understanding of the structures of African culture.

In discussing the Black feminist perspective it is important to be mindful of the fact that we are simultaneously talking about a conceptual system. A conceptual system refers to those philosophical constructs we use to define and structure reality, and is therefore, basic to the way in which we perceive and interpret. It is the basis of our world view. All people have a conceptual system usually shaped for the most part by the culture with which they identify. The relationship of one's conceptual system world view and behavior, are internally consistent.[7] Tragically, the American school system has systematically and deliberately denied its non-white clientele the right to identify with their cultures. Rather, we have students 'thinking white' as a result of the white, male studies programs that have dominated education throughout its beleaguered history.

The Afro-centric conceptual system is not exclusively Black or exclusively African. It is a journey toward wholeness which requires seeing the world not Black or white, but in its full spectrum.

The curriculum in our schools today can correctly be called a 'White studies' and a 'male studies' program, focusing on the achievements, cultures, experiences and perspectives of white men and omitting or distorting the histories, experiences, cultures, and perspectives of people of color, and women of all colors. There have been some changes since the 60s, but much of its has been superficial. A few great men of color and a few women of various colors are now referred to, but little is said of the great movements for social change that countless and nameless women and men have taken part in the USA. There are occasional mentions of discrimination, but students are led to believe it results from the prejudiced attitudes of some misguided folks rather than from the deliberate policies and practices of white and male dominated institutions. Sex-biased language such as 'the pioneer took his wife and family West 'has been changed to 'the pioneer family moved West', but the different experiences of 'pioneer' women in a patriarchal society are no more considered today than are the experiences of Native women and men whose lands are being invaded.

'In order for students, male and female, to understand and be prepared to change this patriarchal capitalist society, they must learn the history of women's experiences in this land, from the Cherokee grandmother on the Trail of Tears, to the Black mother in slavery's chains, from the Chicana fighting her people's dispossession to the Puertoriquena fighting for her nation's independence, from the young white woman newly working in Lowell's mills in the early 1900s, from the middle class 'lady' to that unsurpassable Sojourner Truth! They must learn the similarities and differences among women's experiences and between women and men's experiences.'[8] And they must learn about the Black experience in America as experienced by Blacks, and not as an interpreted from a perspective based on Euro-centric ideological constructs and values.

Black feminist pedagogy as a philosophy of liberation for humankind, is designed to enable students through the social, economic, cultural, moral and religious history of Third World People, to re-examine and see the world through a perspective that would instill a revolutionary conscious liberating ideology. Black feminist pedagogy will be the medium for the message. The art and science of teaching as advocated by Black feminist philosophy involves direct schooling for the future that holds viable options other than slave-slavemaster, or corporate giant-woeful worker, relationships. Students will be the building blocks, the true agents for radical change. The teaching of history from the Black feminist perspective is not to imply a one-sided view of history, for as Raya Dunayevskaya so eloquently states in her essay, 'Women as thinkers and revolutionaries', 'There is no such thing as Black history that is not also white history. There is no such thing as women's history that is not the actual history of humanity's struggle toward freedom.'[9]

In discussing social relations in capitalist America, it is of critical importance to begin to examine the minds of the slave captor, power makers, or corporate monsters (however you wish to call those who control capitalist America) from the Afro-centric perspective. If the conceptual system has any validity, any value, it will be important to be able to compare and contrast for people, two conceptual systems; that of the oppressed and that of the oppressors, because the two systems have different and very real consequences for their adherents.

Intuitively, you can know that by defining reality as spiritual and material at once, your have bought into a system that sees itself as infinite and unlimited. In contrast, to the extent that you have bought into a conceptual system that sees reality as material, you have automatically bought into a conceptual system that is by definition finite and limited and that means self-destruction. As we begin to entertain the reality of the greenhouse effect and acid rain, we are beginning to see evidence of the consequences of a sub-optimal conceptual system, one that has allowed technology to go awry and one that will ultimately end in destruction. We must begin to realize that there is an alternative way to view the world and that will optimize experience. It certainly has allowed Black people to survive the most dreadful kind of slavery that has ever been known to humankind.[10] One of the natural consequences of a faulty conceptual system such as one that leads us to base our self-worth on external criteria and leads us to have an ego that is in a constant state of flux and in constant need of defending, is a lot of stress and anxiety. So much so that in this society we have come to accept stress as normal. Advertisements and sales for coping and reducing stress far outweigh advertising for less stressful ways of living.

Black feminist philosophy incorporates a conceptual system capable of being measured against other conceptual systems; and Black feminist pedagogy will examine the capitalist mentality as well as the history and philosophy of the Native American Indians who believed that one can no more own the land that is a source of provision for humans and animals, than one can own the air above the land. Teachers applying Black feminist techniques do not view students as passive recipients. We need only to review the history of student uprisings worldwide to realize their revolutionary potential. What has been lacking in most of their social movements has been a well formulated ideology — one that has been instilled and internalized from an early age. Schooling in capitalist America has indeed instilled an ideology, but one designed to maintain the status quo. The Black feminist pedagogy will supply students with an ideology that will provide the necessary materials for creating conditions needed for radical change.

Black feminist theory is a theory of change with Black feminist pedagogy being the change agent in and outside of the classrooms — wherever education takes place. Black feminist theory does not see class as the primary contradiction with the working class being the agents for change. Rather it sees the primary contradiction to be power relations between Blacks and whites, males and females with Black women being the change agents. Black feminist theory and Marxism both function on the premise that you have to look at specific historical forms of oppression, and that power has to be reconstituted, reconstructed to help find a weak link. Black feminist theory challenges Marxist theory to consider race as a primary contradiction and it challenges feminists, (white feminist theorists) to recognize the automatic dual oppression of sexism and racism that Afro-American and all women of color in the United States face with a routineness akin to breathing. Black feminists ask Marxist and white feminists, 'Is our liberation going to be a part of your revolution? And if so why is it not a major topic in your theory building — in your literature — in your consciousness?'

Classroom illustrations of Black feminist pedogogy in practise will be helpful at this point. Students bring certain basic assumptions into the classrooms and these assumptions reveal the power of ideology — the American dream ideology. For example, Black students will frequently describe experiences of blatant racial discrimination, then in Yuppy tones declare that 'every one is equal, racial differences don't really matter you can make it if you try hard enough'. Black and white female students will readily relate humiliating examples of sexist treatment, then contradictory to their assertions, proclaim, 'I think that with the proper qualifications women can make it in society today. Things have changed, — look at Indira Ghandi, Geraldine Ferraro and Corazon Aquino'. These students, Black and white, female and male, desperately want to believe in the American ideology that America is the land of opportunity and you can become anything you want if you try and work hard enough — what Bowles and Gintis refer to as the meritocratic ideology. Introduce to these students the more truthful belief that wealth in America is not the result of hard work but rather the result of graft, corruption and protected crime, and the resistance will be overwhelming. Teaching style and radicalized students are of great importance in overcoming such resistance.

The first classroom illustration occurs in a college course on Third World women and feminism.[11] The topic of women and resistance led to the mentioning of Eleanor Bumpers, the Black woman killed by a squad of policemen in SWAT gear. They were evicting her for being behind in her rent for approximately $98.00.

After explaining to the class who Eleanor Bumpers was, the statement was made that negligence in paying her rent had very little to do with her death. The students, predominantly white women, initially could not understand what was meant by such a statement. Using the Socratic method, the students soon understood that Eleanor Bumper's death was an illustration of the general treatment of Blacks and poor people in our society.

It spoke of police brutality and racism in its worse form that of seeing an individual as less than human because that person is non-white, poor and elderly. It spoke of putting material wealth and value over human life. Further discussion concerned the inability of white feminists to identify and express national outrage over this incident. The shared historical experience of the Black feminist instructor informed her/him that Eleanor Bumpers was fighting the same war of resistance against dehumanization and dominance that our ancestors in slavery fought. Later in the course the question of capital punishment came up.

When the instructor said, 'Afro-centric thinking or thinking Black tells me that capital punishment is not primarily a moral issue', students were better prepared to interpret the meaning of the comment. When the instructor continued by saying, 'Experiences inform me that white America is morally bankrupt and as in the past, Blacks and other people of color will be singled out as the victims to fill the quotas for capital punishment' the students were no longer taken aback, or involuntarily shrinking or feeling umbrage.

The second illustration of the implementation of thinking Black in the classroom is in a course on domestic violence. In a small Eastern college the students were asked to compile lists of adjectives which they associated with the Black ghetto, suburbia and Appalachia. The purpose was to compare similarities and differences in perceptions and then discuss the commonality of wife battering. The composition of the class was fifteen white females and three white males, six Black and three Puerto Rican females and one Black male. Interestingly enough the white students glibly offered ghetto characteristics. These included: overcrowding, drugs, muggings, slum areas, poverty, and multiplicity of sexual partners. The last characteristic elicited a perceptible gasp of indignation from a Black student. As the instructor heard the list grow, automatically she knew that accepting these responses was to accept a conceptual system that was inherently blaming the victim. That is to say that it was buying into an ideology that attributes defects and inadequacy to the malignant nature of poverty, injustice, slum life and racial difficulties. The stigma that marks the victim and accounts for her/his victimization is an acquired stigma of social origin. But the stigma, though derived in the past from environmental forces is still located in the victim, inside her/his skin. Within this formation, the liberal humanitarian can have it both ways. She can concentrate her/his charitable interests on the defects of the victim, condemn the vague social and environmental stresses that produced the defect and ignore the continuing effect of victimizing social forces. It justifies a perverse form of social action designed to change not society but rather society's victim. It is this type of thinking that the Afro-centric conceptual system aims to undermine. Armed with such a scintillating weapon for change the Black feminist teacher artfully and skillfully interprets classroom interaction while never veering from the goals of liberation for humankind through the process of an analysis of oppressions.

'The hallmark of oppressive ideology is domination and subordination, viewed socially as well as interpersonally. From the standpoint of the oppressor, this refers to power *over*, as opposed to shared power with another or others, with special attention to the oppressiveness of victims of oppression themselves, the marked inclination to dump on anybody we think is even lower than us. From the standpoint of the oppressed, we refer to passivity and compliance, the conviction that subordination is natural. Since all human liberation depends upon the consciousness of servitude, promoting this consciousness where it is absent becomes psychotherapeutically important.'[12]

This analysis of oppression stresses racial, sexual and heterosexual oppression as well as class. The critical importance of the racial dimension was illustrated in the classroom example being discussed. The Black and Puerto Rican students were asked for their lists of characteristics that they associate with the Black ghetto. Leading the list was police brutality followed by exploitation, slum landlords, worst quality of food in the neighborhood stores with the highest prices, corruption and insensitive city officials. The discussion that followed concerned reality beginning with experience, and how divergent assumptions about the world leads to contrary references on the same event. It is noteworthy that despite the differences in economic backgrounds of the Black and Puerto Rican students, and despite the fact that some were gay others not, inevitably their responses to Black feminist pedagogy intimated that the Black dimension is and has been critically significant in their lives and to their survival in capitalist America.

Comments from white students after exposure to Black feminist pedagogy were uniform: the majority showed visible signs of being uncomfortable, but remained silent in their discontent and amazement. Slowly but surely, after mustering up much courage, they stated that they felt taken aback, silenced, afraid that they would be challenged with questions they were unable to answer because they had never 'thought that way' before. (That way being Afro-centric thought or 'thinking Black'.) In response to their comments the domestic Third World students countered, with assurance and conviction in their voices, expressions such as, 'This is the first time in my school career that I feel comfortable, really comfortable, in a class, because I feel like the teacher understands where I'm coming from'; 'I feel good about the class because all sides of a question are discussed. For once the white way is not the only way or the right way'. Eventually the vast majority of students realize and appreciate the value of being exposed to the consistency of a perspective that gives credence and respect to all peoples of different cultures.

A final illustration of Black feminist pedagogy as an agent for change will be demonstrated by voices of several students after completing a semester of a course taught from the perspective of Black feminist theory and pedagogy. The course title was, 'The Domestic Third World', and the comments are from white, middle and upper class, first year college students. The following excerpts are from student self-evaluations written at the completion of the course.

> I have a whole new picture of my radical WASP upbringing, views and culture. You know the type. I was brought up with MS. magazine, Peter, Paul and Mary, 'Free To Be You And Me', and MASH. I am now constantly, constantly questioning books, movies etc. I can't imagine if I hadn't taken this course how twisted my view would have been on this day. Take 'The Cosby Show'. Their family offers to minorities in this country the 'proof' that myth can come true. They are a wealthy and very definitely employed, and loving family. But most importantly, the Cosby's seem to suggest that with all their prosperity, racism disappears. In this TV world of theirs, Blacks are not exploited and prejudice is never discussed. Once an anti-apartheid poster was added to the walls of the Cosby son's room. In Cosby land there is no suffering of minorities in any nation. Why is it that very few Americans understand or even see the poverty and oppression that goes on right under their noses? I feel it is instilled racism that hides those issues from Americans. Just the other day, I was speaking with a fairly liberal friend of

mine from New York city. To my astonishment, she commented that she felt Asian Americans had just as much opportunity to excell in our country as whites did. Like my friend, people constantly proclaim their neighborhood, school or mind to be 'bias-less'. (White male)

Since I am white and see my primary work as confronting racism with white people, my comments will address white actions and attitudes. At present most whites are so locked into a segregated delusion of 'historical amnesia' that they block rather than initiate progressive changes. Myths that must die: that racism is limited to a few twisted individuals like the Klan and neo-Nazi parties; that people of color are 'deprived victims' that need liberal whites to make legal and policy decisions about their futures; that racism is a 'Black, Asian, etc. problem' and it is the responsibility of Third World people to educate whites about our own racism. People of color so often are forced to bridge the cultural and political differences with white people for their survival. Racism is a white problem and many white people must so dedicate their lives to educating and confronting whites on racist practices and attitudes . . . Protestations of 'I am very liberal . . . I love everybody . . . It's just human nature . . . some of my best friends are . . .' do nothing but block communication and put the burden of proof and action on people of color. There are numerous whites who already work full time to educate and confront whites on racist policies and beliefs. Dr. Robert Moore, from New York city, was an excellent example. Ann Braden is an example of a civil rights activist who faced violent retribution in the south. Adrienne Rich has insightful works that connect racism, patriarchy, compulsory heterosexuality and anti-Jewish behavior. These are people who do their own homework and are pro-active allies to domestic and international Third World liberation struggles. (White female)

I know from my high school and elementary education that the materials my schools used did not address any issues of racism, prejudice or discrimination or eliticism. The only way in which I was informed of racism was through incidents in the newpaper or on television. This ignorance of the problem is nearly as bad as overt racism. This course has been the most important one I have ever taken. Thank you, (professor's name), for your enthusiasm, style and spirit which made the course so valuable. (White male)

Black feminist pedagogy has its roots in Africa, the mother of civilization. The philosophy and practice is applicable and beneficial to people throughout the world. That it holds specific relevancy for racism worldwide is extremely appropriate at this time in the 1980s. Racist mobs of young whites hurling insults and assaulting Blacks, and white police regularly beating and brutalizing Blacks with near impunity, are endemic to male violence and racist mentalities that distinguishes the American landscape. White racist violence is flourishing under the Reagan administration which has gutted civil rights enforcement and slashed social service spending while pouring hundreds of billions of dollars into militarization and his pestiferous pet-nuclear star wars.

The incident in Howard Beach, Queens, New York State, on 20 December 1986, when young whites viciously attacked three Black young men leaving one dead, one seriously injured and the third assaulted, is but a single example of a wave of white racist violence in New York City. Bernard Goetz is a white man who at this time of writing still walks free after shooting four Black teenagers on a subway train two years ago, while one of his victims lies disabled for life. Michael Stewart at age 25 was arrested in 1983 for allegedly writing on a subway wall. This Black talented youth was handcuffed, kicked and beaten to death by a group of white transit police, all of whom still walk free. Also still walking free is the police officer who killed Mrs. Eleanor Bumpers in the process of evicting her from her apartment.

These persons are denied being a part of any work force. And that denial is due to racism. The New York city wave of white racist murders is mirrored nationally. White-run police forces and white racist terrorist forces across white America assault African, Asian, Latino, and Native American women and men on a daily basis while the courts and jails in another racist conspiracy, remove millions of others from the visible face of America.[13]

The racist assaults that occur nationally can be chronicled internationally. In South Africa Black children, women and men are shot down in the streets, imprisoned and tortured for trying to put an end to the Western-backed crime against humanity called apartheid. In the West Bank and Gaza, men, women and children are shot dead in the streets, beaten and jailed for demanding self-determination in their own homeland.

Schooling in white capitalist America nourishes a system that helps to train/teach young white children to carry out their racist violence. It instills its white students with a cultural imperialism and intellectual ethnocentricism which fuels them with a white superiority that implicitly and explicitly encourages racism, sexism and heterosexism. This same educational system fails to educate non-whites, who attend classes with regularity or irregularity.

Black feminist pedagogy has as an end result the development of generations of Black, white, Puerto Rican, Chicano, Asian-American, and Native American people prepared to radically change capitalist white America. It is fitting to have Black feminist pedagogy as the theoretical construct for educational change. Black women historically have been central to educational change as teachers, survival technicians, administrators, and revolutionary thinkers. It is politically sound to listen to the reason and intellect of our ancestral educational role models. A social movement led by Black women — the vanguard — is in order. If and when persons with vision in America have sufficient power to radically change the social relations, Black feminist pedagogy should be the prime blue print for the task.

Notes

1 Bowles, S. and Gintis, H. (1976) *Schooling in Capitalist America*, London, Routledge and Kegan Paul, p. 265.
2 A famous quote by Dr. W.E.B. Dubois, which appears in *Souls of Black Folks*, by Dubois. The quote also appears on posters, postcards and has become a popular adage.
3 Unpublished essay by Dr. Robert Moore from a speech delivered in Toronto, Canada, 1985 at an education conference.
4 Mohanty, C. T. *The Social Construction of Black Feminist Thought; An Essay in the Sociology of Knowledge*, unpublished paper, p. 5.
5 *Ibid*, p.14.
6 *Ibid*, p. 15.
7 For a full discussion of this literature, see Myers, L. *Contributions in Black Studies, How to Think Black: Toni Cade Bambara's The Salt Eaters*, 6, 1983–84, pp. 39–44.
8 Unpublished essay by Moore, R. Panel on Education — Third National Convention of Women for Racial and Economic Equality, May 1984, p. 6.
9 Dunaycuskaya, R. from the essay, 'Women as Thinkers and Revolutionaries', *Women's Liberation and the Dialectics of Revolution*, p. 80.
10 Myers, L. *op cit*, p. 43.
11 The classroom illustrations are based on actual experiences of the author.
12 Rakow, R. (1986) 'Sexual freedom and oppressive ideology' *Academy Forum*, 26, 9, winter.
13 Unpublished and untitled paper by Robert Moore, January 1987.

Part III
The Politics of Bowles and Gintis

10 *Old and New Orthodoxies: The Seductions of Liberalism*

Rachel Sharp

It is a tribute to *Schooling in Capitalist America* (SCA) that debates surrounding its themes are still reverberating in the sociology of education. But history has moved on, and so have Bowles and Gintis. In this chapter I want to examine their current theoretical position and assess the extent to which it offers a way of improving upon, or correcting the deficiencies in their original arguments. Whilst it is more clearly spelt out, more comprehensive in scope and applied to a range of issues beyond the analysis of education, their current position mirrors the theoretical themes which structure the work of most of the prominent Anglo-American elaborators of what I have described elsewhere as the new orthodoxy (Sharp, 1986b). Given the new orthodoxy's significance in defining the terrain of legitimate postures within radical educational discourse a careful examination of the work of two of its leading exponents seems warranted. It is, of course, by no means confined to the sociology of education. In North America, in Europe, in Australia and New Zealand, both in theory and in politics, the majority on the left have decreed that classical Marxism is in terminal crisis. History has failed to vindicate the truth of its major premises. The working class as an agent of social transformation is dead. To grasp adequately the new reality, we must modify, reformulate, restructure both our theoretical lenses and our politics to be true to the socialist project in the present conjuncture.

What points of departure were inscribed in SCA? — how to characterize its enduring contribution? It was, first and foremost, a product of the American New Left, embodying both cultural critique and an emancipatory political project yearning for social and individual liberation. It provided a trenchant exposé of social inequality, authoritarian and repressive social structures, their reproduction through educational forms and a dissection of the contradictions of liberalism. Its organizing concern was a debate with liberal discourse and its explanatory paradigms — a concern which has remained central to its authors' subsequent work.

In SCA liberalism was seen as a mystificatory, misleading, ideological system and subjected to critique both on theoretical grounds and in terms of the social outcomes it claims to predict. The terms: *false*, *incorrect*, *inadequate*, *misleading* pervade the work. Liberalism is portrayed as offering a promise which it cannot hope to make good because of its commitment to capitalism. Consequently, any educational reform movement committed to human equality and positive social development must renounce its fundamental premises and move on. Although it would be an exaggeration to describe the work as a Marxist text, it drew heavily upon the Marxist tradition and its analysis of capitalism for its insights and its themes.

And they *were* and *are* critical themes.

Four stand out as of crucial significance. Firstly, the issue of causal primacy. SCA argued, with few qualifications, that the capitalist system of production and its associated social division of labour is causally prior and central to an understanding of the forms of educational provision and their role in constituting the typical forms of consciousness, interpersonal behaviour and personality attributes required by capitalist work relations. Despite the slippage between 'mirroring', 'reflecting', 'relating to' 'corresponding with', the causal sequence was unambiguous. This is especially clear in the book's second theme: the analysis of educational change and its distinct patterns of periodization. SCA maintains that the normal process of capital accumulation and economic growth is structured by contradictory class relations and class struggle. Furthermore, turning points in educational history coincide with periods of economic and social upheaval and an extension of the wage labour system. These phases of intensified class struggle call into question earlier patterns of power and domination (including those in education) which then become restructured. Thirdly, despite the long run tendency for reproduction and correspondence *if* the social relations governing economic life are not transformed, SCA in its recognition of contradictions, lags, lack of fit, institutional inertia, forms becoming fetters etc. *did* recognize that the reproduction of the social relations of production was not a smooth, uncontested and mechanical process with a predetermined outcome. Finally, they attempted to posit the *mechanism* through which the reproduction tendency occurred. Their concept of 'pluralist accommodation' joins *both* the relatively uncoordinated pursuit of private interests by millions of individuals as mediated through local school boards, the market for private education etc. *and* the changing structure of production determined outside the democratic sphere and marked by the dominant classes' pursuit of profit and class privilege. But it is the ruling class which, through its use of the police and its generalized political and economic power, structures educational values, the articulation of programmatic ideas and information *and* the typical content of struggles in education. The struggle between capital and the key contesting class, labour, sets the framework for pluralist accommodation.

None of these themes is presented in an a priori manner. They are put forward as empirical propositions and backed up with a wealth of historical data which added to their provisional plausibility.

I do not wish to devalue the theoretical and empirical work inspired by a desire to develop further, modify, qualify, or contest the central theses of SCA. Indeed, its publication marked the beginnings of a progressive research programme which at least until the early 1980s contributed to the dislodging of Fabian social democratic reformism from its hegemonic position in the sociology of education and in so doing deepened our understanding of educational forms and processes. My argument is more that the specific directions taken by that research programme had reached an impasse by the 1980s, largely due to the failure to pursue the holistic, structural and historical thrust of Bowles and Gintis' earlier work. Through such an omission a space has been left wide open for the New Right and its educational agenda. Furthermore, however laudable its aspirations for a more genuinely democratic and socialist project, I want to suggest that a number of key assumptions of the new orthodoxy undermine the search for a more progressive politics which can defend social democratic gains against the New Right offensive currently being waged in most western capitalist countries, let alone facilitate an advance towards socialism.

The central proposition which will be developed here is that far from escaping from liberalism's seductive tentacles, the subsequent trajectory of Bowles and Gintis' work is a classic example of what Wood has called a new true socialism. Like their earlier forerunners criticized by Marx in *The German Ideology*, they 'innocently take on trust the illusion . . . that it is a question of the "most reasonable" social order and not the needs of a particular class and a particular time . . . They had abandoned the real historical basis and returned to that of ideology . . . True socialism, which is no longer concerned with real human beings but with "man" has lost all revolutionary enthusiasm and proclaims instead the universal love of mankind' (quoted in Wood, 1986). Marxism, according to Gintis, has become just another political ideology attempting the proselytizing of the masses (Gintis, 1980). It is not a coherent theoretical system, but a mere discourse. True, the concept of class still figures prominently in the work of both authors but now the conception of history as a succession of epoch defining institutions which serve the interests of a dominant class is rejected. Instead, they argue that 'all social systems exhibit institutions allowing the *successful* contestation of power and the pursuit of political and other projects by the subordinate classes' (Bowles and Gintis, 1984a, my emphasis). Their earlier stress on the centrality of the ownership and control of the means of production has given way to a Weberian interest in the multifarious forms of domination in society (Bowles, 1982b). Whilst the *size* and *distribution* of the controllable economic surplus is asserted to be central to the explanation of institutional change (Bowles and Gintis, 1984a), they now maintain that the social relations governing surplus extraction are not exclusively class relations and that other relations of power are 'socially consequent'. [Bowles and Gintis, 1983b]. In fact they are deeply skeptical of the proposition that exploitation, particularly class exploitation, provides a sufficient conceptual foundation for a rigorous and conceptual treatment of the variety of forms of political domination (Bowles and Gintis, 1986). Capitalist societies are marked by a heterogeneity of power (Bowles and Gintis, 1983a) operating in *distinct* areas of social life or sites which are not reducible to or derivative from each other (Bowles and Gintis, 1981a; Gintis and Bowles, 1981). Of these the sites of the patriarchal family, the liberal democratic state and capitalist production, each marked by distinct and characteristic sets of social relations are the most fundamental to the dynamics of advanced capitalism. These sites are articulated with each other, in fact, everything is related to everything else but we are not told how or through what mechanisms.

It seems that Bowles and Gintis, in their legitimate desire to distance themselves from what they see as classical Marxism's tendency to collapse all forms of social domination into class relations, in their insistence on the relative autonomy of sites and the rules which structure or regulate the practices therein, and the articulation of sites, have retreated from a concern to offer a coherent account of social causation and perhaps regard such a project as intrinsically absurd. This I think derives from their conception of social structure which now has decidedly idealist and voluntaristic connotations. Structures are now the *rules* which 'regulate' or 'structure' social practices but in a non determinist or mechanistic way. (Bowles, 1985a). Whilst they take on organizational and discursive forms, the motor of history has become social practices detached from a notion of structures as fundamental irreducible elements. As they say, people produce themselves though their practices (*ibid*) which either stabilize or transform the various aspects of social reality. Thus the social is reduced to mere rules and history is merely the product of individual actions alone or in unison. Endogenous change thus comes from the practices of agents structured by the capitalist relations of production and its articulation with the family, the state and other sites. Although they maintain that they 'embrace the fundamental tenet of structural theories that individual action is highly regulated', they also 'attribute no theoretical status and certainly no causal or explanatory power to the reproductive needs of any structure' (Bowles and Gintis, 1986).

Whilst they accord great significance to the struggles which occur in the various sites of domination, including class struggles, this reluctance to ascribe any *causal* power to structures is manifest in their discussion of the processes of social reproduction. Thus they argue that the reproduction of structures of domination, whether of class, state, race or gender, is not assured by the structure itself ... not guaranteed by the logic of the structure but the contingent result of individual and collective practices taking place throughout the society and these structured by the full variety of social relations. This seems rather akin to the pluralist model of society characteristic of liberal social theory, and in their displacement of *any* of these sites from a position of causal primacy, human history is reduced to the realm of mere contingency. It is not clear whether Bowles and Gintis' classificatory schema of distinct structures, sites and practices is intended as the considered conclusion of an exercise of social analysis of capitalist societies or as an heuristic device which may facilitate the same. If the first, I would argue that it is not borne out by an examination of the history of capitalist social formations. If the second, it is unhelpful, in that it contains no hypotheses about primary causal processes, developmental tendencies or structuring mechanisms. The logic of structural causation is multiform, and inchoate, directionless, trendless, if it exists at all. Practice is primary.

A non mechanistic, non reductivist, non determinist theory of social change which wants to preserve a notion of human agency does not necessarily have to forego a concern with the conditions of historical possibility and the constraining and directional effects of social structures on political and other practices. In conceding that practices can be transformative or reproductive is it illegitimate to enquire of the preconditions for either? Are not particular *patterns* of structural relationships more conducive to reproductive as opposed to transformative practices? If, as they maintain, they are 'interested in the effects of intervention within a given structure to enhance the possibility of structural change' (Gintis, 1980), does this not necessitate an analysis of the real objective constraints on practice and the limits of the feasible? Although they argue that historical change is 'structured, systematic ...' and that it is crucially related to power ('structure of rules empowering or restraining actors in various degrees') they are singularly silent when it comes to specifying in empirical terms an analysis of concrete power relationships in particular historical situations. This is despite their contention that in 'sometimes obscure ways', social structures limit our actions' (Bowles and Gintis, 1986).

Classical Marxism maintains that an essential element of an analysis of the structural constraints on action is an analysis of class interests, conceptualized as prior to the particular social struggles which take place within society and the characteristic forms of consciousness manifested therein. Bowles and Gintis have rejected such a notion of interests seeing it as typical of a pervasive tendency within Marxism, to derive the actions of individual agents from a knowledge of their class position. In their view, interests are not determined independently from practice (Bowles, 1985a). This is, of course, true in the formal sense that objective class interests and the structures which ground them depend on practice for their reproduction and/or transformation. However, Bowles and Gintis would have us believe, in line with their voluntaristic 'politics of becoming' (Bowles, 1982b), that interests are *made* or constituted by practice: 'classes *constitute themselves* by the tools of discourse and the organizational practices they develop'. Interests are *politically* produced through practices and it is illegitimate to assign interests to people and groups 'behind their backs' as it were (Bowles and Gintis, 1985a). By the same logic, people would have no interest, for example, in the maintenance of the language which their discursive practices unconsciously ensure. They also oppose themselves to an economistic conception of interest emanating simply from the site of capitalist production. Social actors are concerned about community, democracy, environmental issues, for example, which extend beyond the mere sphere of economic rationality. Indeed such concerns have been the inspiration for the development of the new social movements, now portrayed as *the* carriers now of an emancipatory future (Bowles, Gordon and Weisskopf, 1986). Yet there exists a certain ambiguity, not to say downright inconsistency, in the conception of interests in their work. They have recently denied that interests are subjective or otherwise lacking in substance (Bowles and Gintis, 1986). Bowles, for example, recognizes the need to separate interests from wants and that there has been no satisfactory way of reconciling wants and a view of interests as being politically produced through practices. He also sometimes wants to maintain that interests do reside in the structure of social relations after all (Bowles, 1985a). His solution is to arrive at a normative concept of interests, projecting the problem into the future in the search for a structure of social relations in which wants can reflect interests, i.e. in democratic social relations where, through democratic procedures extending throughout social life, the possibility exists for the satisfaction both of the reproduction needs of the community and its demands for self actualization (*ibid*).

Indeed, in his writing on economics and politics, Bowles frequently reverts to a notion of interests anterior to social practices. For example, when discussing class alliances he claims that their basis consists of common economic interests. Such interests are not, of course, seen as mechanistically determining specific outcomes: 'political, ideological and other phenomena not specifically encompassed by . . . economic models' play a role. His notion that 'class conflicts fought out not only on the terrain of the economy but in the state and in other social arenas' influence such 'critical variables as the rent share, the wage rate, the allocation of labour among sectors, the rates of productivity increase and relative prices' seems to suggest that class interests are differentially affected by such conflicts. Indeed, it is difficult to make sense of his analysis of class alliances without a notion that the class relationships — of expropriator to worker — the different 'forms in which unpaid surplus labour is pumped out of the direct producers' give rise to different objective class interests. Thus, in his own terms: 'expropriators and workers in one class relationships [are] united and pitted against other classes, coalitions of the have nots against the haves, and more complex alliances' (Bowles, 1984). Likewise in his joint work with Weisskopf and Gordon, the focus on class is held to be 'reasonable in view of the impressive insights gained by historians and other social scientists in analyzing structural change from a class perspective' (*ibid*). Implicit in this work are notions of the short-term and long-term interests of capital and labour, the crucial contending classes whose contradictory relations have structured post-war American history. Whilst the view is taken that interests may or may not be *realized* in politics they are not deemed to be merely constituted thereby. Gintis, too, in his important discussion of the nature of the Accord struck by capital and labour in the first decade of the twentieth century (rather akin to Bowles' use of the term 'social structures of accumulation') seems to believe that this 'reorganization of institutions and the tools of political discourse' is socially consequential for the different social classes. Although he maintains that 'through an accord, classes redefine their interests and their identities so as to produce a new logic of social action', he also seems to believe that the existence of the Accord is better for subordinate classes than, for example, the pattern of class relationships which led to fascism. Does this not imply that the interests of subordinate classes were better accommodated under the Accord than in its absence? Additionally there is the question of *accounting* for the Accord. Gintis' answer is little more than a restatement of known empirical facts. (Gintis, 1980). If as he maintains the bourgeoisie's coalition with popular classes was the crucial factor in facilitating popular participation in politics, how does one *explain* the different pattern of alliances which materialized in various countries without a thorough going class analysis and a notion of objective interest? This seems to be recognized in Bowles and Gintis' most recent work where despite the stress on interests being formed through practices there is also the concession that interests motivate practices (Bowles and Gintis, 1986). Historical possibilities are not completely open but structured by objective interests and social relations which are more than just rules. Class struggles and class alliances do not emerge in vacuums. The retention of a notion of classes having objective interests does not necessarily commit one to a view of history as an inevitable succession of stages in which classes inexorably produce the politics which will realize their interests. This, however, seems to be entailed by Gintis' view that:

> the problem with scientific Marxism includes its explanatory inadequacy, its inability even in principle to deal with a logic of class relations in advanced capitalism as it operates in itself and not as contrasted with the Marxist projector of its ideal form . . . Marxist historiography is convincing on the proposition that historical events are best studied as the process of class struggle, but weak on the forces underlying particular manifestations of class struggle and their transformations across time and space. (Gintis, 1980)

The theoretical weakness of classical Marxism, according to Bowles and Gintis, is that it has neglected politics and culture in its explanatory framework (Bowles and Gintis, 1981b). Marxism is concerned merely with subject-object relations rather than subject-subject relations mediated through communicative discourse (Gintis, 1980; Bowles and Gintis, 1986). They distance themselves from what they call a nomological conception of Marxism in which labour is conceptualized as a use value for capital, a mere commodity leading to a purely structural theory generating laws of motion for the capitalist mode of production without theoretical attention to human intentionality (Bowles, 1985a). In their critique of the labour theory of value they argue that Marxists have failed to recognize the specificity of labour in the distinction between labour and labour power. Labour is represented not as practice, as subject, but as an output or a use value for the capitalist, as a commodity. In its place they want to develop a non-economistic theory of the politics and culture as well as the economics of production. They do not deny the centrality of profits, accumulation and capitalist production but argue that an analysis of the profit rate is to be sought in the variety of power relationships which mediate the relationship of capital to the workers, to the state and to external economic agents. The profit rate, according to them, is affected by political organization, ideology, family structures and other relationships.

Labour power is now just a commodity, they argue, and 'the theoretically necessary and sufficient non commodity aspects of labour power must be located in the distinct, non commodity structuration of its production located at sites distinct from the site of capitalist production': the family and the state (Bowles and Gintis, 1981a; Gintis and Bowles, 1981).

Invoking Gramsci and E.P. Thompson on their side, they assert the primacy of the political, originally reformulating the labour theory of value such that labour becomes an 'ensemble of practices' and the labour theory of value becomes 'a theory of the articulation of appropriative, political, distributive and cultural practices at the site of capitalist production' [Bowles and Gintis, 1981b]. Likewise, (when they were still committed to the labour theory of value), they criticized classical Marxists' inability to provide an explanation for labour market segmentation on the grounds that the determination of the segments and the boundaries thereof depend upon political and ideological as well as economic aspects [Bowles and Gintis, 1977].

As with John Elster (whose work Bowles' commends) (Bowles, 1985b), they 'proceed as if Steedman and the Straffa School have done the job of refuting Marx's most basic concepts of value' (Wood, 1986). They accuse Marx of abstracting from the class nature of capitalist production in his formulation of the labour theory of value (Bowles and Gintis, 1981b). They fail to grasp the significance of Marx's emphasis on the *dual* nature of labour (use value and exchange) value under capitalist production. Marx's distinction between labour and labour power (only the latter becomes a commodity) as the foundation for a theory of exploitation and accumulation under capitalism is deemed to be both inadequate and superfluous (Bowles and Gintis, 1984b).

Although they still want to stress, as we have seen the dominant structures of surplus extraction and the forms of social contestation to which these give rise (Bowles and Gintis 1984a), their theory of crisis includes no role for the labour theory of value, the theory of the falling rate of profit and the rising organic composition of capital (Bowles, 1985b). Instead, crises are seen as merely the result of profit squeezes, brought on by the mobilization of the workers (constituting their interests) and citizens' movements and of struggles within the state which undermine capitalist profitability (Bowles, Gordon and Weisskopf, 1986). This approach to crisis is manifested in the work of Glyn and Sutcliffe, Boddy and Crotty, Weisskopf etc. whom Bowles frequently cites approvingly. These authors are largely post-Ricardians. What they, and Bowles and Gintis, hold in common is a rejection of the labour theory of value and an emphasis on *distributional* struggles. Indeed, Bowles and Gintis both seem to assume that class struggles are merely over distribution (Bowles and Gintis, 1986).

The real thrust of the classical labour theory of value, however, is that it links an analysis of the normal forms of capital accumulation and its inner laws of motion with an analysis of crisis. It in no way abstracts from the reality of class relations nor excludes politics and ideology from their content. To read Volume 1 of *Capital*, with its accounts of struggles over the working day, struggles between various fractions of capital in the state over female and child labour, and struggles within and over the labour process, as an economistic, mechanistic account of the laws of motion of capitalist societies is no mean feat of interpretation. Marx is therein asserting connections between social practices and long term historical tendencies, *and* providing an account of the structures by virtue of which these tendencies operate. Class relations and class struggles are at the centre of the analysis. In their anxiety to assert that everything is much more open and complex Bowles and Gintis have lost any sense of structural primacy, and the logic of system. In place of an analysis of the inner dynamics of social systems we are offered superficially true or hollow slogans: 'the structure of discourse is itself the continual object of class struggle' [Gintis, 1980], or 'the paradigm of subject-subject relation-politics is not the interplay of diverse and irreducible social interests but the coalition, the class, the class alliance.'

Behind this shift in theoretical perspective lies an important shift in social practice: the fact that most class struggles in western capital societies have not been informed by a revolutionary analysis of capitalist society, that popular struggles tend to be articulated in liberal democratic discourse. Gintis dismisses concepts such as 'bourgeois hegemony', 'incorporation', 'false consciousness', 'class betrayal' by working class leaders as indispensible tools for the explanatory analysis of these phenomena. Indeed the very notion that anything requires explanation is dismissed as absurd. 'It cannot be done because there is nothing to explain any more than we can explain why the Trobiand Islanders do not speak English' (Gintis, 1980).

Presumably it is equally futile to try to explain why Marxist discourse exists as a fact in revolutionary movements in the periphery of the capitalist world: in the Philippines, South America, Southern Africa and elsewhere. Fortunately, there *are* Marxists who have engaged in the study of the material conditions for the emergence and reproduction of a set of communicative practices and their organizational forms and can provide an account of the above realities which has at least provisional plausibility. In their more restrained moments our authors themselves inconsistently concede that something requires to be explained. Thus Bowles laments the fact that in the twentieth century capital has managed to marginalize any alternative conceptions of economic logic (Bowles, 1982a). Both in their account of the early Twentieth Century Accord, include the marginalization of revolutionary discourse as one of its attributes. This process, not mechanistically predetermined, is a quite proper object of scientific investigation just as is the problem of explaining why some Trobianders do in fact speak English.

For the most part, however, Bowles and Gintis, in true liberal fashion, cling heroically to the primacy of politics and human agency, and are loathe to see us constrained by anything other than rules which can be changed and discourses which can be transformed. When the Trobianders learned to shout 'bring us Kellogs'! they themselves transformed their whole world!

This brings us to the question of what precisely is their conception of politics. Politics are those aspects of social practices geared to the social relations of a site or its articulation with other sites. Politics are about altering or stabilizing the rules of the game which regulate or structure the practices in the various sites of the social formation (Bowles and Gintis, 1981a; Bowles 1985a). Political practices are thus not confined to the state but are located also in the sites of capitalist production and the family. In fact politics is everywhere. However, each site possesses a political structure distinct from what exists in the others. What then is the relationship between politics in the various sites? Let us first consider the state. The state is 'a distinct structure governed by distinct rules which are irreducible to the social relations of production or the imperatives of reproduction' (Bowles, 1985a). It is in no sense an effect or reflection of class relations. Indeed, we are told that the state apparatus is capable under some conditions of being a major historical actor in its own right (Bowles and Gintis, 1984a). They argue, correctly, that many different forms of state are possible even within capitalist societies. But, in its liberal democratic form, the state, whilst 'central to the reproduction of the conditions of domination and subordinacy in the family and the economy is not itself a site of domination' (Bowles and Gintis, 1981a; Gintis and Bowles, 1981). What then are the armies, police forces and judiciary of liberal democratic states *for*? Have Bowles and Gintis been seduced by liberal democracy's own rhetoric? Do they not observe any connection between the existence of liberal democracy and its rhetoric of 'person rights' in countries like the USA and the lack of it in much of the periphery and the use of the coercive power of the liberal democratic state wherever capitalist social relations are under severe challenge? Only from a provincial nation-state perspective which takes no account of imperialism and which ignores the role of state coercion in cementing the social order in a class society, can the liberal democratic state be defined as not itself a site of domination.

What is it that they want to assert by such formulations? In line with their constitutive theory of politics and their stress on the primacy of politics [Bowles, 1982b] and of discourse ('language use contributes independently to the self constitution of social life') (Gintis, 1980), they want to make space for the autonomy of politics which, despite the frequent use of the term 'relative', in effect — given the primacy of practice over structure and of political over other practices, becomes the prime motor of history. We are not told under *what* conditions the state can be an independent actor, nor what the limits of state intervention are, for example, with respect to the mediation of crisis in the accumulation process. Indeed there do not seem to be any limits, only a number of possibilities. It all depends on the nature of social practices in each site and these are by definition indeterminate. Thus the openness of history is announced.

Bowles and Gintis will doubtless claim that they *are* concerned with limits and structural contraints and that history is not completely open, that I have distorted their arguments setting up a straw person version only, the more easily to undermine straw assumptions. Bowles might quote his own words: 'Egalitarian or economic growth promoting education thus confronts its limits in the imperatives of the reproduction of the class structure, the logic of the accumulation process and the capitalist state'. This, however, is the old Bowles speaking; it is taken from a revised version of an early 1978 paper. If we examine their current (post-1980) position a rather different picture emerges. There are, for example, multifarious forms of domination of which extractive relations are crucial. The social is a mere plurality of 'overlapping assymetrical games'. 'Society is a game without a core' (Bowles and Gintis, 1986). But if extractive relations are not exclusively class relations, and if each of the many sites in which relations of domination occur are articulated with each other (as a result of previous practices which alter or reproduce the rules of the games in a site or in its relations with other sites), and if structures merely regulate or structure practice (but not necessarily so) are we not saying that nothing is causally prior, or that everything is causally prior because everything is articulated with everything else? Bowles and Gintis might respond that the practices in other sites impose limits on any one site, but since practices in any site can be 'transported' or changed and since practices in any case are not structures, I find it hard to discern *any* structural limits. I think that this framework is confusing reflecting Bowles and Gintis' own confusion. Sometimes they seem to want to have it both ways, or all ways at once.

This failure to *theorize* constraints is especially apparent in Bowles' jointly authored work on post-war American history, and the elaboration of the specifics of an alternative economic strategy for the present conjuncture. Like other versions of the alternative economic policy emanating from the left wing of social democracy the proposals are premised on a view of capital and the capitalist state as acting irrationally, on a moral critique of capitalism for its waste, and its inequity, and its lack of democracy, accountability and incompatibility with person rights.

What is advocated to combat the current assertion of capitalist power through attacks on the welfare state and rising unemployment, and the intensification of work discipline as a consequence of capital restructuring is a strategy of wage-led productivity growth, an economic bill of rights institutionalizing security and equity, and a thorough going democratization of economic life extending to workers' control and democratic planning (Bowles, Gordon and Weisskopf, 1986). Such an economic program, depending crucially on the political strength of the labour movement and the new social movements to bring it about, is as utopian as the desire to dissolve in thought the laws of motion of capitalist societies within whose constraints any movement for change necessarily operates. Bowles and his co-workers conceive of such a program as a set of transitional goals, conceding the possibility that it may lead to inflation, middle class opposition, capital exports and capital strikes: the kinds of reactions encountered in Allende's Chile and Mitterand's France (Devine, 1984). But given an adequate degree of political mobilization of subordinate strata they do not see this as inevitable. This is because they do not see the nature of exploitation in capitalist production as always and necessarily involving a zero sum situation (Bowles, Gordon and Weisskopf, 1983). On the contrary, they believe that both capital and labour can benefit from such a strategy. In the short and medium term they do not have incompatible interests. This perspective informs their position too on the ending of the Great Depression of the 1930s. Given their analysis of that crisis as a demand-side crisis, one suspects that they believe (in line with the dominant tradition of the historiography of the period) that, if *only* Keynesianism had been fully implemented, the depression could have been ended without the trauma of fascism, class polarization and war (Bowles, Gordon and Weisskopf, 1986). An alternative, and, I believe, better founded analysis of the 1930s, would argue that given the way in which crises accentuate *both* the conflicts between capital and labour *and* crucially the conflicts within the ruling class, neither the economic nor the political preconditions existed for the institutionalization of Keynesianism. Even in Sweden (which authors sharing Bowles' economic assumptions are frequently prone to hold up as a model) the class alliance which facilitated the implementation of a modified Keynesianism did not produce an end to the recession, as the statistics of Swedish unemployment and economic growth reveal (Higgins, 1985). The problem with Bowles is that he is reluctant to concede that in certain circumstances structures permit few alternatives and that the economic policies being pursued by capitalist states, admittedly in a contradictory totality, might, for the most powerful fractions of capital be the objectively most rational alternative, given the class interests at stake.

As Devine has pointed out, Bowles' supply-side view of the current crisis is little different from that of the Reaganites whose conclusions lead them to attempt to repress the labour movement and stamp on the new social movements and on Third World movements for liberation. A fully democratized economy, as Bowles and Gintis are well aware, is incompatible with the basic dynamic of capital — that of profit. If the former is conceived of as the ideal, perhaps the radical break between capitalism and socialism has to be emphasized and not just in some hoped for future when the appropriate social mobilization has materialized. The issue of locating the forces which are to bring about such a mobilization needs, too, to be addressed. It is here, however, that Bowles and Gintis' pessimism regarding working class agency and its potential role in a socialist transformation becomes problematic. Since interests are constituted merely in struggle and since the labour movement shows, according to them, little sign as yet of challenging capital's power, we are left with no alternative but to place our hope in the citizens' movements. Only they are capable of articulating the 'new universalization of interests that conceives of and permits movement towards an alternative model of economic rationality, community and democracy'. Only they are not contaminated by mere subject-object relations and can represent the cultural and political as well as the economic needs which inspire practices.

The final aspect of their work which I wish to comment on is their conception of socialism. Both view socialism as a process rather than an end state and yet they have some clear ideas as to what is not socialist. They criticize, for example, the view of socialism as property claims to output, or a mere change in the relations of ownership which is not accompanied by a full democratization of the relations of production, which is the way they conceive of the Soviet Union (Bowles and Gintis, 1975). They criticize the state conception of politics which in their view has inhibited a socialist conception of democracy, and yet the positive content of their view of socialism is rather vague, and closely tied in with recurring themes in liberal democracy. Indeed, they no longer identify themselves primarily as socialist, but as post-liberal democrats. Thus they stress the importance of the move towards political equality, majority rule and popular sovereignty and for their extension throughout all the sites of civil society such that democracy becomes something more than a mere system of procedures co-existing with substantive inequality (Bowles and Gintis, 1983b). Precisely what this means however, is unclear. Thus: 'we have not argued that collective property be substituted for private property or that justice requires some specific relationship between the state and the economy. And it needs hardly be said that issues of liberty and personal choice represent critical components of a solution to the problem of economic justice' (*ibid*).

Similarly, the relationship between liberal democratic discourse and socialist discourse is ambiguously defined. The goals of progressive forces should, they repeatedly emphasize, be articulated 'within the structural boundaries of liberal discourse since it is this discourse (neither true nor false) which is a fact in the west' (Bowles and Gintis, 1981a; Gintis and Bowles, 1981). This implies that the concepts of 'rights' holds a focal place in the struggle for a more desirable state of affairs (Bowles and Gintis, 1986). But whether socialism implies a movement beyond capitalism or its humanization and democratization, whether it is simply a question of finding a more equitable mode of surplus labour extraction or bringing to an end all coercion and exploitation is unclear. Bowles' history of the accumulation process in the USA and the contrast that he makes between demand constrained accumulation in the Long Boom, and exploitation led accumulation under Reagan seem to imply a conception of capitalism as not intrinsically based on exploitation but merely wasteful under certain conditions (Bowles, Gordon and Weisskopf, 1986). If socialism 'will be the joint fulfilment and transcendance of the liberal democratic promise and with it the transformation of the tools of communicative discourse of liberal democratic capitalism' (Bowles and Gintis, 1981a), does this denote the end of capitalism? The 'quest for a society devoid of illusion whose transparency facilitates popular and reasoned collective decision making' (Bowles, 1985a), seems to imply more than 'the democratic politicization of capitalist civil society' (*ibid*), . . . more than 'the democratization of the work place and community power' (Bowles and Gintis, 1981a). In their most recent work they have called for the elimination of 'the central institutions of the capitalist economy' but their ambiguity about the nature of property rights in the future society remains (Bowles and Gintis, 1986). 'Community access to capital' and democratic accountability surely has to be thought through, in terms of what property relations could ensure the same.

What is not ambiguous, however, is the failure to tie in the concept of socialism with the interests of a class. Whilst one can reiterate Bloch's adage:— 'Men do not live by bread alone . . . especially when they have none' (Bloch, 1933) — the reluctance to stress the material interests of the working class in gaining control over the basic reproductive necessities for any sort of life at all, let alone the kind of life that is possible where the forces of production are most advanced, is I think, a significant omission. It demonstrates that Bowles and Gintis are more preoccupied by capitalism in one country, than as a complex integrated world system of imperialist domination which denies even the basic material needs of the majority who live under its sway. Capitalist militarism, in this view, is not a mere option, and undesirable possibility, an irrational and wasteful utilization of resources, but an *essential* aspect of capitalism's mode of reproduction (Mandel, 1983). If this point is not grasped by the left in the advanced world in the 1980s, the prospects of averting a horrendous unleashing of the full might of imperialism's military machines seem dim indeed. We are no longer confronting the relative autonomy of the nation state and self contained social formations such as to permit our own more humane way out of the crisis as indicated in the conclusion of *Beyond the Wasteland*. It is not inconsistent to argue both that subordinate classes have achieved some precarious gains within the liberal democratic form of capitalist state *and* that the essence of such a state is an extreme form of class dictatorship and class barbarism, when viewed in terms of its operation on a world scale.

I began this chapter with a reference to the new orthodoxy in radical educational discourse. My survey of Bowles and Gintis' work has elucidated the assumptions which underly this new orthodoxy. Its thrust is to distance itself from the classical Marxist tradition whilst claiming both a common heritage and a common distaste for the multifarious forms of domination, inequality, the lack of participation, the authoritarianism etc. in capitalist society. Its 'bêtes noirs' are 'economism', 'mechanistic determinism', 'class reductionism', 'functionalism', 'naive fundamentalism'; it claims to take account of class *and* race *and* gender, of the possibilities of resistance, of the spaces for progressive intervention within the state, of the existence of contradictions (as well as reproductions) and of the uniqueness and specificity of each social formation and historical conjuncture. History is complex — and open. Hurrah!

Whilst claiming to offer a more sophisticated framework which can grasp multidimensional causality and the flux of events, the new orthodoxy, in the name of human agency, is blind to its own history. That history is the history of liberal discourse and its non-contingent role in articulating capitalist hegemony. From the inception of capitalism, its history has been marked by a class struggle at the level of ideas as well as at the point of production. The struggle between Marxism and bourgeois social theory is an old one, but the debating themes are recurrent. So too is the persistent tendency on the part of its liberal opponents to project Marxism as a mechanistic, deterministic theory of 'the economy', as a theory of subject-object relations which denies human agency. Having demolished the scarecrow, mechanistic determinism, the field is cleared for pluralistic openness. In fact one need not think about 'the economy' any more: that can be left to the appropriate specialist, the economist, armed with an appropriate conceptual baggage of post-monetarist, or post Keynesian, but certainly post-Marxist tools, to lead us to an understanding of that distinct but articulated sphere.

Bowles and Gintis are not complicit in this disregard for economics, and indeed castigate those who, in their anxiety to be rid of Marxist 'economism', have banished the economy completely from their analyses. However, most exponents of the new orthodoxy heed them not, operating instead within the arbitrary construction of disciplinary boundaries — so fitting for a complex world. Yet in their own attempt to respect the irreducibility of levels of analysis, Bowles and Gintis have arrived at an ontology which sees only distinct structures, pluralistic games, and contingent and arbitrary relationships. The search for underlying causal connections and tendencies deriving from the nature of social realities and their laws of development has given way to a view of history which in my judgment *cannot* move beyond description. I do not think that the vital project initiated by *Schooling in Capitalist America can* be completed given Bowles and Gintis' current stance.

What has all this to do with the analysis of education? In the last section of this chapter I want to present a challenge to Bowles and Gintis. Can they demonstrate the superiority of their 'new and better theory' over a classical Marxist theoretical framework in explaining some of the more salient developments in recent educational history (Sharp, 1986a).

It will not have escaped the attention of educators in capitalist societies that the last decade has seen a significant restructuring of educational priorities, the amounts and direction of state educational funding, and the institutions and mechanisms of state control. We may be prone to blame this on Reaganism, Thatcherism, Hawkism or whatever, but we cannot fail to notice a marked discontinuity from the 1960s and early 1970s. What may have escaped our attention, however, is that despite the different unique histories of each educational system, there is a marked *convergence* in the form and content of this restructuring in every advanced capitalist country (including Sweden) (Svennson, 1986) that we care to name.

This structural reorganization of priorities and emphases exhibits a number of recurrent features. Among the most significant are: a growing trend towards centralized control undermining traditionally established autonomies of various kinds; attacks on the social wage affecting both the amount and the direction of educational expenditure; the accentuation of hierarchical and horizontal divisions within education, thus reversing some of the egalitarian and progressive trends of the social democratic settlement of the 1960s and early 1970s; a greater emphasis on vocationalization and instrumentalism; the move towards the commodification of education (voucher schemes, user-pay principles, marketing courses); an increase in privatization often with increased funding for the private sector; enhanced links between the corporate sector and schooling institutions; curriculum differentiation; a heightening of the competitive ethos; the reorganization of state administrative apparatuses; increased deskilling of the teaching force; a reconstitution of the crisis as a crisis of schooling ('young people can't get jobs because the schools have failed'); a reorganization of patterns of teacher education...

These developments are common throughout the 'advanced' capitalist world regardless of whether social democratic or more conservative parties are in office. Progressive students, parents, teachers and state bureaucrats have nowhere allowed them to go uncontested. None has been brought about easily, without resistance, refraction (Freeland, 1986), or, dare I say it, class struggle. In each capitalist state there have been various interventions within the state apparatuses, some more successful than others, some lessening the impact or altering its effects. But everywhere the consequence of the changes have been disastrous for precisely those groups who formed the target of the earlier social democratic advances: working class pupils, blacks, women, the disabled, migrants or guest workers. (Sharp, 1984).

Moreover, if we move back to the 1930s, despite the differences between that depression and the current one, we find that from the late 1920s a rather similar form and pattern of educational restructuring took place. In the three countries I have examined closely, Britain, Australia and Germany, what strikes one most, beyond the pecularities and ideosyncracies, is the convergence, and the similarities with current restructuring.

In my view these recurring trends have a shared structural root: the causal processes at work within *all* capitalist societies stemming both from the mode of *producing* the surplus within definite sets of contradictory class relations and from the mode of *appropriating* the surplus. Bowles and Gintis might not disagree although they would not collapse all relations of appropriation into class relations. Neither would I. I note however that gender and ethnic relations seemed to move in parallel with class relations, with a reassertion and accentuation of gender and ethnic divisions during crises, despite the lessening of such divisions which had occurred in the two decades before the 1930s and the 1970s and 1980s.

I argue that the simultaneity and multi-national character of these changes in the form and content of educational provision is related to the operation of the law of value and the class struggle based on contradictory interests. Such processes generate in *some* historical periods the possibility for significant advances for subordinate groups, but in other periods significant retreats caused by a massive ruling class offensive necessitated by the objective constraints within which class actors manoeuvre. I suggest that in periods of capitalist crisis there are only three logical possibilities: (i) a ruling class offensive rolling back previous gains; (ii) subordinate class militancy which defends previous gains or even facilitates advances, but resulting in a deepening of the crisis; (iii) the abolition of capitalist production relations and their substitution by others (not necessarily socialist).

The operation of the law of value thus generates structural constraints and limits on what is possible. The law of value is not a theory of the economy and how it works but a theory of how the social relations of capitalist production play a key structuring role in every region of the social system, including the state, the family, ethnic relations. I do not accept that Reagan and Thatcher and the forces which they represent are acting irrationally, given the mode of production, any more than I accept the thesis that the fascist version of the capitalist state displayed the primacy of politics. (Mason, 1966). On the contrary what is occurring is the making of rational calculations of what are the real limits to the feasible including the political and other obstacles in the way of pursuing the class interests represented by their policies.

A crisis of capital accumulation which is not merely the result of previous distributional struggles necessitates an offensive by capital to regenerate the economic political and ideological conditions for a new wave of growth. This struggle is simultaneously a struggle to maintain hegemony, necessitating under certain conditions in some countries the forging of new patterns of alliances, in others the consolidation of the old. *If* capitalism is to survive (and with Bowles and Gintis we agree that there is nothing definite about that), all basic social relations have to undergo a continual process of restructuring and renewal. Schooling institutions, strategically placed in terms of their allocative and ideological function in the social division of labour, cannot be analyzed apart from the fundamental processes which derive from the inner logic of capitalist production.

The will to politics cannot, of itself, overthrow the material conditions which constrain us. People do make history, but not in conditions of their own choosing. It is the contradictory inner dynamics of the social structure which define the limits of the possible, including the possibility of their own supercession. To be sure they derive their momentum in the last analysis from social practice but they are never created by it and no amount of 'true socialist' yearning can dispel their causal primacy. This is what Bowles and Gintis seem to reject. Such a view does not entail that we retreat into a position of resigned pessimism and apoliticism, but that we struggle to capitalize on the real objective processes at work within our mode of production which make possible but not inevitable an emancipatory future.

Such a struggle is not advanced in my view by a perspective which, whilst noting the segmentation and heterogeneity of the working class and its labourist and instrumentalist traditions defines this, not as the central challenge to be overcome through political struggle, but as a demonstration of the failures of Marxism. It is not theory which has produced such divisions and forms of political expression but the real movement of history. Bowles and Gintis themselves are too perceptive as commentators not to have noticed these facts. (Bowles and Gintis, 1982b).

Classical Marxism provides the basis for understanding that such divisions are now accentuating because of underlying *value* processes which *constrain* the dominant fractions of capital to intensify the disorganization and fragmentation of subordinate classes. It also provides the pertinent political lesson. An anti-capitalist opposition must confront the revisionist and social democratic illusion. These is no *capitalist* way out of the crisis which will *not* be detrimental to labour. The only defence for labour is for socialists to overcome the *political* obstacles in the way of realizing labour's essentially common interests. The old Sam Bowles may fittingly be given the last word: 'To discuss the egalitarian or growth functions of education . . . in the absence of rebellion against the capitalist order is worse than ideal speculation. It is to offer a false promise, an ideological palliative which seeks to buy time for capitalism . . . (Bowles, 1982b). It is for this reason that I suggest that we reject the New Orthodoxy and urge Bowles and Gintis to return to their original project.

References

Bloch, E. (1933) 'Non synchronism and its obligation to its dialectics', *New German Critique*, 9.

Bowles, S. (1982a) 'The post-Keynesian capital labor stalemate', *Socialist Review*, 65, August.

Bowles, S. (1982b) 'The labour theory of value and the "Primacy of the political"', *Economic Forum*. Fall, 13, 2.

Bowles, S. (1984) 'Class alliances and surplus labour time' in Syrguin, M. Taylor, L. and Westphal, L. (Eds) *Economic Structures and Performance*, New York, Academic Press.

Bowles, S. (1985a) 'State structures and political practices: A Reconsideration of the liberal democratic conception of politics and accountability', in Coe, R. and Wilber, C. (Eds) *Capitalism and Democracy, Schumpeter Revisited*, Notre Dame, University of Notre Dame Press.

Bowles, S. (1985b) 'Post Marxian economics: Labour, learning and history', *Social Science Information*, 24, 3.

Bowles, S. and Gintis, H. (1975) 'Class power and alienated labour', *Labour Monthly Review*, May.

Bowles, S. and Gintis, H. (1977) 'Heterogeneous labor and the Marxian theory of value, *Cambridge Jornal of Economics*, 1, 2.

Bowles, S. and Gintis, H. (1981a) 'Education as a site of contradictions in the reproduction of the capital-labour relationship: Second thoughts on the correspondence principle', *Economic and Industrial Democracy*, 2.

Bowles, S. and Gintis, H. (1981b) 'Practice and structure in the labour theory of value, *Review of Radical Political Economics*, spring.

Bowles, S. and Gintis, H. (1982a) 'Schooling, class conflict and uneven development', in Simmons, J. (Ed) *The Educational Dilemma: Policy Issues in the Developing Countries*, Oxford, Pergamon.

Bowles, S. and Gintis, H. (1982b) The crisis of liberal democratic capitalism: The case of the United States, *Politics and Society*, 11, 1.

Bowles, S. and Gintis, H. (1983a) 'Die Heterogenitat von Macht', *Das Argument*, 140, August.

Bowles, S. and Gintis, H. (1983b) 'The power of capital: On the inadequacy of the conception of the capitalist economy as "private"', *The Philosophical Forum*. summer, XIV.

Bowles, S. and Gintis, H. (1984a) 'State and class in European feudalism', in Bright, C. and Harding, S. (Eds.) *State Making and Social Movements: Essays in History and Theory*, Ann Arbor, MI, University of Michigan Press.

Bowles, S. and Gintis, H. (1984b) 'The labour theory of value and the specificity of Marxian economics' in Resnick, S. and Wolff, R. (Eds) *Rethinking Marxism: Struggles in Marxist Theory*, New York, Praeger.

Bowles, S. and Gintis, H. (1986) *Democracy and Capitalism : Property, Community and the Contradictions of Modern Social Thought*, New York, Basic Books.

Bowles, S., Gordon, D. and Weisskopf, T. (1983) 'Long swings and the reproductive cycle', *American Economic Review* 73, 2.

Bowles, S., Gordon, D. and Weisskopf, T. (1986) *Beyond the Wasteland: A Democratic Alternative to Economic Decline*, London, Verso.

Devine, D. (1984) *Reagan Electionomics: How Reagan Ambushed the Pollsters 1976–84*, Ottawa, Green Hill.

Freeland, J. (1986) 'Australia: Search for a new educational settlement', in Sharp, R. (Ed) *Capitalist Crisis and Schooling: Comparative Studies in the Politics of Education*, Melbourne, Macmillan.

GINTIS, H. (1980) 'Communication and politics: Marxism and the problem of liberal democracy', *Socialist Review*, 50–51, March–June.

GINTIS, H. and BOWLES, S. (1980, 1981 and 1987) 'Contradictions and reproduction in educational theory' in BARTON, L., MEIGHAN, R. and WALKER, S. (Eds) *Schooling Ideology and the Curriculum*, Lewes, Falmer Press; DALE, R. *et al* (Eds) *Education and the State: Volume 1: Schooling and the National Interest*, Lewes, Falmer Press; and chapter 2 of this volume.

HIGGINS, W. (1985) 'Unemployment and the labour movements breakthrough in Sweden, in ROE, J. (Ed) *Unemployment: Are These Lessons From History?*, Sydney, Hale and Iremonger.

MASON, T. (1966) 'The primacy of politics', in WOLFF, S. (Ed) 1968 *The Nature of Fascism*. London, Weidenfeld and Nicolson.

MANDEL, E. (1984) *Ricardo, Marx Sraffa*, London, Verso.

SHARP, R. (1984) 'Urban education and the current crisis', in GRACE, G. (Ed) *Education and the City: Theory, History and Contemporary Practice*, London, Routledge and Kegan Paul.

SHARP, R. (Ed) (1986a) *Capitalist Crisis and Schooling: Comparative Studies in the Politics of Education*, Melbourne, Macmillan.

SHARP, R. (1986b) Review of TROYNA, B. and WILLIAMS, J. *Racism, Education and the State*, *Capital and Class*, 29, summer.

SVENSSON, L. (1986) 'Reschooling society in Sweden's social democracy' in SHARP, R. (Ed) *Capitalist Crisis and Schooling: Comparative Studies in the Politics of Education*, Melbourne, Macmillan.

WOOD, E. M. (1986) *The Retreat from Class. A New 'True Socialism'*, London, Verso.

11 *Reformism Or Revolution: Liberalism And The Metaphysics of Democracy*

John Freeman-Moir, Alan Scott and Hugh Lauder

The struggle for socialism, whatever else it entails, is about the self-emancipatory struggle of the working class. For many people,and not just Marxists, socialism is not an end in itself, but the beginning of a road to a society where, to use Marx's words, 'the free development of each is the condition for the free development of all', and where people work 'according to ability' and receive 'according to need'. Socialism requires collective ownership, production for need rather than commodity exchange, and the development of a classless and stateless society based on the direct democratic participation of all citizens in decision-making, administration and problem solving. The struggle against capitalism has, as its principal immediate objective, however abstractly or obliquely post-Marxists might render it, the smashing of bourgeois productive relations based on the law of value and the destruction of the bourgeois state which, under late capitalism, plays a fundamental, though far from autonomous, role in reproducing capitalist social relations. Throughout the entire history of the socialist movement two approaches have emerged in relation to this struggle: reformism and revolution. Reformism stands for the progressive transformation of capitalism through evolutionary change, and it is precisely this reformist notion of destroying capitalism by extending liberal democracy that is taken up in much of the later work of Bowles and Gintis. It is this work we wish to challenge, for the position is not new; nor could a strategy based on it transcend the contradictions of capitalism.

When Bowles and Gintis published *Schooling in Capitalist America* in 1976 the international crisis of capitalism had begun to turn the high tide of social democracy. Not surprisingly, their book embodies many of the contradictions which such an historical moment represents. In its structural explanation of the relationship of formally institutionalized education to the capitalist mode of production the authors pointed to the pervasive and near intractable ways in which capitalist structures order all our lives. But in their extremely brief discussion of the strategies and prospects for socialism they are altogether more hopeful that capitalism can be transformed in the foreseeable future. It was as if they were still infected with the optimism of the long economic boom which had seen the development of the welfare state, the emergence of various liberation movements — blacks, women, gays — and an explosive, if brief, student radicalism.

The continuing crisis, now more than a decade long, has thrown the naive optimism of social democracy into harsh relief. In the USA alone the so-called new social movements have been pushed backwards, unions are attacked and union membership is in steady decline, the Democratic party has been shown to have no progressive potential, and internationally the full fury of declining imperialist domination, despite the catastrophe of Vietnam, is thrown against Nicaragua and other potentially socialist states.[1] At home democracy is defended by the nuclear bases in Europe and meglomaniacal plans to militarize space. Once again the struggle for socialism is posed directly and urgently. 'Socialism or barbarism' is the question we face.

In this chapter we want to explore some aspects of the strategy for the development of socialism in a hostile environment as posed by Bowles and Gintis. Until recently questions regarding the strategy for socialism have been treated perfunctorily by radicals concerned with education[2]. In our view radical educational theory must focus attention on practice. In this context it is worth noting that most criticisms of *Schooling in Capitalist America* have been directed at the explanatory structure of the correspondence principle rather than at the issues raised regarding the socialist struggle. Nevertheless, these two points are not unconnected. Rejecting the logic of correspondence as underwriting a seamless capitalist domination various leftist critics have tried to situate the possibility for social change in terms of the relative autonomy of politics, the state, ideology, and hence all superstructural phenomena, including schooling. All this is tied to, and is part of, revisionism late-capitalist style. Bowles and Gintis are prominent exponents in the USA of this latest expression of anti-revolutionary 'socialism'. We say 'latest' because, throughout the history of socialism, the illusions of revisionism — expressed variously as 'utopianism', 'social democracy', 'the parliamentary road' or 'democracy' — have been repeatedly advanced. Marx and Engels first criticized the 'true' socialists in *The German Ideology* and *The Communist Manifesto* during the 1840s. In the latter work they speak of 'true' socialism as the position which has '. . . ceased to express the struggle of one class against another'. Consequently the 'true' socialist felt conscious:

> . . . of representing, not true requirements, but the requirements of truth, not the interests of the proletariat, but the interests of human nature, of man in general, who belongs to no class, has no reality . . . True socialism spreads like an epidemic. The robe of speculative cobwebs, embroidered with flowers of rhetoric, steeped in the

dew of sickly sentiment . . . served to wonderfully increase the sale of their goods among the public.[3]

During the early part of this century the great debate over Bernsteinian revisionism raged inside German social democracy. Luxemburg, referring back to the 'true' socialists criticized by Marx and Engels, slammed Bernstein in the following terms:

> Before Marx and independent of him, there also existed a labour movement and various social systems . . . The basing of socialism on the moral notion of justice, on a struggle against the mode of distribution instead of against the mode of production; the conception of class antagonism as an antagonism between the poor and the rich; the effort to graft the 'cooperative principle' on capitalist economy already existed before him [Bernstein] And, in their time, these theories, in spite of their insufficiency, were actual theories of the proletarian class struggle; they were the children's seven league boots, thanks to which the proletariat learned to walk upon the scene of history . . . But after the development of the class struggle itself and its social conditions had led to the abandonment of these theories and to the formulation of the principles of scientific socialism . . . there can be no socialism outside of Marxian socialism . . . Therefore, the return to pre-Marxist socialist theories today does not in the least signify a return to the seven-league boots of the childhood of the proletariat. No it is a return to the puny, worn-out slippers of the bourgeoisie . . . According to Bernstein, for example, democracy is an inevitable stage in the development of modern society. To him, as to the bourgeois theoreticians of liberalism, democracy is the great fundamental law of historical development in general whose realization must be served by all of the active forces of political life. However presented in such an absolute form, this is totally false; it is a petty-bourgeois and superficial schematization of the results of a very short peak of bourgeois development, roughly the last twenty-five or thirty years. We reach entirely different conclusions when we examine more closely the historical development of democracy and at the same time the general political history of capitalism.[4]

During the post-war period social democrats proclaimed the end of ideology, the humanization of capitalism through the welfare state and the triumph of democracy. And, revolutionary rhetoric to one side, Eurocommunists and Stalinists in the West adopted a similar programme. The Eurocommunist strategy explicitly rejects any revolutionary perspective as the following example from the *British Road to Socialism* (1968) demonstrates:

> In this way, by political action, using our democratic rights to transform traditional (i.e. capitalist) institutions, parliament can be made into the effective instrument of the peoples' will, able to carry through legislation to challenge capitalist power, and replace capitalism by socialism.[5]

And through the later 1970s and the 1980s there has been a resurgence of utopian or new 'true' socialism as Wood (1986) has termed it.[6] Class struggle and the building of class unity have been pushed out of view to be replaced by the relative, if not absolute, autonomy of ideology, politics and culture understood in strictly superstructural tems. Wright (1986) captures the shift like this:

> The increasing awareness of the importance of democracy has been one of the hallmarks of recent political debates on the left. Indeed, it would not be going too far to say that, at least in the American context, the problem of democracy has tended to displace the problem of socialism from centre stage of leftist political discourse.[7]

Two recent discussions of revisionism, by Mandel (1979) and Wood (1986) have distilled the essential features which underly the theory of Bowles and Gintis and discussed in this volume in some detail by Sharp.[8] For convenience of reference and summary we set out these two analyses in table form below (table 1).

In our view what is flawed about Bowles and Gintis' writing is that they have attempted to show how the pursuit of liberal democracy can be a sufficient strategy for socialism. In order to show how democracy is related to the development of socialism they have developed a theory of the liberal democratic state in which they see a major contradiction between the rights liberal democracy invests in persons and the rights capitalism invests in private property. For them this contradiction can be exploited through the ballot box as a means of extending persons' rights into the capitalists' sphere of property rights. And in education they draw on the more progressive elements of liberal philosophy of education, as articulated by Dewey for example, to argue for the democratization of educational structures:

> The admirable quality of self-development philosophy of education lies in the power it draws from embracing a central category of the discourse of rights: the right to freedom from unwarranted interference, of which John Stuart Mill was the most eloquent exponent. Its drawback of being incurably a-social, is easily remedied by recourse to the communitarian emphasis on joint democratic control of conditions of social life by affected groups and individuals. No doubt there are formidable obstacles in the development of such a philosophy of educational structure and we are not

Table 1: Characteristics of Reformism

	New 'True' Socialism (after Wood)	*The Strategy of Eurocommunism (after Mandel)*
1	The working class has not produced a revolutionary movement.	Can only achieve socialism in the industrialized countries with the consensus of the majority of the population.
2	Ideology and politics are (relatively? absolutely?) autonomous from economic class relations.	Majority support bourgeois-parliamentary institutions so these must be preserved.
3	The working class has no 'fundamental' interest in socialism.	State is neutral or can be progressively emptied of its bourgeois content.
4	Formation of a socialist movement in principle independent of class.	Head-on class confrontation must be avoided; this would lead to defeat of the working class and destroy parliament.
5	Political force can be organized out of 'popular' elements independently of class.	To win support the workers must fight for structural reforms which will transform the capitalist system by stages.
6	Objectives of socialism are universal human goals which transcend class.	Essential stage now is the democratization of economic life and state institutions.
7	The struggle for socialism can be conceived of as a plurality of 'democratic' struggles.	Must build a wide alliance of workers, peasants, small and middle bourgeoisie. System of private property cannot be fundamentally challenged at this stage.

personally equipped to meet this task. But it remains central to the growth of an effective movement toward socialist education.[9]

If Bowles and Gintis do not feel they are able to now carry through this project at the school level there are others such as Apple and Giroux who have taken up this task. Overall what this approach to strategy amounts to is the attempt to use popular struggles to democratize the institutions of the state, at central or local level: or to put it another way they are reaffirming Rudi Deutschke's commitment to the long march through the institutions.

There are, then, a number of issues associated with this approach to strategy that bear closer examination. These are the cogency and viability of exploiting the contradiction Bowles and Gintis identify between the rights of persons invested by the liberal democratic state and the property rights which the same state protects with force and fosters; the plausibility of the strategy of the long march through the institutions; the role of the working class in this strategy and its relationship to other groups in struggle; and the role of education in the transition to socialism.

Bowles and Gintis' theory of the democratization of the capitalist state rests on the proposition, that there is a fundamental contradiction between the rights of persons and the negation of those rights as instanced in the rights of property. What this means is that people are assigned democratic rights as regards political and civil society but are, under capitalism, subject to the authoritarian demands of the capitalist workplace. For Bowles and Gintis the political mileage to be gained from this contradiction lies in people's recognition that their rights as persons are not consistently applied to all spheres of their lives. But as the basis for the development of a radical political consciousness such a contradiction can only be considered feeble precisely because it refers to a debacle in thought rather than social structure. As such it is a typically idealist strategy and one that Bowles and Gintis have employed before.

In chapter 8 of *Schooling in Capitalist America* they argue that the oversupply of educated labour promotes a similar contradiction in thought because middle class graduates will face proletarianized work conditions. The fact that many graduates will be confronted with work that does not match their expectations for an intrinsically interesting career prompts Bowles and Gintis' view that this will produce a radicalized white collar proletariat. What, of course, they overlook is the discipline imposed by the 'dull compulsion of work'. And what such an oversight suggests is that the basis of revolutionary activity should be located within the contradictions of capitalist social and economic structures not in the contradictions of thought they generate. Unlike the idealist liberalism of Bowles and Gintis it is the ABC of Marxism to locate the revolutionary potential of the working class in the material base of capitalist society. No doubt Bowles and Gintis will dismiss this as crass economism but they effectively leave unexplained the very contradictions in thought which their ameliorative strategies depend on. For a more detailed discussion of their idealism and the retreat from class struggle and exploitation to discourse, subject-subject dialectics and domination we refer the reader once again to Sharp's chapter.

Complementing this view about contradictions in the ideology of the liberal capitalist state is a set of propositions similar to those set out in table 1 above, regarding the nature of the capitalist state which makes plausible the idea that it can be captured by the process of democratization. Here Bowles and Gintis (1982) argue that the state should not be considered a reflection either of capital's dominance or of a balance of class forces forged within the dynamics of accumulation. They reject these Marxian propositions on the state in favour of a view which describes the state as a contradictory totality. In addition, the state is seen as integral to the production of crises as well as to its their resolution. This latter view enables them to side with the New Right, and supply-side economics in claiming that the state has played a seminal role in creating the present economic crisis. In contrast they claim that Marxists and liberals,

> have persisted in treating the tendency toward crisis solely as a

> congenital weakness of capitalist accumulation, to which the state may respond more (liberal) or less (Marxist) effectively.[10]

In consequence they claim that their theory of the state can account for the reproduction and transformation of boundary relations among structures participating in the social totality. Decoded this means that the state not only is in part responsible for the present economic crisis but that it also can have a significant influence on the balance of class forces.

What Bowles and Gintis are trying to do here is to open up the theoretical space which allows for the possibility that the democratization of the state can have a significant effect on class relations, pushing them to the point of socialism. In the context of the present crisis they argue that capital seeks to depoliticize the accumulation process and commodify the state. And it does this by trying,

> to curtail the transportation of practices from the liberal democratic state to capitalist production and to promote a transportation of practices from capitalist production to the liberal democratic state.[11]

What this means is that capital will try to prevent the person rights invested by the state being extended to the sphere of production. And as a counter-attacking measure capital will try to promote the privatization of the state. How then are workers to respond to this? They argue,

> A possible viable response of workers is to politicize the accumulation process and to strengthen and extend democratic control of the state apparatus. While the impetus to politicize and democratize the accumulation process is hardly the dominant strand of labour's defensive programme today, it may be seen as a possible culmination of the post World War II accord. For the 'logic of the process' of class conflict initiated by the accord is precisely the conflict of person rights versus property rights.[12]

It is clear from these quotations that Bowles and Gintis no longer see the state as a capitalist state. Rather, in the language of pluralist liberalism, it is neutral territory to which the protagonists come to scrap for advantage. The metaphor of transportation encourages such a view, prompting the image of the state as an island linked by causeways to the two competing sides. Indeed, the idea that the democratization of the state is possible and that this will lead to the democratization of production relations is only plausible if the state is viewed as neutral, and it basically expresses nothing more than a vague utopian liberalism.

A central problem for Bowles and Gintis is that they make a massive conceptual leap from the claim that the state can be a factor in the development of crises and the balance of class forces to the absolutely illegitimate claim that it can therefore be used as a means to alter the fundamental nature of capitalist society. We would argue that it is quite consistent and more plausible to claim that the state may help create crises and alter the balance of class forces, but that the limits of tolerance to the state's activities are determined by the accumulation process. In other words the state may well be a site of conflict but the conflict and the rules that govern it are fundamentally determined by the conditions of capital accumulation. Furthermore, it is a central tenet of historical materialism that the state is a class state, prepared long before the last instance to use every means of physical repression to ensure the conditions of accumulation. Even a cursory understanding of labour history in the USA not to mention the proclivity of late imperial America to prop up anti-democratic dictatorships, attack and even bomb unfriendly régimes, and to demand access throughout the capitalist world for its nuclear ships and weapons is enough to dispense these naive notions to the wind. To a very large degree American freedoms at home are materially maintained by unfreedoms elsewhere on the globe. We do not deny of course that the state is, to use the language of Bowles and Gintis, a site of struggle. But we also insist that this struggle is determined by the vicissitudes of accumulation — most directly by the rate of profitability.

However, as we have seen, the central strategy recommended by Bowles and Gintis is 'to strengthen and extend democratic control of the state apparatus'. What can be expected from this logic of person rights in conflict with property rights? Bowles and Gintis answer as follows:

> demands posed as universal rights and movements constituted by the universal discourse of liberal democracy are prone to become class demands and class movements. The extension of the suffrage to workers is a prime example of this process. The crisis of capital may thus hasten the realization that the struggle over universal rights — the right to participate in political decisions, the right of a free press — is a class struggle. If we are correct in this conjecture, the ongoing conflict over the reconstitution of the accumulation process may starkly reveal the anti-democratic imperatives of capitalism as a system and thus unify for socialists two of the most powerful potential mass issues in the United States today: the defence and extension of democracy and the defence of living standards. Capitalism may survive the encounter. But liberal democracy may well be radically transformed — either toward a corporate authoritarianism as a condition of capital's survival or toward an instrument, however imperfect, of popular power.[13]

The language of democracy, on this view, has the potential to be transformed into a programme of working class demands. Let us test this hypothesis using the revolutionary Marxist analysis of suffrage made by Clara Zetkin and Rosa Luxemburg. If the Bowles and Gintis theory does not hold up in the central case of suffrage then there is little reason to uphold it in any other area.

First, there can be no question here of not defending and extending the living conditions, political and economic power of the working class. This naturally includes politicizing the state to the highest degree as an arena of struggle through which the working class develops its strength, learns about the struggle for socialism, and builds unity. But this is very different from posing the strategy of socialism as the extension of democracy, as if, bit by bit, the neutral state will be transformed into a state fully responsive to popular demand.

Zetkin, in her well known address, 'Women's right to vote' does not pose suffrage as a universal right grounded in the discourse of liberal democracy. On the contrary,

> we demand it as a social right which is anchored in the revolutionized economic activity and in the revolutionized state and personal consciousness of women.[14]

Far from a universal right being transformed into a class demand, something like the reverse is envisaged by Zetkin's argument. In the first place Zetkin points out that winning the vote does not touch the most significant question for the position of women under capitalism; 'private property in which is rooted the exploitation and suppression of one human being by another'. While winning the vote, and extending the social wage no doubt puts some limits on the ability of the capitalist class to accumulate, suffrage nevertheless does not eliminate the social relations of production. For Zetkin the winning of universal suffrage was important as a way of arming 'female proletarians in their battle against class exploitation and class rule.' Zetkin rejects some 'bloodless principle' of liberal democracy as the basis for socialist struggle in favour of a mass and class demand of the proletariat. What Zetkin is pointing to is the priority of establishing a class demand. So for example, she observes that gains against the bourgeois state in Belgium, Holland, Russia and Austria were only won using mass mobilization and strikes. But further she notes that the female sex does not form 'one phalanx to fight for universal women's suffrage'. Bourgeois women do not stand united and are 'even more reluctant to fight energetically'. In reply, Zetkin suggests a united front (march separately, fight together) with bourgeois suffragettes but always remembering that:

> our demand for the women's right to vote is no suffragettes' request but a mass and class demand of the proletariat.[15]

Luxemburg a few years later in 1912 added to this perspective which clearly rejects any reformist commitment to what Wood (1986) calls the 'transformative effects of liberal discourse'. Luxemburg argues:

> The working class has always had to prove its maturity for political freedom by a successful revolutionary uprising of the masses. Only when Divine Right on the throne and the best and noblest men of the nation actually felt the calloused fist of the proletariat on their eyes and its knee on their chests, only then did they feel confidence in the political maturity of the people, and felt it with the speed of lightning.[16]

Obviously, the argument here does not proceed from demands posed as universal rights within the discourse of liberal democracy to class demands and class movements as the liberalism of Bowles and Gintis supposes. The fighting organization of the working class (in the example considered, the millions of women who can strengthen revolutionary social democracy) sets the goals of socialist democracy to be built 'when the present society falls in ruins under the hammer strokes of the revolutionary proletariat'. Where Bowles and Gintis rely on the transformative power of liberal discourse Luxemburg and Zetkin, look to the force of organized working class struggle to extend the rights of workers, 'keep' the liberal state 'honest' and win unity for the further struggle; all with the simple aim, not of extending bourgeois democracy, but of demolishing it.

Judged against the criterion of historical materialism the Bowles and Gintis hypothesis has both the language and lines of determination of class struggle back to front. Where the Bowles and Gintis position moves from liberal democratic discourse to an ill-defined class movement Marxism insists on moving from revolutionary class movement to socialist democracy. The difference here, as we indicated at the beginning of this chapter, is fundamental and has been part of the wider labour movement since its more self conscious origins. The struggle against the social democratic (modern usage) illusions of the kind perpetrated by Bowles and Gintis is an important task for all socialists though it might be nice to think that such scores were settled by Marx and Engels in 1848, or at the very latest by Luxemburg against Bernstein's reformism and Kautsky's centrism. But unfortunately, such has not been the case.

In *Democracy and Capitalism* Bowles and Gintis extend their analysis of liberal democracies but the core of their argument remains much the same as their earlier works; that in Western capitalist societies, at least, the motor of history is not class warfare but the clash between personal and property rights.[17] Despite the material and psychological stranglehold of a divisive social system the human voice cries out for universal rights; the right to free speech, of association, of suffrage, of religion, and so on. There is, if you like, a popular press for the universal 'rights of man' which goes beyond or cannot be simply explained by peoples' place in the economic order or by the level of their material comfort. Again, this argument has been made before for it lies right at the heart of the philosophy and politics of anarchism. The interesting thing is that a reading of anarchist theory and practice reveals and insight into the very difficulty with Bowles and Gintis' argument that they seem unaware of.

Quite rightly Bowles and Gintis ask why it is that the clash between personal and property rights has not been cataclysmic. If a contradiction is big enough to drive history then it's large enough to blow apart capitalist democracies. What has kept the lid on, they maintain, is a series of accords between capital and labour, the last one of which is the accord of Keynesian economics. In a 'democracy', with the state as arbiter, the workers are able to push their personal rights and win some concessions. The difficulty with this reasoning, as anarchists have long pointed out, is that the surest way to lose rights is to sell them off. If there is a demand for universal freedom they argued, then democracy, rather than being the outcome of the demand, is in fact the very thing that will crush it. Those who hold power use a process of incorporation to effectively deny others their rights, backed up by the legal and military power of the state should the ruse fail. For our purposes it does not matter whether power is viewed psychologically and socially, as many anarchists have suggested, or economically, as Marxists argue. The result is the same. The 'accord' is a victory for one side while the other side thinks it has done well. How this happens is not difficult to understand, but, simple or not, it is precisely the mechanism that sinks the extension of democracy as a method of changing or destroying capitalism.

Personal rights which contrast and clash with property rights, as Bowles and Gintis suggest, are in fact defined within the ideology of the liberal democracies in which they function. They don't stand outside of capitalism, and consequently they are incorporated rights because their use, limits and extension are controlled by the logic of property. To use an example; the right to associate and to combine, to form unions in other words, a right won after prolonged and bitter struggle, was won in exchange for other rights, because an accord is a barter system. Consequently workers can only associate and combine 'reasonably'. To ensure this the state has a plethora of laws which govern union behaviour dealing with registration, control of funds, manner of picketing and so on. Bowles and Gintis would not dispute this; they would say that practices had been transported from capitalist production to the liberal democratic state. However, these laws represent the rights of property, but they are rights expressed ideologically as personal rights. They prevent unions from hindering the right of non-interference, the right of individual capitalists, or non-involved workers, to go about their lawful business. However it is this lawful business which is precisely the issue at stake. The upshot is that unions are often unable to operate effectively because they seem to be abusing the rights of others. In this case the workers' personal rights stand not in contradiction to the rights of property (capital), but rather operate within the framework created by it. The British miners' strike in 1984 showed this most clearly. When the miners attemped to picket effectively in support of their claim for the right to work (which incidentally, Bowles and

Gintis state as the second proposition on which post-liberal democracy should be built) they were then met by the full might of the state. Put simply, the capitalist state resorted to force once it realized that the miners were pressing their personal rights away from the bargaining table and were refusing to accept the state's definition or description of that right. They wanted that right on their own terms (as their class right we would argue) and for that they paid the price. The point is, of course, that as long as personal rights are defined within the framework of capitalist ideology then they are incorporated rights and whatever is won on the strength of them is at best a compromise within capitalism. To struggle through democracy is to struggle in the uniform of the opposition. Inevitably, and this is the real point, if the clash over rights is to have any solid outcome then personal rights have to be taken out of the realm in which they are defined. That means revolutionary action and it is that conclusion that Bowles and Gintis seem determined to avoid.

We could go on and point out other rights which have been incorporated within the capitalist state. The public debate over the miners' tactics was largely constructed by the 'free' press. Freedom of speech is another hard won personal right, but it now hardly stands in opposition to the rights of property. It is doubtful whether there would be any capitalists in liberal democracies who would demand a denial of free speech in order to defend property rights. This is for two reasons. Firstly, the right to free speech has been incorporated: capitalism has taken the right as its own with the result that in controlling the press it controls the paramenters of the public debate. It uses the press to push its own ideology. It could thus use a universal freedom (speech) to seemingly defend other freedoms such as non-interference. In our example above, it could defend the rights of reasonable people to be protected from the miners leaders whom it characterized as anti-democratic madmen and fascists. Secondly, large publishing industries and television corporations make a mint out of free speech. Television in particular depends on revenues from capitalist organizations which it uses to promote stereotyped attitudes ad characters which ultimately support the status quo. In turn, companies depend on advertising to promote their image and increase their profits. It would not be too fanciful to say that Coca Cola, for example, rather than finding 'free speech' antithetical to its property rights, in fact depends upon it for its existence. In a similar vein drug companies in liberal democracies where state health care is assured use the right to health to promote their wares. This has culminated in the Distillers litigation farce or equally farcical and just as tragic, milk powder companies offering their products to third world mothers. The right to freedom from interference continues to be used by gun companies in the USA to defend a citizen's right to bear arms. Further, the arms industries of the liberal democracies, and the foreign policies of their governments, are premised on the personal right of freedom from interference. That is to say, though the motivation be profit it is passed ideologically as the defence of the personal rights of the citizens of the free West. Simply put it is nonsense to suggest that the pursuit of personal rights can be used to exploit a chink in the capitalist armour. Capitalism takes the rights as its own and uses them to defend itself. How the working class and all oppressed people are to work their way out of this conundrum we do not believe Bowles and Gintis resolve at all.

In our view the ballot box of bourgeois democracy is a two-edged weapon. On the one hand it has been used by the working class to further their claims for a social wage, and it has been instrumental in protecting civil liberties — up to a point. On the other hand, while these achievements should be recognized, it is also the case that bourgeois democracy fragments issues and obscures real interests. Herein lies a major problem for theorists such as Bowles and Gintis who seek to democratize the means of production through the ballot box.

An issue within this approach concerns the interests and relationships between the actors in this populist development of democracy. When the question of class interests is raised in connection with a strategy of the long march through the institutions there is a clear danger both in the short and the long term that it is middle class interests that will be served. This is because the state institutions of capitalism are run by the middle class. If these institutions are to be democratized then the main thrust will come from those who have the knowledge and skills to do the job — the middle class. Now insofar as this strategy is flawed the long march will amount to no more than reforms which will create a greater degree of autonomy for the middle class. Moreover, within this scenario it is unclear what role the working class will play. Their role is made problematic by the fact that they do not vote as a class in a bourgeois democracy, rather the issues that would unite them as a class are fragmented and their interests obscured. How then are they to act as a class to protect and further their interests? But of course the logic of bourgeois democratic politics which fragments class issues also obscures the relationship between class exploitation and gender and racial oppression; and more specifically, their common interest in socialism. And so we now find post-Marxist theorists of class, race and gender, reflecting the pluralist appearance of liberal democracies by arguing that the causes of the various oppressions are different, and hence the interests of the various oppressed groups are also separate. Given the centripetal force of bourgeois democracy the question remains as to the theoretical rationale by which these groups can be united. And this in turn raises the spectre of middle class reformism because if these groups are not united, it will be the middle class, of whatever gender or race, that will gain.

As we have just indicated the fragmentation of issues and interests which occurs in bourgeois democracy has been reflected in the theories of post-Marxists. These theorists argue that economic exploitation is causally no more basic than other forms of oppression and that action against oppression is action against causes which are distinct from economic causes. In other words the relationship between class exploitation and gender and racial oppression are contingent. As such the much vaunted pluralism of liberal democracy reproduces itself at the level of theory.

What is clearly needed at the level of theory is an analysis which shows that the relationships between exploitation and the various forms of oppression are necesssary and not contingent; so that if class exploitation is directly generated from the framework of the capitalist mode of production, then the latter also produces significant aspects of gender and racial oppression. The practical political corollary to such an argument is the development of a revolutionary party which harnesses the apparently disparate issues and interests of the mass working class in the drive to socialism.

It is important, therefore, that the necessary connections between class exploitation and gender and racial oppression are made. In doing so, however, we are concerned not to make the category mistake of reducing all forms of oppression to class exploitation. In this respect the work of Milton Fisk has been helpful and it is upon this we draw to sketch out the connections we think are necessary to the building of a genuinely socialist party.

In his paper 'Feminism, socialism and historical materialism' Fisk sets out to develop a view of historical materialism that,

> does not commit us either to the subordination of the feminist struggle, the class struggle or to the complete separation of the one from the other. On this view of historical materialism both struggles are to be set within a common materialist framework. This framework, made up of basic economic tendencies, is primary, and in relation to it the factors of class and sex are given equal status.[18]

In order to develop such a view Fisk attacks the idea that historical materialism can be appealed to in order to eliminate or blur the autonomy of struggles against oppression. Such a view presupposes that there is a direct link between economic changes and all other changes in society. This ignores the fact that causes can be identified at two levels. The first and primary level of causation is that of underlying causal structures which create a framework within which the secondary level of stimulus causes are connected within an overall pattern. What Fisk then goes on to show is that the stimulus causes of class and gender oppression are intimately connected by the framework of capitalism. For example, in the nineteenth century the division between home and work and the attendant socialization of labour by capitalism created a contradiction between the demands of patriarchy and those of capitalism. This is because patriarchal control over the household was loosened by women working. This break in the control of the father over the household had a revolutionary significance because it created the space for the emergence of feminism. At the same time capitalism buttressed the emergence of new forms of patriarchy in the way it has created categories of work which are set aside as 'women's work'. Fisk warns that it is a mistake to claim that capitalism has produced this contempory version of patriarchy because,

> Capitalism socialized labor, but it did not socialize the control of women's labor. It was patriarchy's response to the challenge of socialized labor that led directly to the socialized control of women's labor and reproductive activity. Capitalism was certainly the framework within which this response could be effective in the way it was . . . in view of the latent tendencies (of capitalism) to encourage any divisions in the workforce in the capitalist workplace.[19]

This, then, provides an example of the framework model in which the independent tendencies of patriarchy are limited and channeled by the framework set down by the tendencies produced by capitalism. In recognition of the limits and possibilities placed on patriarchy by capitalism Fisk argues that a critique of capitalism and a socialist strategy against it are an integral part of a consistent feminism. But this does not mean that the feminist struggle must be collapsed into the class struggle for,

> . . . the present struggle for cultural hegemony against patriarchy is a condition for sexual equality later. Winning sexual equality is not just a matter of eliminating the class context that puts limits on the struggle for sexual equality; the potential for feminist struggle opened up by the division of patriarchal control has to be realized all along the way.[20]

In this way the struggle against patriarchy can be seen as at once autonomous and intimately related to the struggle for socialism. In our view a similar argument can be mounted for the struggle against racism. Fisk, following a long tradition, is arguing once again for the development of a revolutionary party drawn from all members of the working class, including women and blacks, and all those who have an interest in the struggle for socialism against capitalism. What is more, it is a struggle which must overthrow capitalism for anything less will ensure a continuation of bourgeois democracy. For this reason the class struggle and socialist revolution remain the necessary conditions for the building of socialist democracy. Bowles and Gintis might well agree with Marxism that capitalism is the first stage of socialism, but this does not mean that socialism can be built by a gradual wearing down of capitalism or an evolutionary attenuation of capitalist social relations. To base a strategy on this premise is to give away any chance of guaranteeing the kind of freedom for future human development Bowles and Gintis claim to be so concerned about. It is, more immediately, to deny any real efficacy to, or success for, the great movements committed to liberation, whether of women, of racial minorities, or against war. And that, let us all be warned, is to weigh the balance of history in favour of barbarism as the outcome, rather than socialism.

Notes

1 For a discussion of these points see, for example: Davis, M. (1986) *Prisoners of the American Dream: Politics and Economy in the History of the Working Class*, London, Verso; Moody, K. (1985) 'Stumbling in the dark: American labor's failed response', and Brenner, R. (1985) 'The paradox of social democracy: 'The American case', Pfeif, F. Davis, M. and Sprinkler, M. (Eds) *The Year Left*, pp. 32–108; Chester, E. (1982) 'Revolutionary socialists and independent political action', *Against The Current*, 2, 1, pp. 33–7.

2 Lauder, H., Freeman-Moir, D. J., and Scott, J. A. (1986) 'What is to be done with radical academic practice?, *Capital and Class*, 29, pp. 83–110.

3 Marx, K. (1848) 'The communist manifesto', *Collected Works* (1976), vol 5, New York, International Press, p. 467.

4 Luxemburg, R. (1908) 'Social reform or revolution' in Howard, D. (Ed), (1971) *Seclected Political Writings of Rosa Luxemburg*, New York, Monthly Review Press, pp. 130—1.

5 British Communist Party (1968) *British Road to Socialism*, p. 49.

6 Wood, E. M. (1986) *The Retreat From Class: A New 'True' Socialism*, London, Verso.

7 Wright, E. O. (1986) *Classes*, London, Verso, p. 287.

8 Mandel, E. (1978) *From Stalinism to Eurocommunism: The Bitter Fruits of Socialism in One Country*, London, NLB.

9 Gintis, H. and Bowles, S. (1980, 1981 and 1987) 'Contradiction and reproduction in educational theory' in Barton, L., Meighan, R. and Walker, S. (Eds) *Schooling, Ideology and the Curriculum*, Lewes, Falmer Press; Dale, R. *et al* (Eds), *Education and the State: Volume 1: Schooling and the National Interest*, Lewes, Falmer Press, p. 58; and chapter 2, p. 30 in this volume.

10 Bowles, S. and Gintis, H. (1982) 'The crisis of liberal democratic capitalism: The case of the United States,' *Politics and Society*, 11, 1, p. 60.

11 *Ibid.*, p. 92.

12 *Ibid.*

13 *Ibid.*, pp. 92–3.

14 Zetkin, C. (1907) 'Women's right to vote', in Foner, P. S., and Davis, A. Y. (Eds) *Clara Zetkin: Selected Writings*, New York, International Publishers, pp. 99–100.

15 *Ibid.*, p. 105.

16 Luxemburg, R. (1912) 'Women's suffrage and class struggle,' in Howard, D. (Ed) (1971) *Selected Political Writings of Rosa Luxemburg*, p. 218.

17 Bowles, S. and Gintis, H. (1986) *Democracy ad Capitalism*, London, Routledge and Kegan Paul. This book arrived too late for any detailed consideration in this chapter. However, the authors plan a critique of its essentially reformist positions in the near future.

18 Fisk, M. (1981) 'Feminism, socialism and historical materialism, *Praxis International*, p. 118.

19 *Ibid.*, p. 132.

20 *Ibid.*, p. 134.

12 *Can There Be a Liberal Philosophy of Education in a Democratic Society?*

Samuel Bowles and Herbert Gintis

Our recent critique of Marxism as the basis for a theory of democracy has prompted some, in this volume and elsewhere, to suggest that we have embraced liberalism as a political philosophy. This impression, however, is quite misplaced. It thus may be fruitful to address the relationship of liberalism and educational theory and practice somewhat more directly than we did in *Schooling in Capitalist America*.

Two fundamental partitions are central to the liberal philosophical tradition spanning the three centuries from the contributions of Thomas Hobbes and John Locke in the seventeenth century to the great liberal thinkers of the twentieth century.[1] First, social space is divided into a private and a public realm. The public realm of social space is considered to be the state, whereas the private realm is constituted by the family and the capitalist economy. Second, individuals are partitioned into two groups: rational agents whose intentions and choices are the subject of the explicit political and economic theory of liberalism, and those who for reasons of age, incapacity, or citizenship are excluded from this privileged category. The logic of liberal political philosophy may be underlined if we term the first *choosers* and the second *learners*.

Liberalism is a discourse — a way of talking and writing — which makes essential use of the private public partition of social space and of the learner chooser partition of social agents.

As a result of the partition of individuals into learners and choosers, liberal political philosophy has a defect which renders its model of choice incompatible with a democratic theory of education. This is the assumption that the individual enters into a choice situation with externally constituted goals — the 'preferences' of neoclassical economics, and the 'interests' of political science. Thus where the problem of intentional action — agency — arises, and hence where considerations of liberty and democratic accountability apply, individuals can be taken as given. This handy fiction makes the argument for individual liberty extremely simple and elegant — consider, for instance, the following well-known passage from John Stuart Mill's *On Liberty*:

> The only purpose for which power can be rightfully exercised over any member of a civilized community against his will is to prevent harm to others. His own good . . . is not a sufficient warrant.[2]

But by the same token it undermines the defense of popular sovereignty. For taking preferences as given, while allowing us to recognize democracy's contribution to the proper aggregation of wants, obscures the contribution of democratic institutions to human development — their unique capacity to foster in people the ability intelligently and creatively to control their lives. Liberalism tells us that people make decisions. But the liberal conception of action must be reconstructed to recognize that decisions also make people.[3]

Of course the liberal model of the individual recognizes that preferences and capacities are formed somewhere. Its error is to assume that where individuals are in the process of becoming, problems of agency and choice are absent. For instance, Mill's famous proclamation of the involability of individual preferences cited above is followed immediately by the less frequently cited proviso:

> It is, perhaps, hardly necessary to say that . . . we are not speaking of children or of young persons below the age which the law may fix as that of manhood or womanhood . . . (who) . . . must be protected against their own actions . . . For the same reason we may leave out of consideration those backward states of society in which the race itself may be considered as in its nonage . . . Despotism is a legitimate mode of government in dealing with barbarians, provided the end be their improvement.

Mill here erects an opposition between 'choosers' on the one hand and 'learners' on the other, and justifies a system of relations of domination and subordination between the former and the latter. This opposition is characteristic of liberal discourse in general. Choosers are the knights in shining armor of liberalism, while learners represent a residual category — individuals whose statuses do not include, and whose behavior does not support (be it temporarily or *in perpetuum*) the right of free choice; in short, those who are not deemed to be rational agents.[4]

The status of 'chooser' has always applied in liberal discourse to educated, propertied, white male heads of households, and variously through history to others as well. The status of 'learner' has always applied in liberal discourse to children, prisoners, the insane, and the uncivilized. It has also applied variously to women, servants, workers, as well as specific races and cultures which, by virtue of their biological constitution or social station, are deemed to be more or less permanently denied the status of rational agent.

The learning/choosing opposition, in addition to permeating liberal consciousness, is reflected in the very taxonomy of the traditional social sciences. Economics and political science deal with 'choosers', and exhibit scant concern for the formation of wills, while sociology, anthropology, and psychology deal with 'learners' in the process of formation of wills, hence lying outside the logic of choice. Perhaps it is for this reason the maximizing models of economics found a ready welcome in political science but are yet to make serious inroads into the other social sciences.

If we combine the learning/choosing partition with the private/public distinction, we arrive at four basic types of action accessible to liberal theory: learning in the private sphere, choosing in the private sphere, learning the public sphere and choosing in the public sphere. Contemporary liberals prescribe a set of favored social institutions for the regulation of each type of action, some of which are illustrated in figure 1.

Figure 1: The Liberal Partitions and Favored Social Institutions

	Social Sphere	
Action	*Private*	*Public*
Learning	Patriarchal families	Hierarchical schools
Choosing	Competitive markets	Democratic elections

The crux of the liberal learning/choosing partition can be summarized by reference to figure 1. First, institutions deemed educational or correctional are exempted from scrutiny according to the principles of rational agency, freedom, and choice. Within the liberal discourse one does not ask. for instance, whether schools are democractic. Since such favored institutions of learning as families and schools are not required to be accountable to their participants, central forms of domination governing personal development are obscured. Second, liberalism relegates choice to an arena of personal autonomy ostensibly devoid of developmental potential. While liberal institutions — market and ballot box — are praised as sensitively attuned to expressing the wills of consumers and citizens, this sensitivity fails to extend to a most central area of personal control: the choice as to how individuals are to develop their preferences, their capacities for social participation, and their abilities to make critical and informed choices. Liberalism claims that the market place and the ballot box allow people to get what they want. But liberalism is silent on how people might get to be what they want to be, and how they might get to want what they want to want.

This defect in the liberal model of action helps us understand how the golden age of free trade and the 'democratic revolution' also saw the birth of systems of institutional dependence (for example, compulsory education) and social control (for example, conscription) to an extent unparalleled in human history. Our point here is hardly to mourn some fictitious idyllic past when popular forces impresses upon society a free and democratic structure of personal development. Forms of domination (class, ethnic, patriarchal, religious, and other) clearly underlay personal formation in pre-capitalist society. Indeed, the expansionary tendency of personal rights has doubtless undermined many such ancient forms of oppression. We suggest, rather, that it is in the nature of the learning/choosing partition systematically to obfuscate the issue of domination in human development; that the liberal state cannot account for its own manner of imposing preferences is simply a case in point.

In our view, learning and choosing represent polar categories of a more general form of social action. In place of the archetypal 'child' and 'adult' of liberal theory, we say that the individual constitutes preferences and develops personal powers through acting in the world. This model thus supplements Mill's vision of the rational chooser with Marx's conception of the formative power of action. For it was the Marx of *Capital* who stressed that labor is

> a process going on between man and nature, a process in which man, through his own activity, initiates, regulates, and controls the material reactions between himself and nature. He confronts nature as one of her own forces . . . By thus acting on the external world and changing it, he at the same time changes his own nature.[5]

Using this becoming-by-acting model, schools, families, workplaces, the electoral process, playgrounds, town meetings, sports arena, markets, and hospitals can all be assessed according to the same criteria: those of liberty, popular accountability, and contribution to personal development.

Our unification of learning and choosing, in rejecting the traditional status of the child, also thereby rejects the status of adult. Those traditional liberal defenses of liberty based on the sanctity of individual preferences are thus severely compromised. When individuals are at once choosers and learners, the boundaries between liberty, popular sovereignty, and legitimate authority become blurred. A simple example should illustrate our point here. Ought the producer or consumer determine the nature of a service delivered? If the consumer is considered a 'chooser,' the service is called a commodity, and consumer sovereignty is deemed to hold. If, by contrast, the consumer is considered a 'learner' (for example, a child), the preferences of others count. Schools, for instance, teach what children *should* know, not what they *wish* to know. If we reject the learning/choosing dichotomy, however, we must search for new principles to resolve the issue. How do we deal, for example, with the case of the craft which considers not only what consumers want, but what will also contribute to the development of consumers' capacities to appreciate? Or, again, students who fully accept the notion of learning and perhaps even revere the superior wisdom of their teachers, but wish to participate in making educational policy? These, we submit, are not anomalous cases. They are the rule, not the exception to the rule.

The use of a becoming-by-acting model of individual choice provides educational philosophy, not with a set of ready made political slogans, but rather with a challenging intellectual enterprise: how might the centrality of individual choice and the commitment to liberty and popular sovereignty be preserved, while at the same time the myths of the autonomous individual and the fully-formed chooser are rejected?

We address this problem by recognizing that personal development is in general best served through an interaction of two strategies: exercising one's freedom to choose independently of collective sentiment, and entering into mutual, reciprocal, and participatory action with others to achieve commonly defined goals. These two strategies are precisely Albert Hirschman's twin notions of 'exit' and 'voice'.[6] The critique of the liberal model of action in terms of exit and voice is then simply stated. By taking preferences and interests as pre-given, liberalism equates agency with exit. Individuals exercise their rights either through market and ballot box. Both involve presenting a 'menu' of alternatives, of which the preferred can be chosen by the individual in social isolation. The power of the chooser, then, is limited to his or her ability to abandon a product or a political party — i.e., to 'exit'. The market economy and the liberal democratic state, then, stress exit to the virtual exclusion of voice, and representation as opposed to the virtual exclusion of participation. The balance of exit and voice upon which personal development depends, is thus not permitted to develop.

The instrumental theory of action of course simply bypasses these concerns, for it cannot accommodate the insight that we become who we are in part through what we do. According to the principle of learning through choosing, by contrast, individuals and groups in general participate not merely to meet pre-existing ends, but also to constitute themselves, or to reaffirm themselves, as persons and groups with particular and desired attributes.[7] It follows that preferences are as much formed as revealed in the exercise of choice. Individuals choose in order to become, and the nature of the opportunities given for the expression of choice will affect the formation of wills. One thus does not merely register one's preferences in giving to charity or voting; rather, one constitutes and reaffirms oneself as a charitable person or a good citizen. Similarly, in volunteering for combat the soldier is not merely registering his preference for victory, nor even expressing his status as a brave man; rather, he is constituting and reaffirming his character as brave. Finally, the worker joining with others to overcome class oppression is not simply opting for one social outcome as opposed to another; he or she is in addition affirming his or her status in social life, and his or her dignity by virtue of, or even despite, that status.

The great liberal thinkers themselves did not pretend that choice based on instrumental action could form the universal model of social practice. Obligation, loyalty, love, shame, civic virtue, and a host of other sentiments and commitments, were variously held to be essential influences upon social action. Even Bernard Mandeville, who shocked his eighteenth century readers with *The Fable of the Bees* did not envision that private greed would yield public virtue in all realms of society, but rather focused on the economy. Early liberal economic thinkers — notably Smith and Bentham — showed a lively interest in both the learning and choosing aspects of economic life, pondering the kinds of human beings that the emerging capitalist system would produce and advocating institutions to guide and correct this process. The celebrated ability of markets to reconcile individual interests and collective rationality — or at least to substantially attenuate the contradiction between the two was always viewed as conditional on a kind of morality and moral action. We could hardly agree more with Denis Obrien on this point:

> . . . while the classical writers were the earliest fully to appreciate the allocative mechanism of the market, and the power, subtlety and efficiency of this mechanism, they were perfectly clear that it could operate only within a framework of restrictions. Such restrictions were partly legal and partly religious, moral and conventional; and they were designed to ensure the coincidence of self and community interest.[8]

The early liberals recognized that the perpetuation of these moral, religious, and conventional commitments could not taken for granted. But later views, particularly those inspired the instrumental conception of action exemplified by neoclassical economics, came to embrace a much simpler view of the nature of the individual as exogenous to social life. Custom, community, and commitment might still be the bedrock of social interaction, but liberal thinkers — rejecting the activism on behalf of tradition of Edmund Burke and other conservatives — increasingly saw these as the result of a more or less historical legacy rather than the outcomes of ongoing projects of cultural reproduction. Thus the problem of the reproduction of a culture consistent with the workings of the market, the ballot box, and the other institutions advocated by liberalism dropped from theoretical debate.

To some extent the eclipse of cultural practices as a theoretical concern has flowed from the logic of liberal discourse itself. By couching its fundamental principles in terms of an individual and asocial conception of rights, liberal discourse makes difficult the expression of solidarity and cooperation as goals of political practices. With the ascendency of liberalism, observed Otto Gierke, the 'sovereignty of the state and the sovereignty of the individual were steadily on their way towards becoming the two central axioms from which all theories of social structure would proceed, and whose relationship to each other would be the focus of all theoretical controversy'.[9] The sole forms of social solidarity explicitly sanctioned in liberal discourse are nationality, based on common citizenship, and kinship, based on the family. It is perhaps for this reason that among the most effective forms of 'the politics of becoming' in some advanced capitalist countries today are nationalism and the anti-feminist defense of the patriarchal family.

Paradoxically the disappearance from theoretical discussion of this problem of cultural reproduction in the nineteenth century coincided with a growing awareness that heightened labor mobility, urbanization, economic dynamism, and other upshots of the growth of capitalist economy itself had undermined many traditional bases of morality and social control. Thus just as the issue of cultural reproduction fell from theoretical view, it began to assume immense practical importance in the minds and work of the growing army of reformers and administrators who since the nineteenth century have attempted to construct (mostly state) surrogates for the rapidly eroding family, neighborhood community, craft guild, church, community, and the like. The result was the construction of compulsory schools, asylums, and prisons during an era which prided itself on tearing down other walls in the interest of economic freedom.

A fundamental problem of liberal social theory, then, is that it takes as axiomatic the reproduction of those cultural, moral and economic conditions which are necessary to make good the normative claims made on behalf of its favored institutions. The task of cultural reproduction falls in important measure to schooling, but schools are arenas of learning not of choosing, and thus, as we have seen lie almost totally outside the boundaries of the explicit liberal theory itself. Schools, of course, are only a part of the process of social reproduction: we become who we are as much through what we learn in our economic and political activities as through our schooling. But liberalism — either as a philosophy or as an approach to social science — is not only temperamentally ill-disposed but conceptually ill-equipped to address the problem of the forms of learning promoted by the spread of markets and elections as the dominant framework for choosing.

Thus we may broaden considerably the assessment of liberal educational theory offered in *Schooling in Capitalist America*. In our consideration of the educational theory of John Dewey, for example, we limited our critique to a single point: we argue that the triple objectives of human development, equality, and preparation for adult occupational tasks are simply inconsistent in a capitalist society. We also note the improbable liberal assumption that individual development is exogenous to social processes. But beyond this we did not question the philosophical foundations of liberal educational theory. Yet the reasoning of this brief easay bears the unavoidable implication that a viable theory of education in a democratic society requires the rejection of the fundamental liberal partition of individuals into learners and choosers and its replacement by a theory which takes account of the manner in which class relationships, the state, the family and other structures regulate our own individual and collective projects to shape who we are.

Notes

1 We have developed this reasoning in some detail in our (1986) *Democracy and Capitalism: Property, Community, and the Contradictions of Modern Social Thought*, London, Basic Books and Routledge and Kegan Paul.

2 In COHEN, M. (Ed) (1961) *The Philosophy of John Stuart Mill*, New York, Modern Library, pp. 197–8.

3 The reader may be surprised that we limit our critique of the liberal model of individal action to this one point. We are, of course, aware that the major criticisms leveled against the liberal model of the individual lie elsewhere — in its purported attribution of such traits as rationality, egotism, hedonism, subjectivism, instrumentalism and atomism to the individual actor. We contend, however, that such critiques are either invalid, or can be more pointedly argued in terms of the liberal presumption of the givenness of wants. For an insightful exploration of the liberal model of choice complementary to that presented below, see ELSTER, J. (1979) *Ulysses and the Sirens*, Cambridge, Cambridge University Press; and ELSTER, J. (1983) *Sour Grapes*, Cambridge, Cambridge University Press.

4 The logic of Mill's argument in no way depends upon the particular examples he has chosen — children and barbarians — and is scarcely discredited by what we might now consider a racist choice of terminology in apparently referring to non-European societies.

5 MARX, K. (1977) *Capital*, Volume 1, New York, Vintage, p. 283.

6 HIRSCHMAN, A. (1970) *Exit, Voice, and Loyalty*, Cambridge, MA, Harvard University Press. Liberal theory typically does not even address the remaining term of Hirschman's trilogy: loyalty.

7 Though quite foreign to the structure of liberal theory *per se*, this common sense idea is hardly novel. It has been taken in interesting directions by FAY, B. 'How people change themselves: The relationship between critical theory and its audience' in HALL, T. (Ed) *Political Theory and Praxis*, Minneapolis, University of Minnesota Press, among others.

8 OBRIEN, P. (1975) *The Classical Economists*, Oxford, Oxford University Press, p. 272.

9 GIERKE, O. (1958) *Political Theories of the Middle Ages*, translated by F. W. Maitland, p. 87.

Part IV

Bowles and Gintis Reply to Their Critics

13 *Schooling in Capitalist America: Reply to our Critics*

Samuel Bowles and Herbert Gintis

Schooling in Capitalsit America was conceived in the belief that the formal educational systems of contemporary capitalist societies are, at one and the same time, critical bulwarks of privilege and fruitful arenas of struggle for progressive social change. We are pleased that others who share this belief have taken our contribution sufficiently seriously to offer careful assessment and critique over the years since it publication. A respected writer once commented that the only judgment he really feared was the gnawing criticism of the moths. If *Bowles and Gintis Revisited* is any indication, *Schooling in Capitalist America* has apparently so far escaped this final judgment.

The insight and spirit of comradely criticism evident in this volume only reaffirm our faith in the openness and creativity of the political left. While a mood of conservatism persists in the advanced capitalist countries, the pendulum will once again swing, as it has so often in the past, in the direction of progressive change. When this occurs, educators will be called upon to provide feasible, effective, and emancipatory alternatives to our current system. Our goal here is thus not to defend *Schooling in Capitalist America* (although we will not hesitate to do so), but rather to stress issues relevant to developing these alternatives. Accordingly, rather than dealing with our critics point by point, we shall isolate some general areas of contention upon which to concentrate.

Schooling in Capitalist Amercia upheld a simple criterion for an adequate educational system in a good society. Such a system, we argued, must simultaneously meet three objectives. First, education should foster the personal development of each member of society. Personal development, we stressed, is not limited to the acquisition of knowledge and cognitive skills. Equally important, we noted, are those affective and interpersonal skills which allow individuals to control their lives, and foster the self-esteem and sense of personal dignity which lead them to demand the resources to exercise such control. Second, education should act as an equalizing force, removing obstacles to substantive social equality and tempering the tendency for social privilege, and more importantly social deprivation, to be transmitted from generation to generation.

Finally, education should be a stabilizing force in the good society, fostering what John Dewey called the social 'continuity of life', by training youth to accept and affirm dominant culture and its institutional expression. Indeed we might judge a good society by the extent to which the success of its educational system in assuring the social continuity of life would simultaneously promote the personal developmental and egalitarian objectives of schooling. Educational systems of advanced capitalist society fail to perform their developmental and egalitarian functions, we argued. Indeed, we attempted to show that in the process of performing its *stabilizing* function, schools consistently thwart full personal development and legitimate rather than attenuate social inequality. This failure, we suggested, lies not so much in the schools themselves as in the type of society in which these schools are embedded. Only a *democratic* society, we held, would the personal development of individuals at the same time promote social equality and affirm dominant social institutions and their cultural forms. Yet capitalist societies, even liberal democratic ones, fail to be democratic in the strict sense that their economies are systems in which decision makers (the owners and controllers of wealth) remain *unaccountable* to the individuals who implement, and are affected by, their actions. Lacking a democratic economy, and assuming dominant groups are sufficiently powerful to ensure the stabilizing function of education, schooling in capitalist society will necessarily remain antithetical to social equality and personal development.

We must stress that these are the *major* conclusions of *Schooling in Capitalist America*, that they have not been subject to what we consider damaging criticism, and hence we continue to hold that they are correct. Indeed, we hold that these conclusions both identify the *precise* limitations placed by the capitalist economy upon the development of an adequate educational system, and establish *necessary prerequisites* for an economic alternative within which these limitations may be removed.

Our stance has often been subjected to the criticism of economism and reductivism, on the grounds of ignoring racism, sexism, and other non-class forms of oppression, as well as slighting the central political and cultural forces shaping education in capitalist society. Yet we do not claim, and we do not believe we have *ever* claimed, that these necessary prerequisites are in addition *sufficient* for an adequate educational system. Nor do we pretend that the economy is the *only* social force placing serious obstacles to the educational system's serving as an emancipatory force. Our readers would do well to take *Schooling in Capitalist America* not as a comprehensive theory of contemporary schooling, but rather as a theory of the linkage between education and the economy. In this context the suggestion that our work is economistic and reductivist loses much of its force. That overcoming racial, sexual, and other forms of oppression imposes additional goals for educational change fails to temper the thrust or question the veracity of our analysis.

The reader will note, however, that the so-called 'correspondence principle' plays no explicit role in conclusions set forth above in our general summary of *Schooling in Capitalist America*. Indeed, we originally conceived of the linkage between education and economy in terms of Marxian base-superstructure terms, rather than in terms of functionalist sociology à la Talcott Parsons. Only after recognizing the methodological limitations of these two approaches did we begin to search for a causal mechanism between the educational system and the world of work. Thus the correspondence principle was a late development in our thought on the subject.

The correspondence principle contains two distinct assertions. First, it holds that to the extent that the educational system reproduces the capitalist economy, it does so by virtue of a correspondence between the social relations of education and the social relations of production. That is, the division of labor in education, as well as its structure of authority and reward, mirror those of the economy. Second, it holds that in any stable society in which a formal educational system has a major role in the personal development of working people, there will tend to emerge a correspondence between the social relations of education and those of the economic system.

The first of these assertions has been taken by some readers to imply that education is a system of *uncontested domination*, in which students face the educational system passively, submitting placidly to their socialization into compliant workers. That this inference can be drawn from our work no doubt indicates a certain expositional weakness in *Schooling in Capitalist America*. We have, however, never even remotely entertained such a notion. The view of education as a system of uncontested domination is surely not a *logical* implication of our work. If the capitalist division of labor were *itself* a system of uncontested domination, then the correspondence principle would, by default, imply the same of the educational system. But we have *not* treated capitalism in this manner.

The conception of the social relations of capitalist production developed in *Schooling in Capitalist America* has appeared to many as similar to that of Harry Braverman, as presented in his well known *Labor and Monopoly Capital*.[1] This similarity, however, is purely superficial and misleading. Our own framework was grounded in a quite divergent framework stressing that the organization of production was, and is, the product not of class *domination*, but rather of class *struggle*.[2] This conception of capitalist production treats the capitalist division of labor as what our colleague Richard C. Edwards calls a 'contested terrain'.[3] In addition, the contested nature of capitalist work relations holds a central theoretical position in our new book *Democracy and Capitalism*, where we suggest that the costs of enforcing labor discipline in an undemocratic economy represent a progressively deepening threat to capitalism, and major source of capitalist inefficiency.

Schooling in Capitalist America did not develop a comparable theory of educational contestation, and our silence on this issue may have been misread. Indeed, our conception of the capitalist social relations of production, together with the correspondence principle, would lead us to expect that educational contestation might be a critical explanatory factor in understanding the structure of schooling. In fact, our critics in this area have generally limited themselves to demonstrating the existence of a *culture of resistance* to the impositions of formal education on the part of exploited groups. Such cultural dynamics, far from contradicting the correspondence principle, in fact reinforce it. We would welcome (although there does not appear to exist) a strong argument to the effect that the *structure* of education is the product of contested class, gender, racial, and other relationships.

The second part of the correspondence principle, asserting a long run accommodation of educational structure to the economic division of labor, has also been received with skepticism on the part of some of our readers. It has been argued, both in this volume and elsewhere, that the correspondence prinicple in this strong form is deterministic, mechanical, and simplistic. Far from promoting progressive educational change, it is argued, our formulation invites pessimism and discouragement on the part of activists within the educational system. We respond by reminding the reader of two points. The first is that if this aspect of the correspondence principle is true (and we believe it is), then it is important that it be taken into account in a strategy for social change. Second, we consider the principle to be a tendency which asserts itself *only in the long run*, although the effects of a dislocation between the social relations of education and those of economy are likely to have persistent short-run effects.[4] Indeed, we stress this point in *Schooling in Capitalist America*:

> [Our] study of historical change in the US school system reveals not a smooth adjustment of educational structure to the evolution of economic life, but rather a jarring and conflict-ridden course of struggle and accommodation. In this course, the school system has, for substantial periods, been orgainzed along lines which, far from corresponding to the developing organization of economic life, appear as bizarre or anachronistic throwbacks to earlier times.[5]

This may however be insufficient for our critics. Might we not also entertain the possibility of educational innovation *leading* rather than *lagging* economic change? Is it not, after all, a fact that in even the most repressive societies, and even in the most repressive spheres of advanced capitalist societies, students and teachers have been in the forefront of social change? Is it not also a fact that access to information and commitment to universalist principles on the part of many teachers and students have rendered, and may continue to render educational institutions extremely dangerous to despots, racists, capitalists, patriarchs, and other oppressors?

Yes, these are indeed familiar facts. Indeed they are a staple of the largely apologetic liberal notion of education against which we wrote. If we have inadequately stressed the disruptive and potentially liberating aspects of schooling in our work, we invite others to repair the fault. We cannot see, however, that these principles are either in conflict with, or diminish the importance of, the principle that there is a tendency for a long run correspondence between social relations of education and economic life.

The reader of this volume will note that the comments of its contributors have not been limited to *Schooling in Capitalist America*, but rather has covered our later study 'Contradiction and reproduction in educational theory' (republished in this volume as chapter 2) as well our subsequent work outside the area of education. We shall now move on to deal with reactions to this work.

In 'Contradiction and reproduction in educational theory', we suggested that the correspondence principle expresses the *reproductive linkages* between education and economic life, yet leaves the nature of their *contradictory linkages* unanalyzed. We there argued that the major contradictory linkages in liberal democratic capitalism flow from the educational system's location at the intersection of two distinct social systems: the liberal democratic state and the capitalist labor market. The person rights and democratic accountability operative in the state sphere contrast sharply with, and may clash with, the rules of the game of the capitalist economy, which are grounded in property rights, contract, and unaccountable power.

We continue to affirm that the location of education and economy in distinct sites governed by distinct rules of the game accounts for the major contradictions between the two. However, we now believe that the site/practices framework upon which our account was erected in 'Contradiction and reproduction in educational theory' was not sufficiently developed to serve as an adequate alternative to the base/superstructure model of the relationship among spheres of social life, and does not make sufficiently clear the nature of the interaction between the structures of social life and the practices of individuals and groups which transform these structures.

In *Democracy and Capitalism* we attempted to repair this gap. We there argue that the notion of a *site* with a set of characteristic social relationships is better expressed by that of a *game* with a set of rules governing the actions of participants. Mike Cole in chapter 3 of this volume, is quite correct in stressing our debt to Althusser in developing our notion of a 'practice'. Our conception of a 'site', however, was never adequately captured by either traditional sociological notions of social subsystems or the more sophisticated but similar notions of 'structure' in contemporary

European neo-Marxism. The notion of a sphere of social life as a *game* whose rules govern the behavior of participants is, however, hardly unique. Indeed it is more directly inspired by Max Weber and Ludwig Wittgenstein. We extend the metaphor of these thinkers considerably, however, by rendering the rule as much the effect as the source of power, and by linking the concept of a game to the Marxian idea of domination and, more specifically, of exploitation.

The conception of society as a game, we argue, solves a major problem which has plagued Marxian theory for the better part of the twentieth century: that of theorizing the relationship between action and structure in such manner as to maintain the irreducible, yet mutually determining character of each. By recognizing that the game exists independent of, and prior to, the actions of its participants, we affirm the materiality and causal determinacy of social life. Yet by equally affirming the autonomy of social actors as participants treating social life as means towards the achievement of their goals and the satisfaction of their needs, the irreducible and determinate character of individual and collective choice is maintained.

The notion of a 'game must of course be purged of its popular connotation with play, voluntarism, and frivolity. The games we have in mind are quite serious, as they determine the life, death, and life chances of individuals and groups. We have argued that society is composed of a set of asymmetric, recursive, constitutive, and overlapping game (arco games). The notion of an *asymmetric* game incorporates the Marxian notion of exploitation: in social games, not all individuals are equally situated; there are lords and serfs, men and women, masters and slaves, bosses and workers, white and black, despots of state and the disenfranchized. The notion of a *recursive* game recognizes that the rules are not pre-given (the most serious error of structuralist social theory, we believe, is to treat structures as eternal and self-reproducing), but rather are transformed by the actions of the participants. The rules of the game, we hold, are part of the stakes of the game. The concept of a *constitutive* game recognizes that the participants are not pre-given, but rather are constituted by their acts.

These three principles together allow us to treat society as a system in which actors and their social environment are mutually determining (they are recursive and constitutive), while maintaining the important insight that *contesting and protecting social asymmetries* accounts for critical forms of social action and solidarity. The notion of *overlapping* games adds to our repertoire of theoretical tools the element needed to understand the relationship between distinct spheres of social life. While there is a strong tendency in all of social theory (Marxian and non-Marxian alike) to conceive of society as a unified expression of a single underlying logic, the notion of society as a set of overlapping games recognizes the irreducible heterogeneity of such distinct areas of society as state, family, education, economy, and community. These sites, rather than expressing an underlying unity, we suggest, articulate as overlapping and heterogeneous games.

The notion of distinct and mutually irreducible forms of domination (state, class, gender and race) also flow naturally from this perspective.

In *Democracy and Capitalism* we suggest that the notion of social games as overlapping and asymmetrical provides a compelling foundation for the treatment of power as irreducibly heterogeneous, yet structured and accessible to systematic analysis. We there argue that while the various forms of social power have effects which reverberate throughout society, their origins lie in the diverse way distinct sites structure their internal political, cultural and other social relationships. We thus argue that the economy is inextricably political and cultural, and generalize this insight by suggesting that *each* site of social practice structures *all* the various characteristic forms of social expression. The heterogeneity of power derives from the fact that politics and culture, like production and reproduction, are central to the operation of *each* of the distinctly structured sites of which society is composed.

This framework has appeared to some readers as unmanageably complex and indeterminate. The unitary character of power in traditional Marxism, it is often argued, lends a coherence to social theory which the heterogeneous conception of society in our alternative sorely lacks. However, we believe there are synthesizing principles accounting for social coherence in the face of the centrifugal forces of heterogeneous power, and in the face of the fact that the rules of the game are, both in principle and in fact, continual objects of contestation and change. We thus argue for a conception of society as a *reproductive and contradictory totality*. In this conception, where social cohesion is secured, it flows from the mutual dependency of sites: the various centers of power are generally unable to secure their own conditions of existence, and hence are forced to reproduce forms of power to which they would otherwise be unalterably opposed. Social change in such a system stems in part from ecological, demographic, natural, technical and social changes in the social infrastructure. But it flows more critically from the distinct forms taken by the asymmetrical exercise of power on which social domination depends. Society is in general a contradictory totality, we argue in *Democracy and Capitalism*, in that fundamental social change normally takes the form of the application of rules of the game generic to one site of social practice to another where it undermines the dominant forms of power and forces structural change. Thus the women's movement deploys principles from the liberal democratic state to transform the patriarchal family; workers insist on due process and popular accountability in production; and capitalists invoke the concept of personal liberty to extend and enhance the property rights of the capitalist corporation. This conception of reproduction and contradiction has allowed us to understand the historical trajectory of liberal democratic capitalism.

One of the most direct offshoots of our concept of arco games is the notion of the contradictory relationship between person rights and property rights in the liberal capitalist system. We argued in 'Contradiction and reproduction in educational theory' and *Democracy and Capitalism* that liberal discourse, whatever its ostensible role in serving to obfuscate socialist consciousness and legitimate capitalist hegemony, in fact has been consistently (and successfully) exploited by subordinate groups towards undermining the asymmetries on which their subordination depends.

The various criticism of our conception of arco games and its related treatment of liberal discourse as an effective tool of social struggle have not induced us to alter our insistence upon the importance and applicability of these new concepts. Rachel Sharp, for instance, in chapter 10 of this volume, apparently misunderstands our position when she claims that we fail to theorize constraints, that we take practice as primary, that we reduce social history to the realm of mere contingency, and that we refuse to ascribe any causal power to structures. The arco game conception argues for a perfect duality of structural determination and the contingency of human history upon social practices. Indeed, in *Democracy and Capitalism* we outline a logic of social development based on various stages of accommodation of the rules of the game to the contradiction of person rights and property rights.

In addition, we have by no means claimed that the use of liberal discourse is socially 'neutral'. Rather we argue that it is an objective material reality upon which the struggles of oppressed groups have been based. Liberal discourse is of course amply and effectively used by the defenders as well as the opponents of capitalism, racism, patriarchy, and imperialism. Clearly the use of this as opposed to a different discourse entails that certain types of goals are more easily articulated than others, and hence that a specific logic of social struggle will materialize therefrom. Indeed, we clearly stated that the particular character of demands (and successes) of working class, feminist, national liberation, and anti-racist movements in advanced capitalist countries flows from the prevalence of liberal discourse.

Traditional Marxists may of course not be happy with our conclusion. To some, it may seem 'idealist' or 'voluntarist' to hold that practices have any independent causal efficacy in the determination of the historical trajectory of society. Yet until someone shows how practices of individuals and groups are fully and uniquely determined by environmental structures (and we are as far from doing that today as we were in Marx's time), it is only reasonable to assume that they are not. We are thus prepared to accept Marx's credo that people make history, but not under circumstances of their own choosing. Like Rachel Sharp we prefer the clean lines and parsimony of expression in the formulation of historical materialist principles Marx and his intellectual heirs. Yet these principles, however elegant, appear to us an insufficient guide to understanding or affecting the political, cultural, or even economic conflicts and possibilities of our epoch.

It is not unreasonable to assume that society, and social change, are more complex than can be captured in some simple, comprehensive theory. The principle of arco games must be considered not as a social *theory*, but rather as a *method* within which social theory can he developed — a flexible framework avoiding the major errors which have plagued social theorists in the past,[6] leading us to formulate and research problems more fruitfully and efficiently.

As an example of the power of the approach, consider its capacity to clarify the concept of 'interests' in social theory. We argue in *Democracy and Capitalism* that interests are *objective*, and hence amenable to analysis on the basis of their determination by structural parameters of society. On the other hand, we argue that interests are *constituted through social action*, in the sense that the character of group interests are contingent upon the character of group formation and action, rather than vice-versa. A group (for example, the working class) may thus have pre-constituted *material needs*, such as for biological subsistence, a healthy work and natural environment, and the like. But its *interests*, in the sense of the concrete objects of the social practices of the group, are not similarly pre-constituted. For there are clearly many ways a given need can be met, and which will be successful is both subject to uncertainty and the actions of other groups.

It is thus clear that workers *have* a need for, and *recognize* a need for, the conditions under which they may lead lives of dignity, material adequacy, and personal fulfillment. But it is simply wrong to say that the working class has an 'interest in fighting for socialism', unless the term 'socialism' is taken in the purely tautological sense of that which will satisfy this need. Armed with the concept of false consciousness it has been all to easy for some to assume that they know what is best for the workers, and hence to effect a quick transition from 'need' to 'interest'. Freeman-Moir, Scott and Lauder, for instance, in chapter 11 of this volume treat it as crystal clear and elementary that socialism consists of collective ownership, the replacement of production for profit with production for need, the withering away of the state, and the abolition of representative government. The history of Western capitalism attests, of course, to the fact that working class movements have widely rejected this notion of their 'interests'.

It would be misleading to think that if this conception of 'working class interests' is wrong, there might be another which is correct. The search for 'socialism' is a futile one, simply because there is no unique optimal strategy for the working class (or any other oppressed group, most probably). Indeed, in arco game theory, as in game theory in general, the payoff of any strategy of a participant (individual or group) depends upon the strategies taken by others. Where coalitions of players are possible, where the rules themselves can be altered through the play of the game, and where the participants constitute themselves through their actions, this indeterminacy is even more pronounced than in the simple games analyzed in economics and political science. Arco games, as we have stressed elsewhere, have no unique solutions.

In closing, we would like to stress here, as we have stressed throughout our work, that history is on our side. The spirit of dedication to and struggle for the emancipation of the oppressed peoples of the word is no less strong today than in any period in history. If by socialism we mean the society in which no person's freedom is won by another's servitude, then Freeman-Moir, Scott and Lauder are correct in insisting that our choice is 'socialism or barbarism'. For nothing but totalitarian despotism or nuclear cataclysm is likely to stem the progressive realization of dignity, personal freedom and political democracy for the oppressed. For education these demands translate into the quest for schools which, by promoting the full development of the student's personal powers and capacity for collective action, provide individuals and groups with the intellectual and spiritual means of controlling their lives, and the will to be satisfied with nothing less than a world in which the exercise of this power is each person's right.

Notes

1 Braverman, H. (1974).
2 See Marglin, S. (1974) and Gintis, H. (1976).
3 Edwards, R. C. (1979). See also Edwards, R. C. Gordon, D.and Reich, M. (1981); and Lazonick, W. (1978).
4 This of course was the message of chapters 6–9 of *Schooling in Capitalist America*. It has been suggested that we overstated the correlation between the development of the factory system and the emergence of the common school, and understated the importance of political culture as opposed to economic organization in the impulse towards universal mass education. We cannot assess these claims, since we have largely abandoned research in educational history in the years since the appearance of *Schooling in Capitalist America*. We are generally open to such alternatives, however, and have developed similar themes in *Democracy and Capitalism*. See also in this regard the recent works of Gareth Stedman Jones (1983) and Eric Hobsbawn (1983). We consider such research to be a substantial contribution to a balanced treatment of education in liberal democratic capitalism, and we welcome amendments to our interpretation of educational history deriving therefrom.
5 *Schooling in Capitalist America*, p. 151.
6 We therefore endorse the efforts of John Roemer (1982 and 1986), Jan Elster (1985), Adam Przeworsky (1985) and others to erect game theory to a central position in political economy. We stress, however, that the recursive, constitutive, and overlapping nature of social games renders the theory more complex and wide-reaching than these theorists appear willing to admit.

References

Bowles, S. and Gintis, H., (1986) *Democracy and Capitalism: Property, Communtiy, and the Contradictions of Modern Social Thought*, New York, Basic Books.

BRAVERMAN, H., (1974) *Labor and Monopoly Capital*, New York, Monthly Review Press.

EDWARDS, R.C., (1979) *Contested Terrain: The Transformation of the Workplace in the Twentieth Cenury*, New York, Basic Books.

EDWARDS, R.C., GORDON, D. and REICH, M., (1981) *Segmented Work, Divided Workers: The Historical Transformation of Labor in the United States*, New York, Cambridge University Press.

ELSTER, J., (1985) *Making Sense of Marx*, Cambridge, Cambridge University Press.

GINTIS, H., (1976) 'The nature of the labor exchange and the theory of capitalist production', *Review of Radical Political Economics*, 8.

HOBSBAWM, E., (1983) 'Mass-producing traditions: Europe, 1870–1914' in HOBSBAWM, E. and RANGER, T., (Eds) *The Invention of Tradition*, Cambridge, Cambridge University Press.

JONES, G.S., (1983) *Language of Class: Studies in English Working Class History, 1832–82*, Cambridge, Cambridge University Press.

LAZONICK, W., (1978) 'The subjugation of labor to capital: The rise of the capitalist system', *Review of Radical Political Economics*, 10.

MARGLIN, S., (1974) 'What do bosses do?', *Review of Radical Political Economics*, 6.

PRZEWORSKY, A., (1985) *Capitalism and Social Democracy*, Cambridge, Cambridge University Press.

ROEMER, J., (1982) *A General Theory of Exploitation and Class*, Cambridge, Cambridge University Press.

ROEMER, J., (1986) *Analytical Marxism*, Cambridge, Cambridge University Press.

List of Contributors

Mike Cole taught in Inner London schools for five years and has been lecturing at Brighton Polytechnic, England since 1976, during which time he also taught at St Thomas University in Canada and Macquarie University in Australia in 1980–81 and 1985–86 respectively. Currently he is Senior Lecturer in Sociology ad teaches courses on class, 'race' and gender. He has published widely in these areas both in academic and committed journals and books. He is the editor of *The Social Contexts of Schooling* and *Education for Equality: Some Guidlines for Good Practice* (forthcoming 1988). An active trade unionist, he is the secretary of NATFHE — the lecturers' union – at Brighton Polytechnic. He is also joint-coordinator of ARTEN (the Anti-Racist Teacher Education Network) for London and the South East.

Samuel Bowles is Professor of Economics at the University of Massachusetts. He has also taught at the University of Havana, Harvard University, and the Center for Popular Economics. In addition to *Schooling in Capitalist America*, he and Herbert Gintis have recently published *Democracy and Capitalism*. He is also author (with Richard Edwards) of *Understanding Capitalism: Competition, Command and Change* and (with David Gordon and Thomas Weisskopf) *Beyond the Waste Land: A Democratic Alternative to Economic Decline* and (with the Center for Popular Economics) *The Economic Report of the People*. He is currently engaged in teaching economics to rank and file trade unionists and other political activists through the Center for Popular Economics, as well as continuing his research in economic and political theory.

Herbert Gintis is Professor of Economics at the University of Massachusetts. He has taught at Harvard University and the University of Paris and has been a Member of the Institute for Advanced Study at Princeton University. His books include *Inequality* (with Christopher Jencks and others), *Schooling in Capitalist America* and *Democracy and Capitalism*, co-authored with Samuel Bowles. He is currently working on problems of international capital mobility with the World Institute for Development Economics Research, a branch of the United Nations Institute.

Robert Moore is Senior Lecturer in the Sociology of Education and Multicultural Education at Homerton College, Cambridge. He is especially interested in the relationship between educational and social inequality and in the effects of educational reform upon social inequality and differentiation. As a co-contributor to Schooling For The Dole? ((Bates I *et al*, 1984), and in various articles, he has been particularly concerned with the role of vocationalism in educational ideologies.

Peter MacDonald is Assistant Professor in the Department of Social Sciences at St. Thomas University in Fredericton, Canada. His graduate work was in the sociology of education at the Ontario Institute for Studies in Education. His research interests are in the area of the origins of state schooling, particularly at the comparative level.

Michael W. Apple is Professor of Curriculum and Instruction and Educational Policy Studies at the University of Wisconsin-Madison. He has been president of a teachers' union and a political activist, and has written extensively on the relationship between education and economic, political, and cultural power. He is the author of *Ideology and Curriculum* (1979), *Education and Power* (1982, revised edition 1985), and *Teachers and Texts: A Political Economy of Class and Gender Relations in Education* (1986). Among his many edited books are *Cultural and Economic Reproduction in Education* (1982), *Ideology and Practice in Schooling* (1983) (with Lois Weis), and *The Curriculum: Problems, Politics and Possibilities* (1988) (with Landon Beyer).

AnnMarie Wolpe is Senior Lecturer in Sociology at Middlesex Polytechnic where she is Set Co-Ordinator of Women's Studies on the Modular Scheme. Her teaching is now exclusively in this area. Her main interests are in Feminist Theory and the Sociology of Education. She has published widely in this area: apart from a number of articles she has co-edited *Feminism and Materialism* (with Annette Kuhn) and *Is There Anyone Here from Education?* (with James Donald). Her book *Within these Walls* on gender differentiation in a secondary school will be published shortly. She is a founder member of the collective which publishes *Feminist Review*.

Dennis Carlson is an Assistant Professor of Education at Rutgers University in Newark, New Jersey. Before joining the Rutgers faculty in 1983, he taught at Hobart ad William Smith Colleges in upstate New York and completed his doctoral work in Educational Policy Studies at the University of Wisconsin-Madison in 1978. He has been published in the *Harvard Educational Review*, *Curriculum Inquiry*, and *Interchange* among other journals and is now engaged in the preparation of a book on teachers as political actors, based partially on a longitudinal study of an urban teachers union.

Gloria I. Joseph is a Professor in the School of Social Science at Hampshire College in Amherst, Massachusetts, USA. She has taught at the University of Massachusetts in the School of Education. During that time she founded an Alternative Elementary School, The Che Lmumba School for Truth. She has also taught at Cornell University, Ithaca, New York, in the African Studies and Research Center. She is co-author (with Jill Lewis) of the book, *Conflicts in Feminist Perspectives: Black and White*. In addition, she has contributed to many publications in the fields of sociology, education, feminism and Black Studies. Her current research on South African women's self-help groups, is an outgrowth of the organization, Sisterhood in Support of Sisters in South Africa, (SISA) which she founded in 1984. Other areas of interest include studies on Malcolm X, Sojourner Truth and pioneering work on 20th century Black Feminists.

Rachel Sharp is Professor in the Sociology of Education, Macquarie University, Sydney. She co-authored *Education and Social Control: A Study in Progressive Primary Education*, is the author of *Knowledge Ideology and the Politics of Schooling* and the editor of *Apocalypse No: An Australian Guide to the Arms Race and the Peace Movement*. and *Capitalist Crisis and Schooling: Comparative Studies in the Politics of Education*.

John Freeman-Moir is Senior Lecturer in Education at Canterbury University, New Zealand. He has published numerous articles on marxist educational theory. With John Broughton he edited a book on genetic and evolutionary epistemology. He is active in the socialist movement in New Zealand, married, and the father of two children.

Hugh Lauder is Senior Lecturer in Education at Canterbury University University, New Zealand. He has published articles on the sociology of education in various journals and edited collections. He is co-editor, (with Phil Brown) of *Education: in Search of a Future*, Falmer Press (forthcoming) — a collection of papers on educational policy. He is co-editor of the New Zealand Literary Journal *Landfall*; has published a collection of poems *Over the White Wall*; and currently undertaking a quantitative and qualitative study of origins and destinations in New Zealand.

Alan Scott is Senior Lecturer in Education at Christchurch Teachers College, New Zealand. His major interests are in the Sociology and Politics of Education and in Drama in Education. He has published work on the ideology of school time, and (with John Freeman-Moir and Hugh Lauder) co-authored 'What is to be done with radical academic practice', (*Capital and Class*, No. 29, Summer 1986). He is the television critic for *Monthly Review*, New Zealand's independent socialist journal.

Index